FOOD & WINE

MAGAZINE'S

Wine
Guide
2003

produced by
gonzalez defino
7 east 14th street, new york, ny 10003

editorial director **Joseph Gonzalez**
art director **Perri DeFino**
volume editor **Tara Q. Thomas**
copy editor **Anne O'Connor**
chief researcher **Kathleen L. Kent**
researchers **Kae Denino, A. Gregory Finkell, Sharon Kapnick**
indexer **Andrea Chesman**

AMERICAN EXPRESS PUBLISHING CORPORATION
senior vice president/chief marketing officer **Mark V. Stanich**
vice president, marketing/publisher **Bruce Rosner**
director, branded services & retail sales **Marshall Corey**
marketing manager **Bruce Spanier**
marketing coordinator **Richard Nogueira**
business manager **James R. Whitney**
production manager **Stuart Handelman**
newsstand coordinator **Hanif Harris**

cover photograph **Colin Cooke**

FOOD&WINE
MAGAZINE'S

Wine
Guide
2003

by Jamal A. Rayyis

American Express
Publishing Corporation
New York

contents

foreword

by Lidia Matticchio Bastianich

A table at its best is not complete without wine; the best food preparation without the right glass of wine to accompany it always falls short. For a chef, the preparation of a dish, which involves the harmony of flavors, textures, and aromas, inevitably ends with a poignant question: "And what wine should I serve with it?"

It is thrilling for me as a chef to see the ever-growing interest in the values and pleasures of wine paired with food—something that I recall was always a part of our family table and certainly has a big emphasis at our restaurants.

The beautiful world of wine is wide and complex, but there is much assistance at hand: from wine directors and sommeliers at restaurants, well-prepared wine merchants, and reference books and guides.

FOOD & WINE Magazine's Wine Guide 2003 is a portable source full of excellent information. It is accessible and easy to navigate—always steering you to the delightful end of enjoying a glass of wine—by itself or together with food.

Lidia Bastianich

Owner: Felidia, Becco, and Esca restaurants in New York City;
    Lidia's Pittsburgh and Lidia's Kansas City restaurants
Cookbook Author: *La Cucina di Lidia, Lidia's Italian Table,*
    Lidia's Italian-American Table
PBS TV Host: *Lidia's Italian Table, Lidia's Italian-American Kitchen*

introduction
by Jamal A. Rayyis

Even if Dionysus had the power and prestige of Zeus, it would be hard to imagine that he could have created as many wines as are on the market today. Though Chardonnay and Cabernet Sauvignon have spread everywhere, wines from rare varieties and obscure regions are finding their way into wine shops throughout the country. Without guidance, all but the most experienced wine lovers would get lost. This book will help you navigate the sea of wine, with useful information as well as recommendations for specific bottles. As much as possible, I tasted wines blind, that is, with their identities hidden until I made an evaluation. From the thousands of wines tasted, I chose bottles based on quality, value, availability, and, sometimes, interest. I have suggested wines from as many producers as possible to increase the chances that you'll be able to find a wine for any occasion. That said, within the 1,400-plus wines recommended here, there is plenty of room for the esoteric. Part of what makes wine fun is discovering uncommon bottles. So don't think of this as a library reference, but as a tool to use in wine shops and restaurants. Carry it with you and choose your wines with confidence.

key to symbols

This guide is different from most: it's up to date. Our recommendations are for the exact wines being released for sale this year. Recommendations include the following symbols:

Type	🍷 / 🍷 / 🍷	red wine / white wine / rosé wine
Quality	★★★★	**Outstanding** Worth a search
	★★★	**Excellent** Top-notch example of its type
	★★	**Very good** Distinctive
	★	**Good** Delicious everyday wine
Price	$$$$	over $50
	$$$	$26 to $50
	$$	$15 to $25
	$	under $15

wine tasting terms

With so many wines and so little space, tasting notes are necessarily short, but to the point, offering a quick overview of what to expect from a wine, whether through mention of specific flavors, occasions to which the wine would be appropriate, or simply the feeling evoked by its taste. Putting wine flavors into words is tricky, and the terms I use to describe them are meant as analogies. All the wines described in this guide are made from grapes, but grapes have a unique ability among fruits to evoke the flavors of other fruits, herbs, minerals, or substances. A wine said to taste like "blackberries" isn't made from, or flavored by, blackberries. Rather, it evokes the flavor of blackberries.

While I have diligently tried to avoid obscure wine jargon in these pages, some of the terms commonly used to describe wine may be unfamiliar. Here's a selective mini-glossary:

Balance The harmony between acidity, tannin, alcohol, and sweetness in a wine. If one or more of these elements dominate others to their detriment, the wine is said to be unbalanced.

Body How heavy or thick a wine feels in the mouth.

Dry A wine without perceptible sweetness. A dry wine can, however, have powerful fruit flavors; they just don't taste sweet.

Earthy An earthy wine evokes the soil in which the grapes were grown or related flavors like mushrooms, leather, or damp straw.

Fruity Wines that have an abundance of fruit flavors, whatever the kind, are often described as "fruity."

Mineral Flavors that evoke the minerals in the soil in which certain grapes are grown. "Steely" is a subset of mineral.

Oaky Wines that carry the flavors of the oak barrels in which they were aged are said to taste "oaky." For more on oak, see page 187.

Powerful Full-flavored, heavy in tannin, acid, and/or alcohol.

Rustic A "rustic" wine tastes a bit rough and unsophisticated, but these can be charming attributes.

Tannin A component of grape skins, seeds, and stems, as well as oak barrels, tannin is found most notably in red wine. It's what gives the mouth a dry, cottony feel, much like the feel that over-steeped black tea will give, as it, too, contains tannin.

guide to grape varieties

Wine is made from thousands of different grape varieties, but about twenty of them seem to dominate American wine racks. Many of these are grown around the world; others are specific to a certain place. Here's a short, concise guide to the most common grape varieties:

♟CABERNET FRANC

Cabernet Franc is an important grape in Bordeaux (p. 95), where it adds peppery, red cherry flavors to blends. To find it solo look to the Loire Valley (p. 121), where it makes light reds with spicy herb and red cherry flavors, as well as California (p. 36) and Long Island (p. 79).

♟CABERNET SAUVIGNON

Cabernet Sauvignon is revered for its cedary black currant flavors bolstered with strong tannin that allows the best examples to age for years. It finds its best expression in Bordeaux (p. 95) and California's Napa Valley (p. 36), though examples show up all over the world, including South America (p. 253) and Lebanon (p. 229).

♟CHARDONNAY

Chardonnay seems to grow everywhere. It reaches its apex in France's Burgundy (p. 100), where it makes elegant, mineral-laden wines, but it can also turn out corpulent, tropical fruit bombs (see p. 232 for Australia; p. 22 for California), toasty Champagnes (p. 264), and nectarous dessert wines. You'll find an example in every chapter of this Guide.

♟CHENIN BLANC

Chenin Blanc's lush fruit and high acidity makes for some of France's greatest wines, like the Loire Valley's full-bodied, long-aging dry wines (p. 116), sumptuous dessert elixirs (p. 281), and charming sparklers (p. 268). Look also to South Africa (p. 258) and California (p. 31) for lighter but eminently enjoyable wines.

guide to grape varieties

GEWÜRZTRAMINER 🍷

Pink-skinned Gewürztraminer offers more flamboyant flavors than Carmen Miranda. These range from honeysuckle, rose, and lychee to apricot, mineral, and sweet spice. Gewürztraminer is especially important in Alsace (p. 88) an parts of Germany (p. 207). New York State (p. 74) and California (p. 31) also make excellent examples.

GRENACHE/GARNACHA 🍷

Grenache is essential to many southern French wines for its fresh cherry and spice flavors, especially those from Châteauneuf-du-Pape and the Côtes du Rhône (p. 136). Many Spanish winemakers rely on Grenache ("Garnacha," in Spanish), especially in Priorat (p. 189). It is also important in Sardinia (where it's called "Cannonau") and shows up in California (p. 57) and Australia (p. 240).

MARSANNE 🍷

Most at home in France's Rhône Valley (p. 133), Marsanne is prized for its honeyed almond flavors and full body. Good versions are also found in California (p. 31) and Australia (p. 234).

MERLOT 🍷

Typically easy to drink, Merlot, with its plum and chocolate flavors, has become one of the world's most popular grapes. At its best, it makes some of the greatest wines in the world, such as the examples from Bordeaux's Pomerol (p. 95) and Washington State (p. 70). There are also terrific examples from California (p. 45) and northeastern Italy (p. 148).

NEBBIOLO 🍷

Though grown in a few different areas of Italy, as well as California (p. 57), Nebbiolo shows its glorious black cherry, cedar, tar, and tobacco flavors best in Italy's Piedmont (p. 151), particularly in Barolo and Barbaresco (p. 152).

PINOT BLANC 🍷

Alsace (p. 85), California (p. 31), and Italy all make wines from Pinot Blanc, but it's most important in Austria (p. 214) where, under the name Weissburgunder, it takes on more character than its medium-bodied, mild-flavored wines usually have.

PINOT GRIS/
♥PINOT GRIGIO

In France's Alsace (p. 85) and Oregon (p. 63), Pinot Gris produces full-bodied, nutty-tasting wines. All over Italy (p. 144),
where the grape is known as Pinot Grigio, it produces light, brisk
white wines.

♥PINOT NOIR

Called the heartbreak grape, Pinot Noir is difficult to grow and
difficult to make. But when made right, it is as seductive as wine
can be, with elegant aromas and flavors like roses, red fruits,
and smoke, complemented by a haunting earthiness. Burgundy
is held up as its ultimate expression (pp. 107 and 110), but
excellent, if different, Pinot Noir also comes from Australia (p. 240),
California (p. 49), the Loire (p. 121), New York State (p. 79), New
Zealand (p. 247), and Oregon (p. 65).

♥RIESLING

Riesling can make wines of incredible complexity with high acidity and lots of mineral flavors, in styles that range from bone-dry
to sumptuously sweet (p. 284). The finest Rieslings are found in
Alsace (p. 88), Germany (p. 202), Austria (p. 213), and New York
State (p. 74). Australia (p. 234) is producing excellent examples
of the grape as well. Many Rieslings can age for more than a
decade.

♥ROUSSANNE

Roussanne finds its home in the northern Rhône, where its
nutty, unctuous flavors are often combined with Marsanne for
the white wines of Crozes-Hermitage, Hermitage, and St-
Joseph (p. 132). It's also occasionally grown in California, with
some good results (p. 31).

♥SANGIOVESE

Called the "blood of Jove," Sangiovese is the life-blood of Italian
winemaking, prized for its tart red cherry, leather, and balsamic
flavors balanced by lots of acidity. It's most common in Tuscany
(p. 163), where it makes up large portions of the wines of
Chianti, as well as many of the exalted Super Tuscans.
Sangiovese has also spread to California, which offers a different take on the grape (p. 57).

SAUVIGNON BLANC 🍷

Sauvignon Blanc finds its greatest expression in the lemony, herbaceous wines of France's Sancerre and Pouilly-Fumé (p. 120), though New Zealand's pungent grapefruit, green pepper, and boxwood-flavored wines have become wildly popular, too (p. 242). South Africa (p. 258), California (p. 29) and Austria (p. 214) also make excellent Sauvignon Blancs.

SEMILLON 🍷

The second of Bordeaux's great white grapes, Semillon finds its glory as the main component of the region's luxurious sweet Sauternes (p. 281), but it is presented on its own or blended with Sauvignon Blanc to make some great, full-bodied dry wines in Bordeaux (p. 94) and Australia (p. 234).

SYRAH/SHIRAZ 🍷

Typically full-bodied and tannic with berry, pepper, and smoky flavors, Syrah offers power—but not without finesse. Its most renowned domain is France's Rhône Valley (pp. 133 and 136), but California's Central Coast (p. 57), Washington State (p. 72), and Australia, where it's called Shiraz (p. 237), also produce great versions.

TEMPRANILLO 🍷

Grown throughout Spain, Tempranillo is best known as the grape responsible for Rioja reds. Tempranillo wines tend to have spicy aromas, full, plummy flavors, and medium body. See p. 185 for examples.

VIOGNIER 🍷

The basis of the nectarous white wines of France's northern Rhône Valley (p. 132), Viognier has become a favorite of California winemakers for the peach, citrus, and floral aromas and flavors of its wines (p. 31).

ZINFANDEL 🍷

California's own great red grape (by way of Italy and/or Croatia), Zinfandel assumes many different forms, from a pale rosé and a quaffable spaghetti red to a full-bodied, tannic wine filled with blackberry and spice flavors (p. 53). Zinfandel also makes thick, Port-style dessert wines (p. 291).

wine style finder

It's white, but will it be too full-bodied to go with trout? Or the recipe calls for a full-bodied red like a Barolo from Piedmont, but you don't want to spend the money for that illustrious wine? This handy guide to wine styles will help you find just the wine you're looking for and plenty of alternatives within each category.

white wines

light-bodied, dry whites

Argentina Torrontés, 252

Austria Grüner Veltliner *(Federspiel)*, 212; Muskateller, 215

California Chenin Blanc, Malvasia Bianca, Muscat, Pinot Gris, 32; Sauvignon Blanc, 29

Chile Riesling, Sauvignon Blanc, 255

France
Bordeaux Entre-Deux-Mers, 94
Loire Valley Muscadet, 119
The Midi Provence whites & blends, 129
Southwest Gascogne, 142

Germany Müller-Thurgau, 208; Riesling (QbA & Classic), 203

Italy
Abruzzi Trebbiano d'Abruzzo, 173
Lazio Frascati, 173
Piedmont Arneis, Gavi, 150
Southern Italy Sicilian blends, Vermentino, 176
Trentino/Friuli Chardonnay, Pinot Grigio, 146
Tuscany Pinot Grigio, Vernaccia, 162
Umbria Orvieto, 173
Veneto Pinot Grigio, Soave, 158

New York State Chenin Blanc, Riesling, Tocai Friulano, 76

New Zealand Chardonnay, 246; Sauvignon Blanc, 244

Portugal Vinho Verde, 196

South Africa Chenin Blanc, Riesling, Sauvignon Blanc, 260

Spain Rioja, 183

medium-bodied, dry whites

Argentina Chardonnay, Sauvignon Blanc, 252

Australia Chardonnay, 233; Riesling, Sauvignon Blanc, Semillon, 235

Austria Furmint, Grauburgunder, 215; Grüner Veltliner, 212; Pinot Blanc, 215; Riesling, 213; Sauvignon Blanc, 215

California Chardonnay, 24; Gewürztraminer, Pinot Blanc, Pinot Gris, Riesling, 32; Sauvignon Blanc/Fumé Blanc, 29

Chile Chardonnay, Sauvignon Blanc, 255

Eastern Europe Chardonnay, Pinot Grigio, Riesling, Sauvignon Blanc, 223

France
Alsace Gewürztraminer, 89; Pinot Gris, 86; Riesling, 89
Bordeaux Bordeaux whites, Pessac-Léognan, 94
Burgundy Chablis, 104; Côte Chalonnaise, 110; Côte d'Or, 105; Mâcon, 111
Loire Valley Chenin Blanc (Anjou, Vouvray), 117; Muscadet, 119; Sauvignon Blanc (Pouilly-Fumé, Quincy, Sancerre), 120
The Midi Languedoc-Roussillon whites & blends, 125
Rhône Valley Châteauneuf-du-Pape, Côtes du Lubéron, Côtes-du-Rhône, 137; Crozes-Hermitage, 133
Southwest Bergerac, Jurançon, 142

Germany Chardonnay, Müller-Thurgau, Pinot Gris, 208; Riesling *(Kabinett),* 203; Silvaner, 208

Greece Assyrtiko, Retsina, Roditis, 220

Italy
Piedmont Arneis, Chardonnay, Gavi, 150
Southern Italy Fiano di Avellino, Greco di Tufo, 176
Trentino/Friuli Gewürztraminer, Pinot Grigio, Sauvignon Blanc, Sylvaner, Tocai Friulano, 146
Tuscany Chardonnay, Malvasia, Vernaccia, Vermentino, 162

New York State Chardonnay, Gewürztraminer, Riesling, Sauvignon Blanc, Semillon, Seyval Blanc, Tocai Friulano, 76

New Zealand Chardonnay, 246; Gewürztraminer, Riesling, 247; Sauvignon Blanc, 244

Oregon Chardonnay, Gewürztraminer, Müller-Thurgau, Pinot Blanc, Pinot Gris, 64

Portugal Bairrada, Bucelas, 196

South Africa Chardonnay, Sauvignon Blanc, 260

Spain Penedès, Priorat, Navarra, 190; Rioja, 183; Rueda, 192

Switzerland Chasselas, regional blends, 217

Washington State Chardonnay, Sauvignon Blanc, 69

full-bodied, dry whites

Argentina Chardonnay, 252

Australia Chardonnay, 233; Marsanne, Semillon, Verdelho, Viognier 235

Austria Grüner Veltliner *(Smaragd)*, 212; Riesling *(Smaragd)*, 213;

California Chardonnay, 24; Marsanne, Roussanne, Viognier, 32

Chile Chardonnay, 255

France
Alsace Gewürztraminer, 89; Muscat, 91; Pinot Gris, 86; Riesling, 89;
  Sylvaner, 91
Bordeaux Bordeaux whites, Pessac-Léognan, 94
Burgundy Côte d'Or, 105; Mâcon, 111
Loire Valley Chenin Blanc (Savennières), 117
Rhône Valley Condrieu, Hermitage, St-Péray, 133

Germany Scheurebe, 208

Greece Moscofilero, 220

Italy
Piedmont Chardonnay, 150
Southern Italy Fiano di Avellino, 176
Trentino/Friuli Ribolla Gialla, 146
Tuscany Vermentino, 162

Middle East & North Africa Chardonnay, regional blends, 228

Spain Rías Baixas, 192; Rioja, 183

Washington State Chardonnay, Semillon, 69

red wines

light-bodied reds

France
Burgundy Beaujolais, 113
Loire Valley Cabernet Franc (Anjou, Bourgueil, Saumur, Touraine), 121

Italy
Piedmont Friesa, 156
Tuscany Chianti, 164

wine style finder

medium-bodied reds

Australia Pinot Noir, 241; Shiraz, 237

California Merlot, 46; Pinot Noir, 49; Sangiovese, Syrah, 58

Chile Cabernet Sauvignon, Carmenère, Merlot, Syrah, 256

Eastern Europe Cabernet Sauvignon, Merlot, Pinot Noir,
Plavac Mali, 224

France
Bordeaux Bordeaux Supérieur, Canon-Fronsac, Côtes de Castillon, Lalande
de Pomerol, Listrac-Médoc, Haut-Médoc, Margaux, Médoc, Pauillac,
Pessac-Léognan, Premières Côtes de Bordeaux, St-Estèphe, 97
Burgundy Beaujolais, 113; Côte Chalonnaise, 110; Côte d'Or, 107
Loire Valley Cabernet Franc (Anjou, Bourgueil, Chinon, Menetou-
Salon, Sancerre, Saumur, Touraine), 121
The Midi Languedoc-Roussillon reds & blends, 126; Provence reds &
blends, 130
Rhône Valley Côtes-du-Rhône, 138; Crozes-Hermitage, St-Joseph, 134

Italy
Abruzzi Montepulciano d'Abruzzo, 174
Piedmont Dolcetto, 154; Gattinara, Rosso delle Langhe, 156
Trentino/Friuli Pinot Noir, Refosco, Schioppettino, Teroldego Rotaliano, 148
Tuscany Carmignano, 169; Chianti & Chianti Classico, 164; Morellino
di Scansano, 169; Rosso di Montalcino, 166; Rosso di Montepulciano, 169
Veneto Valpolicella, 159

Middle East & North Africa Red blends, 229

New York State Cabernet Franc, Merlot, Pinot Noir, 79

New Zealand Pinot Noir, 248

Oregon Pinot Noir, 66

Portugal Alentejo, Beiras, Estremadura, Palmela, Ribatejo, Terras
do Sado, 197

Spain Rioja, 186

Switzerland Dôle, Merlot, 217

Washington State Lemberger, Sangiovese, 72

full-bodied reds

Argentina Barbera, Cabernet Sauvignon, Malbec, Merlot, Syrah, 253

Australia Cabernet Sauvignon, 240; Grenache, Merlot, red blends, 241; Shiraz, 237

California Bordeaux styles, 43; Cabernet, 37; Merlot, 46; Pinot Noir, 49; Rhône and Italian styles, Syrah, 58; Zinfandel, 54

Chile Cabernet Sauvignon, Carmenère, Syrah, 256

Eastern Europe Cabernet Sauvignon, Merlot, 224

France
Bordeaux Grand Cru wines, Haut-Médoc, Pauillac, Pessac-Léognan, Pomerol, St-Émilion, St-Estèphe, St-Julien, 97
Burgundy Côte d'Or, 107
The Midi Bandol, 130; Collioure, Corbières, Languedoc-Roussillon blends, 126; Provence blends, 130; St-Chinian, 126
Rhône Valley Châteauneuf-du-Pape, 138; Cornas, Côte-Rôtie, 134; Côtes du Ventoux, 138; Crozes-Hermitage, 134; Gigondas, 138; Hermitage, 134; Lirac, Vacqueyras, 138
Southwest Béarn, Bergerac, Cahors, Madiran, Marcillac, 142

Greece Agiorgitiko, Xinomavro, 221

Italy
Le Marche Rosso Cònero, Rosso Piceno, 174
Piedmont Barbaresco, 152; Barbera, 154; Barolo, 152; Dolcetto, 154; Nebbiolo blends, 156
Southern Italy Aglianico del Vulture, Copertino, Primitivo, red blends, 178
Tuscany Carmignano, 169; Chianti Classico, 164; Brunello di Montalcino, 166; Super Tuscans, 170; Vino Nobile di Montepulciano, 169
Umbria Sagrantino di Montefalco, 174
Veneto Amarone, 159

Middle East & North Africa Cabernet Sauvignon, red blends, 229

New York State Cabernet Franc, Cabernet Sauvignon, Merlot, 79

New Zealand Cabernet Sauvignon, Merlot, Syrah, 249

Oregon Pinot Noir, 66

Portugal Alentejo, Beiras, Dão, Douro, Estremadura, Terras do Sado, 197

South Africa Cabernet Sauvignon, Merlot, Pinotage, Pinot Noir, Shiraz, 262

Spain Navarra, 190; other regions, 192; Penedès, Priorat, 190; Ribera del Duero, 188; Rioja, 186

Washington State Cabernet Sauvignon, Merlot, 71; Syrah, 72

vintage chart

You've ordered a wine that's supposed to be great—but isn't? Maybe it's the vintage. This chart, which covers the wines that are commonly aged, will aid you not only in ordering wine but in

	1985	1986	1987	1988	1989	1990	1991
Bordeaux							
Right Bank	★★★★	★★★	★	★★★	☆☆☆☆	☆☆☆☆	o
Left Bank (Médoc)	★★★★	★★★★	★★	☆☆☆	☆☆☆☆	☆☆☆☆	★
Red Graves	★★★★	★★★★	★★	☆☆☆	☆☆☆☆	☆☆☆☆	★
Burgundy							
Côte d'Or Reds	☆☆☆☆	☆☆☆	☆☆	★★★	★★★	☆☆☆☆	★★
Chablis	☆☆	★★★	★★	★★	★★★	★★★	★★
Loire							
Chenin Blanc	★★	☆☆☆	★	★★★	☆☆☆☆	★★★★	o
Cabernet Franc	★★★	☆☆	★	★★★	★★★★	★★★★	o
Rhône							
Northern Reds	★★★★	★★★	★★	☆☆☆☆	☆☆☆☆	★★★★	☆☆☆☆
Southern Reds	★★★★	★★	★★	★★★★	☆☆☆☆	☆☆☆☆	☆
Italy							
Barolo & Barbaresco	★★★★	★★	☆	★★★★	☆☆☆☆	☆☆☆☆	★★★
Chianti	★★★★	★★★	☆☆	★★★	★★	★★★★	☆☆☆
Spain							
Rioja Reds	★★★★	★★	★★★	☆	★★★	☆☆☆	★★★
Ribera del Duero	★★★	o	★★★	☆☆	★★	★★★	★★★★
Germany							
Riesling	★★★	☆☆	☆☆	★★★	★★★	☆☆☆☆	☆☆
Other Whites	☆☆☆	☆☆	☆☆	★★★	☆☆☆	☆☆☆☆	★★
California							
Cabernet Sauvignon	☆☆☆☆	☆☆☆☆	★★★★	☆☆	★★★	★★★★	★

o = Very bad vintage; a disaster
★ = Poor to average vintage; only the best wines are good quality
★★ = Good to very good vintage
★★★ = Excellent vintage
★★★★ = Outstanding vintage

evaluating those you already have and in choosing recent wines to purchase. The quality of the wine is indicated by the number of stars, just as in the "What to Buy" sections of this book. The color of the stars tells you where the wine is most likely to be in its progress, from "not ready" through "well past peak." For example, ★★ indicates a good wine at its peak, while ★★★ signals an excellent wine whose time has almost passed.

1992	1993	1994	1995	1996	1997	1998	1999	2000	2001
★	★★	★★★	★★★	★★★★	★★	★★★★	★★★	★★★★	★★★
★	★★	★★★	★★★★	★★★★	★★	★★★	★★★	★★★★	★★★
★	★★★	★★★	★★★	★★★	★★★	★★	★★	★★★★	★★
★★	★★★	★★	★★★★	★★★	★★★	★★★	★★★	★	★★
★★★	★★	★★★	★★★★	★★★★	★★★	★★★	★★★	★★	★★
★★	★★★★	★★★★	★★★★	★★★★	★★★	★★★	★★	★★	★★★
O	★★★★	★★	★★★★	★★★★	★★★	★★★	★★	★★★	★★
O	★★	★★★	★★★★	★★★	★★★	★★★	★★★★	★★★	★★★
★	★★	★★	★★★★	★★	★★★	★★★★	★★★	★★★★	★★★
★	★★★	★★	★★★★	★★★★	★★★★	★★★	★★★	★★★	na
★★	★★★	★★★	★★★★	★★★	★★★★	★★★	★★★	★★★	★★
★★	★★	★★★★	★★★★	★★★	★★★	★★★	★★	★★	★★★
★	★★	★★★★	★★★★	★★★★	★★★	★★★	★★★	★★	★★
★★	★★	★★★★	★★★★	★★★★	★★★	★★★	★★★★	★★	★★★★
★★	★★★	★★★	★★	★★★	★★★	★★★	★★★★	★★	★★★★
★★★★	★★★	★★★★	★★★	★★★	★★★	★★★	★★	★★★	★★★★

★ = Not ready; needs more time   ★ = Past peak but still enjoyable
☆ = Can be drunk or held   ★ = Well past peak
★ = At peak; perfect for drinking now   na = Not yet available

how to handle a wine list

Few things cause diners as much anxiety as the presentation of a wine list. But you can conquer any list with a few easy steps:

Assess the list A good list is diverse or it specializes in a certain region. There should be wines in different price ranges, with a few priced under $30. If you see a Riesling—not popular in the U.S., but an excellent complement to many dishes—the restaurant is probably serious about wine. A poor list might be limited in selection (not necessarily in number: fifty California Chardonnays and a handful of other whites can be trouble), have too many wines from one producer, or fail to list vintages. If the list is poor, order the least expensive thing that you recognize as being reasonably good.

Ask questions A wine list is just a menu. You can ask how tannic the Cabernet is just as you inquire how the salmon is prepared. Very few people can look at a list and know exactly what all the wines taste like at that moment. It's the restaurant's job to explain them to you.

Taste the wine When the bottle arrives, make sure it's exactly what you ordered—the vintage, the producer, the blend or varietal. If not, say so. If the listed wine is out, you might prefer to choose something else. You may be presented with the cork. Ignore it. We've had fine wines with spoiled corks and bad wines with sound corks. Sniff the wine in your glass. If it smells like sulfur, cabbage, or skunk, say that you think the wine might be off and request a few minutes to see if the odors dissipate. If they remain, the wine is probably bad. Another problem: About 5 percent of wines, in all price ranges, are "corked"—the cork was improperly processed, and the wine tastes like musty cork or wet cardboard.

Send a bottle back if necessary If the wine is off, the server should take it away and offer a new bottle. The restaurant gets credit for bad wines anyway. Disliking a wine is not a reason to send a bottle back unless a server described it quite inaccurately, as light and fruity when it's heavy and tannic, for instance.

pairing wine with food

We used to hear, white wine with fish and red with meat. The modern adage seems to be, drink whatever you like with whatever you want. Both approaches have advantages, but you're bound to encounter pitfalls by adhering too closely to either. The trick is to pair food and wine so that neither overwhelms or distorts the other. Some suggestions to help you on your way:

Be body-conscious Pair light bodied, delicately flavored food with similar wine and heavy-bodied, full-flavored dishes with matching wine. The subtle flavors of sole meunière are going to get lost if washed down with a hearty Napa Cabernet.

Balance extremes If a dish is rich and creamy, you need a tart wine as a counterpoint—and to cleanse your palate. A bit of sweetness in wine balances salty or spicy foods. If you can't wait to drink those young, astringent Bordeaux, Barolo, or California Cabernets, the protein and fat of meat will moderate their tannin.

Dance to the same beat Peppery meat dishes work well with spicy Rhône Valley reds. Dishes with fruit sauces are great with richly fruity wines from southern Italy. California Chenin Blanc and Loire Valley or New Zealand Sauvignon Blanc have the right mineral and herbal nuances to stand up to asparagus and artichokes, which can make other wines taste metallic.

Do as the Romans People have been pairing locally made foods and wines for centuries. Wines from a particular region are often just the thing to drink with foods from the same place.

Mix and match Though the "red with meat, white with fish" rule is too sweeping, tannic reds do taste metallic when drunk with oily fish like mackerel or sardines. If you want to drink red with them, select one that is low in tannin and high in acidity.

For more specific food and wine pairing recommendations, see the Food & Wine Pairing Chart on page 292.

21

california

With its bright sunshine, ocean-cooled breezes, and varied terrain, California is the promised land of American winemaking, both in terms of quality and diversity. California vineyards supply 90 percent of the country's wine production and three of every four bottles bought in the U.S. Though California is famed for its rich, full-bodied wines, its vintners make more delicate wines as well.

on the label

Californian vintners usually highlight the grape variety on the wine label rather than the region where the grape was grown, as is usual in many European countries. By California law, a wine labeled by variety must contain at least 75 percent of that grape. If the label includes a place name as well (for example, Sonoma or Napa Valley), then 85 percent of the grapes in that wine must have come from that area. If the label mentions a specific vineyard, 95 percent of the grapes must have been grown there. Don't be seduced by terms such as "Reserve" or "Proprietor's Blend"; while vintners often choose better grapes for these wines and age them longer, the terms have no legal meaning.

white wines

CHARDONNAY

Chardonnay is California's most widely planted white wine grape. Though the grape is most esteemed for the austere, mineral-tinged wines it produces in the Burgundy region of France,

Mendocino
— Potter Valley
— Anderson Valley
— Alexander Valley
— Dry Creek Valley
Sonoma Napa • SACRAMENTO
Amador
Carneros
— Russian River Valley
SAN •
FRANCISCO
Contra Costa
Alameda
Santa Cruz Mountains
MONTEREY •
— Chalone
Monterey
— Paso Robles
— Edna Valley
— Santa Maria Valley
Santa Barbara
Santa Ynez   LOS ANGELES
Valley   •

SAN DIEGO •

Featured
Wine-Growing
Regions

California versions tend toward exuberant, rich, tropical flavors and more than a hint of vanillin as a result of oak aging. Tastes are changing, however, and many winemakers have tweaked their techniques to produce wines with more finesse. Today, there is a wide range of styles at all prices, from fruity Central Valley versions to leaner, sophisticated wines from the cool Sonoma Coast.

at the table

Big, oaky Chardonnays can overwhelm fish and fowl dishes traditionally paired with white wines, but they work beautifully with smoked salmon, lobster, or pork or veal, especially with a fruity sauce. Light and lemony versions, on the other hand, are easy to match with everything from snapper to roast chicken or even mild, creamy cheeses like Brie.

23

california **whites**

the bottom line Noteworthy California Chardonnays that cost less than $12 are getting as rare as the California condor. Between $13 and $25, things get more interesting; at the upper end (nearing $100), price can reflect rarity as much as it might quality.

what to buy CHARDONNAY

1999	2000	2001
★★	★★★	★★★

recommended wines

1999 Joseph Phelps Ovation, Napa Valley ★★★★ $$$
dry, medium-bodied, medium oak, high acidity   drink now–12 years
Subtle fruit, mineral, and oak flavors are tightly wound in a Burgundian style.

1999 Robert Mondavi Winery Reserve, Napa Valley ★★★★ $$$
dry, medium-bodied, heavy oak, medium acidity   drink now–10 years
Classic Chardonnay, with lemon curd, smoky oak, and spicy mineral flavors.

2000 Qupé Reserve Bien Nacido, Santa Maria Valley ★★★★ $$
dry, medium-bodied, light oak, high acidity   drink in 1–8 years
Qupé is known for Rhône-style wines, but this mineral-laden Chardonnay points directly to Premier Cru Burgundy.

1999 Rutz Cellars Maison Grand Cru,
Russian River Valley ★★★★ $$
dry, medium-bodied, light oak, high acidity   drink now–10 years
Almost Chablis-like, with a quarry's worth of mineral flavors joined by floral grapefruit notes and smoke.

2000 Far Niente, Napa Valley ★★★ $$$$
dry, full-bodied, medium oak, high acidity   drink now–8 years
Big, smoky, but graceful, too, with flavors reminiscent of the season's first figs.

2000 Beringer Sbragia Limited Release, Napa Valley ★★★ $$$
dry, full-bodied, medium oak, medium acidity   drink now–8 years
Smoky oak plays up the peach nectar flavors, for a generous, complex wine.

2000 Cakebread Cellars, Napa Valley ★★★ $$$
dry, medium-bodied, medium oak, high acidity   drink now–8 years
Spicy orange flavors mixed with a wisp of floral oak against a mineral backdrop.

BUGGED OUT

California winemakers are blessed with good weather, a varied terrain, and an eager market. But these advantages are being threatened by an invader smaller than the end of a pinkie finger: the glassy-winged sharpshooter. The insect is a carrier for Pierce's disease, which weakens vines to the point of death in about two years. The disease isn't new—in fact, it destroyed around 40,000 acres of vines in southern California in the 1880s (back when it was known as Anaheim's disease). However, until the glassy-winged sharpshooter arrived on an ornamental plant brought in from outside the state, the disease was carried primarily by the less efficient leaf-hopper sharpshooter. Today, even garden-variety patio plants that have been shipped to California have to undergo vigorous inspections before they are allowed into wine areas.

2000 Carpe Diem Firepeak Vineyard, Edna Valley   ★ ★ ★ $ $ $
dry, medium-bodied, medium oak, medium acidity   drink in 1–8 years
Late spring in a bottle, with lavender aromas wafting though fresh fig and strawberry flavors. Good minerality, too.

**1999 Franciscan Oakville Estate Cuvée Sauvage,
Napa Valley**   ★ ★ ★ $ $ $
dry, full-bodied, medium oak, high acidity   drink now–10 years
Wild yeast fermentation brings complex scents and flavors of herbs, minerals, and flowery fruit.

**1999 Fritz Winery Shop Block Dutton Ranch,
Russian River Valley**   ★ ★ ★ $ $ $
dry, full-bodied, heavy oak, high acidity   drink now–10 years
A powerful wine, with layers of peach, melon, mineral, and oak flavors, this will get even better with time.

2000 Saintsbury Reserve, Carneros   ★ ★ ★ $ $ $
dry, medium-bodied, medium oak, high acidity   drink now–10 years
Ripeness in restraint, with orange, almond, and stone flavors.

2000 Shafer Red Shoulder Ranch Carneros, Napa Valley ★ ★ ★ $ $ $
dry, full-bodied, medium oak, high acidity   drink now–8 years
Ripe as pineapple, structured with mineral and smoothed with smoky oak, this is big, generous Chardonnay.

california **whites**

2000 Babcock Grand Cuvée, Santa Ynez Valley ★★★ $$
dry, medium-bodied, medium oak, medium acidity   drink now–8 years
Wonderfully complex, with ripe autumn fruit flavors accented by light lavender
and smoke notes.

2000 Cambria Katherine's, Santa Maria Valley ★★★ $$
dry, medium-bodied, medium oak, medium acidity   drink now–6 years
Fine, silky Chardonnay, with peach and pear flavors touched by smoky oak
and mincrals.

2000 Chalone Vineyard Chalone, Monterey County ★★★ $$
dry, medium-bodied, light oak, medium acidity   drink now–8 years
Inside its mineral shell there's an abundance of soft fruit flavors balanced by
very good acidity.

1999 Gallo of Sonoma Laguna Vineyard,
Russian River Valley ★★★ $$
dry, medium-bodied, medium oak, high acidity   drink now–6 years
Ripe peach and pear flavors are brightened with crisp acidity and rounded by
a nuance of oak.

2000 Geyser Peak Reserve, Alexander Valley ★★★ $$
dry, medium-bodied, medium oak, medium acidity   drink now–4 years
Wine is said to be good for the heart, but this is so smoky and rich with bacon
and lemon curd flavors it might clog the arteries.

2000 Ledson, Russian River Valley ★★★ $$
dry, medium-bodied, light oak, high acidity   drink now–6 years
This Chardonnay's citrus flavors are made chewy and rich by an appetizing,
baconlike smokiness.

2000 Peju Province, Napa Valley ★★★ $$
dry, medium-bodied, light oak, medium acidity   drink now–5 years
Fresh applesauce flavors meld with honey and blossom notes for an unusual
and delicious Chardonnay.

2000 Sterling Vineyards Winery Lake Vineyard Carneros,
Napa Valley ★★★ $$
dry, full-bodied, medium oak, medium acidity   drink now–8 years
Light honey notes play up the tropical, floral, and strawberry flavors of this ripe
Chardonnay.

2000 William Hill Winery Reserve, Napa Valley ★★★ $$
dry, medium-bodied, light oak, medium acidity   drink now–5 years
Ripe fruit flavors are balanced by a judicious amount of toasty oak and smoky
mineral elements.

JUST WHEN THEY THOUGHT IT WAS SAFE TO GO OUT WITHOUT AN UMBRELLA

The cool, damp summer and warm winter El Niño and La Niña brought in 1997–1998 put a damper on a decade of excellent harvests in California, but winemakers quickly bounced back when normal, stellar weather returned in 2000 and 2001. However, the National Weather Service declared in July 2002 that El Niño will visit again this fall. Fortunately, it is expected to be milder than it was last time. And, as every cloud has a silver lining, winemakers in the Pacific Northwest are bound to be happy: the last El Niño provided some of their finest harvests ever.

2000 Jordan, Russian River Valley ★★ $$$
dry, medium-bodied, medium oak, high acidity   drink now–5 years
A slimmer Jordan than usual, following a stony, lemon- and violet-lined path.

1999 Sanford Barrel Select, Santa Barbara County ★★ $$$
dry, medium-bodied, medium oak, high acidity   drink now–5 years
Rich, smoky, baked apple flavors are refreshed by a spearmint sharpness.

2000 Arrowood Grand Archer, Sonoma County ★★ $$
dry, medium-bodied, light oak, medium acidity   drink now–3 years
Arrowood's second label offers juicy summer fruit flavors, some minerals and a touch of oak for a fraction of their estate wine.

2000 Benziger Family Winery, Carneros ★★ $$
dry, full-bodied, medium oak, medium acidity   drink now–4 years
For fans of buttery, oaky, and pineapple-laden Chardonnays.

2000 Byington, Sonoma County ★★ $$
dry, medium-bodied, medium oak, medium acidity   drink now–5 years
Ribbons of oak and mineral flavors wrap around ripe pear fruit for a delicious package.

2000 Byron, Santa Maria Valley ★★ $$
dry, medium-bodied, medium oak, medium acidity   drink now–3 years
Cool-climate Chardonnay, with light citrus flavors, minerals, and good acidity.

2000 Jekel Vineyards Gravelstone, Monterey ★★ $$
dry, medium-bodied, light oak, high acidity   drink now–3 years
Truth in advertising, with gravel-like mineral notes joined by peach flavors.

2000 Hess Select, California   ★★ $
dry, medium-bodied, medium oak, medium acidity   drink now–1 year
With a mélange of fruit and smoky oak flavors, this is a bargain at the price.

1999 Peirano Estate Vineyards, Lodi   ★★ $
dry, medium-bodied, light oak, high acidity   drink now–4 years
Gold Country prospectors would be happy to find this honey-scented nugget.

2000 Firestone Vineyard, Santa Barbara County   ★ $$
dry, medium-bodied, light oak, high acidity   drink now–2 years
This hits all the buttons: citrus, butter, and mineral. Simple but effective.

2000 Beaulieu Vineyard, Sonoma   ★ $
dry, medium-bodied, light oak, medium acidity   drink now–2 years
Charming lemon, nut, and grassy flavors go down easily with a light chill.

2000 Fetzer Vineyards Sundial, California   ★ $
dry, medium-bodied, light oak, medium acidity   drink now
Sundial is pleasantly consistent, with tropical fruit flavors and a peck of oak.

2000 Kendall-Jackson Vintner's Reserve, California   ★ $
dry, medium-bodied, medium oak, medium acidity   drink now–2 years
Always reliable, with ripe, buttery tropical flavors and lots of oak.

2000 Robert Mondavi Woodbridge, California   ★ $
dry, medium-bodied, light oak, medium acidity   drink now
Justly popular, for its price and its subtle pineapple and green herb flavors.

WINES WE WISH WE HAD MORE ROOM FOR
1999 Mer Soleil, Central Coast ★★★★ $$$ dry, full-bodied, heavy
oak, high acidity, drink now–10 years; **1999 Rudd Bacigalupi Vineyard,
Russian River Valley** ★★★★ $$$ dry, medium-bodied, medium oak,
high acidity, drink now–10 years; **2000 Joseph Swan Vineyards Trenton
Estate Vineyard, Russian River Valley** ★★★ $$$ dry, medium-bod-
ied, medium oak, high acidity, drink in 2–8 years; **1999 Matanzas Creek,
Sonoma Valley** ★★★ $$$ dry, medium-bodied, light oak, high acidity,
drink now–6 years; **2000 Landmark Overlook, Sonoma County/
Monterey County** ★★★ $$ dry, medium-bodied, medium oak, medium
acidity, drink now–6 years; **2000 Acacia, Carneros** ★★ $$ dry, medium-
bodied, medium oak, high acidity, drink now–4 years; **2000 Cuvaison
Carneros, Napa Valley** ★★ $$ dry, medium-bodied, medium oak, high
acidity, drink now–3 years; **2000 Frog's Leap, Napa Valley** ★★ $$ dry,
medium-bodied, medium oak, medium acidity, drink now–4 years; **2000
Morgan, Monterey** ★★ $$ dry, medium-bodied, medium oak, medium
acidity, drink now–4 years; **2000 Meridian Vineyards, Santa Barbara
County** ★ $ dry, medium-bodied, medium oak, medium acidity, drink now

SAUVIGNON BLANC

Although Sauvignon Blanc has soared to exemplary heights in France's Loire Valley and New Zealand, it always earns silver to Chardonnay's gold in California. When good, California Sauvignon Blancs are wonderfully aromatic, with flavors that bring to mind freshly cut grass, honeydew melon, and lemon with mouth-tingling acidity. Oaked versions are often labeled Fumé Blanc, a moniker invented by Robert Mondavi in 1968 for his oak-aged Sauvignon Blanc, to evoke a connection with France's famed Pouilly-Fumé.

at the table

Light-bodied with lemony, herbal flavors and good acidity, Sauvignon Blanc is a natural with shellfish and mild fish like trout. For cheese, think light and fresh, such as an ash covered goat cheese. Richer Fumé Blanc requires something more assertive, smoky even, like grilled fish or vegetables.

the bottom line Frequently ignored in favor of Chardonnay, Sauvignon Blanc can be a bargain. Many non-oaked versions sell for $8 to $14; richer styles run $25 to $35.

recommended wines

**1999 Robert Mondavi Winery To Kalon Vineyard
Fumé Blanc Reserve, Napa Valley** ★★★★ $$$
dry, medium-bodied, medium oak, high acidity   drink now–8 years
One of the most luxurious Sauvignon Blancs available.

2001 Mietz, Sonoma County ★★★★ $$
dry, medium-bodied, no oak, high acidity   drink now–3 years
Bright, grassy, grapefruity notes play off golden apple richness. Exceptional.

2000 Chateau Potelle, Napa Valley ★★★ $$
dry, medium-bodied, no oak, medium acidity   drink now–4 years
Fruit flavors as bright as an Indian summer day. Delicious.

**2001 Dry Creek Vineyard DCV3 Fumé Blanc Limited Edition,
Dry Creek Valley** ★★★ $$
dry, medium-bodied, no oak, high acidity   drink now–4 years
Old vines bring intense flavors to this excellent Sauvignon Blanc.

29

california **whites**

2000 Duckhorn Vineyards, Napa Valley ★★★ $$
dry, medium-bodied, medium oak, medium acidity   drink now–6 years
Richly textured, with kiwi, berry, and grapefruit flavors.

**2000 Iron Horse Vineyards T bar T Vineyard Fumé Blanc Cuvée R,
Alexander Valley** ★★★ $$
dry, medium-bodied, no oak, high acidity   drink now–3 years
A dash of Viognier adds flower and spice notes to limey Sauvignon.

2000 Matanzas Creek Winery, Sonoma County ★★★ $$
dry, medium-bodied, no oak, high acidity   drink now–3 years
One of the state's best Sauvignon Blancs, with nut, lemon, and mineral flavors.

2000 Merryvale Juliana Vineyards, Napa Valley ★★★ $$
dry, medium-bodied, medium oak, medium acidity   drink now–4 years
As flinty and mineral-laden as Sauvignon Blanc from France's Loire Valley.

2000 Beckmen Vineyards Estate, Santa Ynez Valley ★★★ $
dry, medium-bodied, light oak, medium acidity   drink now–4 years
A wonderful blend of citrus and peach flavors joined by minerals.

2001 Navarro Vineyards, Mendocino ★★★ $
dry, medium-bodied, no oak, high acidity   drink now–5 years
Layers of fruit flavors make this a superbly enjoyable any-day favorite.

2000 Cakebread Cellars, Napa Valley ★★ $$
dry, medium-bodied, light oak, high acidity   drink now–3 years
Tropical fruit aromas speak of the islands, while grass and pine notes evoke
an alpine meadow.

2001 Eleven Oaks, Santa Barbara County ★★ $$
dry, medium-bodied, no oak, high acidity   drink now–3 years
Santa Barbara's cool climate is reflected in tangy citrus flavors.

2001 Frog's Leap Rutherford, Napa Valley ★★ $$
dry, medium-bodied, no oak, high acidity   drink now–2 years
Lemon augmented by yeasty flavors add up to a complex Sauvignon Blanc.

2001 Adler Fels, Russian River Valley ★★ $
dry, medium-bodied, no oak, high acidity   drink now–1 year
Grapefruit and light strawberry flavors joined by an appealing grassiness.

2000 Alderbrook, Dry Creek Valley ★★ $
dry, medium-bodied, no oak, medium acidity   drink now–2 years
A break from a world of herbal Sauvignon Blancs, this one offers pure, tropical
fruit scents and flavors.

2000 Fritz Winery, Sonoma County   ★★ $
dry, medium-bodied, no oak, medium acidity   drink now–5 years
A richer, more honeyed take on Sauvignon Blanc with marmalade-like flavors.

2000 Honig, Napa Valley   ★★ $
dry, medium-bodied, no oak, high acidity   drink now–3 years
Floral, green and yellow apple flavors, with a bit of spice and mineral make this (almost) like Sancerre.

2001 Kunde Magnolia Lane, Sonoma Valley   ★★ $
dry, medium-bodied, no oak, high acidity   drink now–2 years
Viognier adds the floral and minty flavors and Semillon the lushness to Sauvignon's citrusy oomph.

2000 Shenandoah Vineyards, Amador County   ★★ $
dry, medium-bodied, light oak, high acidity   drink now
Another treasure from California's Gold Country, with crisp fruit flavors that hint of smoke.

2001 Geyser Peak, California   ★ $
dry, medium-bodied, no oak, high acidity   drink now
Grassy and refreshingly crisp green apple flavors make this one to keep on hand in the fridge.

WINES WE WISH WE HAD MORE ROOM FOR
2000 Page Mill Winery French Camp Vineyard, San Luis Obispo County ★★★ $$ dry, medium-bodied, medium oak, medium acidity, drink now–8 years; **2001 Rochioli, Russian River Valley** ★★★ $$ dry, medium-bodied, no oak, high acidity, drink now–6 years; **2000 Flora Springs Soliloquy, Napa Valley** ★★ $$ dry, medium-bodied, no oak, high acidity, drink now–3 years; **2000 Beringer Appellation Collection, Napa Valley** ★★ $ dry, medium-bodied, light oak, medium acidity, drink now–4 years; **1999 Peirano Estate Vineyards, Lodi** ★ $ dry, medium-bodied, light oak, medium acidity, drink now–3 years

OTHER WHITE WINES

California winemakers are always experimenting with different grape varieties. Currently, the vogue is for grapes traditionally grown in France's Rhône Valley, such as Viognier, Marsanne, and Roussanne, which tend to produce heady, rich wines in the California climate. Pinot Blanc has also gained favor with the Chardonnay-like qualities (of the good sort) it attains in the Golden State, while Pinot Gris pleases with its dual personality:

luscious and spice-scented in the Alsatian style or light and fresh like Italy's Pinot Grigio, which is the same grape. On the other hand, Gewürztraminer, Riesling, and Chenin Blanc seem to be losing ground in California, even though they grow well in the state's cooler reaches.

at the table

The richness of Rhône-style wines complements full-flavored dishes like garlic-laced roast chicken or seafood stews like bouillabaisse. Pinots Blanc and Gris are excellent with grilled salmon or swordfish, lighter Pinot Grigios with steamed clams, while Rieslings and Gewürztraminers were made for Asian-inspired dishes.

the bottom line Good Rhône-style wines run from $12 to $25; a few luxury bottles can go as high as $70. Fine bottles of Chenin Blanc, Riesling, and Gewürztraminer often cost less than $12.

recommended wines

**2000 Navarro Vineyards Dry Gewürztraminer,
Anderson Valley** ★★★★ $
dry, light-bodied, no oak, high acidity   drink now–10 years
Tension to great effect—powerful floral, mineral, and fruit flavors at a standoff.

2000 Joseph Phelps Viognier, Napa Valley ★★★ $$$
dry, medium-bodied, light oak, high acidity   drink now–5 years
Phelps is a Rhône specialist, and it shows in the floral, mineral, fruit, and nut flavors of this Viognier.

**2000 Tablas Creek Vineyard Clos Blanc,
Paso Robles** ★★★ $$$
dry, medium-bodied, light oak, high acidity   drink now–6 years
The Perrin family of Châteauneuf-du-Pape fame grow this subtle, sophisticated blend of five Rhône varieties in south-central California.

2000 Caymus Conundrum, California ★★★ $$
dry, full-bodied, light oak, medium acidity   drink now–5 years
The macedoine of fruit flavors from this unique mix of grape varieties makes this one of California's most distinctive white wines.

2000 Equus Roussanne, Paso Robles ★★★ $$
dry, full-bodied, light oak, medium acidity   drink now–10 years
Honey-rich flavors with almonds and spice. Excellent.

2000 Freemark Abbey Carpy Ranch Viognier, Napa Valley ★★★ $$
dry, full-bodied, light oak, high acidity   drink now–8 years
Thick and rich, with nutty peach and marmalade-like flavors that last.

**2001 Iron Horse Vineyards T bar T Viognier,
Alexander Valley** ★★★ $$
dry, medium-bodied, no oak, high acidity   drink now–6 years
An exemplary California Viognier, full of fruit, mineral, and spice.

**2000 Long Vineyards Laird Family Vineyard Pinot Grigio,
Carneros** ★★★ $$
dry, medium-bodied, no oak, high acidity   drink now–3 years
One of the finest Pinot Grigios from California—or anywhere—with deep fruit
and mineral flavor.

2000 Rosenblum Cellars Marsanne, Dry Creek Valley ★★★ $$
dry, full-bodied, light oak, medium acidity   drink now–5 years
Luxuriously textured, this Marsanne evokes Provence with flavors of peach
jam and scents of lavender and herbs.

**2001 Au Bon Climat Bien Nacido Vineyard Pinot Gris-Pinot Blanc,
Santa Barbara County** ★★★ $
dry, medium-bodied, no oak, medium acidity   drink now–4 years
Pinots Blanc and Gris combine for a mélange of light fruit and mineral flavors.

2000 Chappellet Dry Chenin Blanc, Napa Valley ★★★ $
dry, medium-bodied, light oak, medium acidity   drink now–6 years
A delicate balance of citrus and apple flavors with peppery minerality.

**2000 Claiborne & Churchill Alsatian-Style Riesling,
Central Coast** ★★★ $
dry, medium-bodied, no oak, high acidity   drink now–10 years
Rarely is California Riesling so full of citrus, lime zest, and mineral flavors. Wow!

2000 Curtis Heritage Blanc, Santa Barbara County ★★★ $
dry, medium-bodied, no oak, medium acidity   drink now–3 years
A blend of Rhône grape varieties gives appealingly rich fruit flavors with a
honeyed, almond edge.

2000 Navarro Vineyards Dry Muscat Blanc, Mendocino ★★★ $
dry, light-bodied, no oak, high acidity   drink now–4 years
Impressively subdued Muscat, with subtle floral, citrus, and mineral flavors.

california **whites**

2001 Bonterra Vineyards Viognier, Mendocino County ★★ $$
dry, medium-bodied, light oak, high acidity   drink now–2 years
A touch of oak spices up this citrus- and peach-scented wine made from organically grown grapes.

2000 Borgo Buon Natale Primogénito/First Born,
Santa Maria Valley ★★$$
dry, medium-bodied, light oak, high acidity   drink now–4 years
Three Italian grapes, including Tocal Friulano, blend into a nutty, flinty, citrus-flavored pleasure.

2001 Qupé Marsanne, Santa Ynez Valley ★★ $$
dry, medium-bodied, no oak, high acidity   drink now–4 years
A spicy, aromatic wine, full of fruit and mineral flavors.

2001 Zaca Mesa Roussanne, Santa Ynez Valley ★★ $$
dry, medium-bodied, no oak, high acidity   drink now–5 years
Tropical fruit flavors from a Rhône variety via the jungles east of Santa Barbara.

2001 Babcock Pinot Grigio, Santa Barbara County ★★ $
dry, medium-bodied, no oak, high acidity   drink now–2 years
Juicy citrus flavors matched by racy acidity are softened by a smoky edge.

2001 Ca' del Solo Big House White, California ★★ $
dry, medium-bodied, no oak, high acidity   drink now–2 years
Juicy citrus, berry, and pear flavors from a unique blend of four grape varieties.

2001 Chateau St. Jean Gewürztraminer, Sonoma County ★★ $
dry, medium-bodied, no oak, high acidity   drink now
Zippy fruit and lightly floral flavors make this a good choice with Thai seafood dishes or curried scallops.

2001 Frog's Leap Leapfrögmilch, Napa Valley ★★ $
dry, medium-bodied, no oak, medium acidity   drink now–1 year
A playful blend of Riesling and Chardonnay offers a fruit basket of flavors.

2001 Ironstone Vineyards Symphony Obsession, California ★★ $
dry, light-bodied, no oak, high acidity   drink now
Symphony, a hybrid of Grenache Gris and Muscat of Alexandria, performs light, summery airs of lime and floral flavors here.

1999 Peirano Estate Vineyards Viognier, Lodi ★★ $
dry, full-bodied, light oak, high acidity   drink now–3 years
Here's a rare opportunity to enjoy the floral, peachy charms of Viognier at a relatively low cost.

2001 Wild Horse Malvasia Bianca, Monterey ★★ $
dry, light-bodied, no oak, high acidity   drink now–2 years
As light and refreshing as a Pacific breeze coming through the wildflower- and herb-laden hills of California's Central Coast.

WINES WE WISH WE HAD MORE ROOM FOR
2000 Bonny Doon Vineyard Viognier, California ★★★★ $$ dry, medium-bodied, light oak, high acidity, drink now–6 years; **2000 Sable Ridge Vineyards Viognier, Russian River Valley** ★★★ $$ dry, full-bodied, no oak, medium acidity, drink now–8 years; **2000 Navarro Vineyards White Riesling, Anderson Valley** ★★★ $ dry, medium-bodied, no oak, high acidity, drink now–8 years; **2000 La Famiglia di Robert Mondavi Pinot Grigio, California** ★★ $$ dry, medium-bodied, no oak, high acidity, drink now–1 year; **2001 Rancho Zabaco Reserve Pinot Gris, Sonoma Coast** ★★ $$ dry, medium-bodied, no oak, medium acidity, drink now–2 years; **2001 Adler Fels Gewürztraminer, Russian River Valley** ★★ $ off-dry, medium-bodied, no oak, medium acidity, drink now–2 years; **2001 Ca' del Solo Malvasia Bianca, Monterey** ★★ $ off-dry, medium-bodied, no oak, high acidity, drink now; **2001 Daniel Gehrs Chenin Blanc, Monterey County** ★★ $ dry, medium-bodied, no oak, high acidity, drink now–2 years; **2001 Dry Creek Vineyard Dry Chenin Blanc, Clarksburg** ★★ $ dry, light-bodied, no oak, medium acidity, drink now–1 year; **2000 Handley Gewürztraminer, Anderson Valley** ★★ $ dry, light-bodied, no oak, high acidity, drink now–3 years

rosé wines

While White Zinfandel is still the most popular pink wine in the U.S., there are many other choices. Rosés made from other grape varieties like Pinot Noir, Grenache, Sangiovese, and Carignane can be more than summertime thirst quenchers, with drier fruit flavors and a hint of spice.

at the table
Rosés are great summer aperitifs, but try them anytime with chicken fajitas or grilled shrimp. Take the more serious examples to the table over the holidays: they go exceptionally well with roast turkey and ham.

the bottom line Fine rosés run from $10 to $28.

recommended wines

2000 Tablas Creek Vineyard Rosé, Paso Robles ★★★★ $$$
dry, medium-bodied, high acidity   drink now–3 years
This rosé of Rhône grape varieties is one of California's best ever, with true cherry flavors, herb notes, and profound minerality.

2001 Iron Horse Vineyards T bar T Rosato dl Sanglovese, Alexander Valley ★★★ $$
dry, medium-bodied, medium acidity   drink now–2 years
Tart cherry flavors plus a twist of orange make a great summer sipper.

2001 Bonny Doon Vineyard Vin Gris de Cigare Pink Wine, California ★★ $
dry, medium-bodied, high acidity   drink now
Perfect sipping for UFO patrols on warm summer nights, with graceful fruit and flower flavors.

2001 Saintsbury Vin Gris of Pinot Noir, Carneros ★★ $
dry, medium-bodied, high acidity   drink now–2 years
This may be almost too red to be called rosé, yet its berry and citrus flavors are light and refreshing.

2000 Sanford Vin Gris Pinot Noir, Santa Barbara County ★★ $
dry, medium-bodied, medium acidity   drink now
Smoky, toasty, and deeply flavorful: a summer wine for hard-core Pinot lovers.

red wines

CABERNET & KIN, PLUS BORDEAUX BLENDS

In California, Cabernet Sauvignon is king. It produces the biggest, most tannic wines, with flavors that range from cassis to eucalyptus to tobacco and mint. Cabernets from Napa Valley and some parts of Sonoma rank among the best wines in the world. These can age beautifully for years, though the almost chewy texture of young Cabernet is prized by many. Cabernet Franc, a close relation also from Bordeaux, is a bit softer, with smoky fruit flavors and a note of black pepper. Winemakers frequently blend it with Cabernet Sauvignon to make a more complex wine, though increasingly they present Cabernet Franc by itself. Since the 1980s, many wineries use the term "Meritage" to identify blends of traditional Bordeaux grapes—the Cabernets often dominate, but they can include Merlot, Malbec, Petit Verdot, St. Macaire, Gros Verdot, and Carmenère. However, several top wineries such as Opus One and Dominus prefer to use their own proprietary names.

at the table
America's steak houses sell tremendous amounts of tannic Cabernets for good reason: they cry out for meat, grilled T-bones, sirloin strips, or prime rib. Vegetarians can pair Cabernets with grilled vegetable kebabs or portobello steaks.

the bottom line Paying court to kings is costly. Serviceable Cabernet Sauvignon starts at a little under $10, but the excitement begins at $30 and goes way up: the $100 bottle is not a rarity. Cabernet Franc is more modestly priced at $15 to $75. Blends can be found in all these ranges.

what to buy CABERNET SAUVIGNON

1997	1998	1999	2000	2001
★★★	★★★	★★	★★★	★★★

recommended cabernets

1998 Altamura, Napa Valley ★★★★ $$$$
dry, full-bodied, heavy tannin, medium acidity   drink in 2–12 years
Exceptionally good, with spicy fruit flavors encased by minerals.

1997 Heitz Cellar Martha's Vineyard, Napa Valley ★★★★ $$$$
dry, full-bodied, heavy tannin, high acidity   drink in 2–15 years
Martha's Vineyard was replanted several years ago because of phylloxera, but Heitz's example, in its second year back, is as great as in years past.

1999 Kathryn Kennedy Winery, Santa Cruz Mountains ★★★★ $$$$
dry, full-bodied, heavy tannin, medium acidity   drink in 2–10 years
Full of fragrant blueberry flavors with spicy oak and bitter herb notes.

california **reds**

1998 Peju Province Reserve Rutherford, Napa Valley ★★★★ $$$$
dry, medium-bodied, medium tannin, medium acidity drink 1–10 years
Napa Cabernet with Provençal flair; wild herb notes augment its berry flavors.

1999 Ridge Monte Bello, California ★★★★ $$$$
dry, full-bodied, heavy tannin, high acidity drink in 2–20 years
Pine and cedar aromas waft through a sea of wild berries.

1998 Arns, Napa Valley ★★★ $$$$
dry, medium-bodied, heavy tannin, medium acidity drink in 1–10 years
A deliciously juicy cabernet with nutty nuances from Sandi Belcher, winemaker
for Long Vineyards.

**1999 B.R. Cohn Special Selection Olive Hill Estate Vineyards,
Sonoma Valley** ★★★ $$$$
dry, full-bodied, full tannin, medium acidity drink in 1–10 years
Deep blackberry flavors with earthy Mediterranean—even olive—notes.

1998 Chateau Potelle Mt. Veeder, Napa Valley ★★★ $$$$
dry, full-bodied, heavy tannin, medium acidity drink in 3–12 years
Mountain-grown fruit makes for intense smoke, mineral, and black cherry flavors.

1998 Far Niente, Napa Valley ★★★ $$$$
dry, full-bodied, medium tannin, medium acidity drink in 3–15 years
Dusty cassis, sweet wood, and vanilla flavors combine in excellent balance.

1999 Flora Springs Wild Boar Vineyard, Napa Valley ★★★ $$$$
dry, full-bodied, heavy tannin, medium acidity drink in 2–12 years
The lavender's in bloom in this dense wine, full of floral and ripe cassis flavors
with spicy oak.

**1997 Freemark Abbey Sycamore Vineyards,
Napa Valley** ★★★ $$$$
dry, full-bodied, medium tannin, high acidity drink in 1–12 years
This big, dense cabernet, structured to age, is one of the better '97 examples.

1998 Gallo of Sonoma Estate, Northern Sonoma ★★★ $$$$
dry, full-bodied, heavy tannin, medium acidity drink in 2–15 years
Great Cabernet flavors are all present and accounted for, but this will only get
better with time.

**1999 Kathryn Kennedy Winery Small Lot Cabernet,
Santa Cruz Mountains** ★★★ $$$$
dry, full-bodied, medium tannin, high acidity drink in 1–10 years
This has all the violet-scented, blackberry, mineral, and spicy flavors that most
"banner" Cabs would love to claim.

1998 Robert Mondavi Winery Reserve, Napa Valley ★★★ $$$$
dry, full-bodied, heavy tannin, medium acidity   drink in 2–15 years
Classic Napa Cabernet, with cassis, chocolate, and black pepper flavors in perfect harmony.

1998 Silver Oak, Alexander Valley ★★★ $$$$
dry, full-bodied, full tannin, medium acidity   drink in 2–12 years
Silver Oak's trademark herbaceousness melds into lush cherry-vanilla flavors.

1998 Arrowood, Sonoma County ★★★ $$$
dry, full-bodied, heavy tannin, medium acidity drink in 1–10 years
A study in black: black fruit, black mineral, black smoke.

1999 Chimney Rock, Stags Leap District ★★★ $$$
dry, full-bodied, medium tannin, medium acidity   drink now–10 years
Rich and spicy as a Christmas pudding, yet as graceful as a stag leaping through the woods.

1999 Duckhorn Vineyards, Napa Valley ★★★ $$$
dry, full-bodied, medium tannin, medium acidity   drink now–10 years
So beautifully balanced with fruit, oak, and mineral flavors, it's hard to believe this is Duckhorn's most modest Cabernet.

1998 Grgich Hills, Napa Valley ★★★ $$$
dry, full-bodied, heavy tannin, high acidity   drink in 3–12 years
Beautifully balanced Cabernet, full of dark berry and smoky tobacco flavors.

A GLASS (OR TWO) A DAY WILL KEEP THE DOCTOR AWAY

The French paradox is old news, but reports supporting the health benefits of wine continue to pour in. One study claims red wine can prevent the development of tumors; another says moderate consumption can prevent dementia in the elderly, and yet another suggests that wine-drinking women suffer strokes less frequently. How much to drink? Well, one to three glasses per day is said to reduce the risk of osteoporosis in elderly women (though more than three glasses has the opposite effect), and white wine drinkers have healthier lungs. All impressive claims. But none beat a Spanish report that suggests that people who drink fourteen glasses of red wine a week are 40 percent less likely to catch the common cold.

39

california **reds**

1999 Groth Oakville, Napa Valley ★★★ $$$
dry, full-bodied, heavy tannin, medium acidity   drink now–10 years
Groth's basic Cabernet might be lighter than their reserve, but with a berry patch of flavors, no one is complaining.

1999 Joseph Phelps Vineyards, Napa Valley ★★★ $$$
dry, full-bodied, medium tannin, medium acidity   drink in 2–8 years
More affordable than Phelp's Insignia, yet just as delicious.

1998 Markham, Napa Valley ★★★ $$$
dry, medium-bodied, heavy tannin, high acidity   drink now–5 years
Absolutely delicious, full of zesty black cherry flavors and a little spice.

1999 Newton Unfiltered, Napa Valley ★★★ $$$
dry, full-bodied, heavy tannin, medium acidity   drink in 2–10 years
Full, rich cassis flavors are supported by smooth mineral notes.

1999 Provenance Vineyards Rutherford, Napa Valley ★★★ $$$
dry, full-bodied, heavy tannin, medium acidity   drink in 2–10 years
Great Napa fruit flavors joined by a "dusty" mineral quality typical of wines from Rutherford.

1999 Shafer, Napa Valley ★★★ $$$
dry, full-bodied, heavy tannin, high acidity   drink in 2–12 years
Roasted coffee, meat, and pepper notes join sweet berry and vanilla flavors.

1998 Stuhlmuller Vineyards, Alexander Valley ★★★ $$$
dry, full-bodied, full tannin, high acidity   drink in 2–15 years
With plenty of acidity and ripe fruit flavors, this is a beautifully balanced wine.

1999 Laurel Glen Counterpoint, Sonoma Mountain ★★★ $$
dry, medium-bodied, heavy tannin, medium acidity drink in 2–10 years
Earthy, with excellent fruit flavors harmonized by lots of minerals and herbs.

1998 Burgess, Napa Valley ★★ $$$
dry, medium-bodied, medium tannin, medium acidity drink now–10 years
A mineral-laden, blackberry nectar with lots of finesse.

1999 Cakebread Cellars, Napa Valley ★★ $$$
dry, full-bodied, heavy tannin, medium acidity   drink in 2–10 years
Wait for the tannins to soften, and the cassis and mineral flavors will show more clearly.

1997 Kunde Estate Winery, Sonoma Valley ★★ $$$
dry, full-bodied, heavy tannin, medium acidity   drink 1–8 years
Brown sugar and bitter mineral notes spice up cassis and blackberry flavors.

1999 Merryvale Reserve, Napa Valley ★★ $$$
dry, medium-bodied, heavy tannin, medium acidity drink in 2–10 years
Meaty berry and green peppercorn flavors suggest a match with steak *au poivre.*

1997 Rodney Strong Reserve, Northern Sonoma ★★ $$$
dry, full-bodied, heavy tannin, high acidity drink now–8 years
Right on the mark, with dense berry, mint, coffee, and mineral flavors.

**2000 Alexander Valley Vineyards Weitzel Family Estate,
Alexander Valley** ★★ $$
dry, medium-bodied, medium tannin, high acidity drink now–6 years
Ready for dinner this evening, with fine fruit flavors balanced by high acidity.

1999 Arrowood Grand Archer, Sonoma County ★★ $$
dry, full-bodied, medium tannin, medium acidity drink now–8 years
Classical California Cabernet for a good price.

1999 Beaulieu Vineyard, Rutherford ★★ $$
dry, full-bodied, heavy tannin, medium acidity drink in 2–10 years
A classic that never seems dated, BV's Rutherford offers all the herbal, cassis,
and peppery flavors you could ask from Cabernet.

1999 Carmenet Winery Dynamite, North Coast ★★ $$
dry, medium-bodied, heavy tannin, high acidity drink now–5 years
Moderately priced, well made Cabernet, fine for everyday.

1999 Clos du Bois Reserve, Alexander Valley ★★ $$
dry, medium-bodied, medium tannin, medium acidity drink now–8 years
Textbook Cabernet, with black currant, green peppercorn, and herb flavors.

1999 Kendall-Jackson Vintner's Reserve, California ★★ $$
dry, medium-bodied, medium tannin, medium acidity drink now–5 years
Easy to find, easy to drink. Good Cab for the money.

1999 Rutherford Hill, Napa Valley ★★ $$
dry, full-bodied, full tannin, medium acidity drink in 1–10 years
Lavender notes thread through juicy black berry fruit, chunky with tannin.

1999 Simi, Sonoma County ★★ $$
dry, full-bodied, heavy tannin, medium acidity drink in 3–10 years
Give Simi's famously tough-tannined Cabernet time so that its dense, delicious fruit flavors can emerge.

2000 Echelon, California ★★ $
dry, medium-bodied, medium tannin, medium acidity drink now–5 years
A lot of Cabernet for not a lot of money.

IS IT THE DE-PROGRAMMERS, OR IS IT THE ECONOMY?

Until the economy slowed last year, bands of oenophiles whispered names like Harlan, Colgin, Dalle Valle, Marcassin, Pahlmeyer, and Screaming Eagle with a reverence usually reserved for God and Country. With exceptionally concentrated flavors and miniscule quantities —often just a few hundred cases a year—these wines gathered cultlike followings. To indulge, one either had to join an impossible-to-get-on mailing list or shell out big bucks at auction. But, as the fast cash days of the nineties and early zeros came to an end, the buzz was off. This isn't to say that they've gone on sale—miniscule supplies assure that won't happen. But, as restaurateurs across the U.S. report, people just don't ask for them like they used to.

1999 Foppiano Family Riverside Collection, California ★★ $
dry, medium-bodied, medium tannin, medium acidity   drink now–4 years
Fun, fruity wine with a peak of summer cherry flavors and pretty floral notes.

1999 Hess Select, California ★★ $
dry, medium-bodied, medium tannin, medium acidity   drink now–3 years
With juicy, tart cherry flavors and an appealing bitterness, this ranks among California's best-value Cabernets.

1999 Fetzer Vineyards Valley Oaks, California ★ $
dry, medium-bodied, medium tannin, medium acidity   drink now–3 years
Always reliable, always a good value.

1999 Talus, California ★ $
dry, medium-bodied, medium tannin, high acidity   drink now–5 years
Have this fruity, affordable Cabernet on hand for a simple, mid-week steak.

WINES WE WISH WE HAD MORE ROOM FOR
1998 Groth Reserve Oakville, Napa Valley ★★★★ $$$$ dry, full-bodied, heavy tannin, medium acidity, drink in 2–12 years; **1998 Clos du Val Reserve, Napa Valley** ★★★ $$$$ dry, full-bodied, medium tannin, medium acidity, drink in 1–8 years; **1999 Flora Springs Rutherford Hillside Reserve, Napa Valley** ★★★ $$$$ dry, full-bodied, heavy tannin, medium acidity, drink in 1–10 years; **1998 Sterling Reserve, Napa Valley** ★★★ $$$$ dry, full-bodied, medium tannin, medium acidity, drink now–12 years; **1999 Stonestreet, Alexander Valley** ★★★ $$$ dry,

medium-bodied, heavy tannin, medium acidity, drink in 2–10 years; **1998 William Hill Winery Reserve, Napa Valley** ★★★ $$$ dry, full-bodied, medium tannin, medium acidity, drink now–8 years; **1999 Byington Bates Ranch Vineyard, Santa Cruz Mountains** ★★ $$$ dry, full-bodied, heavy tannin, high acidity, drink in 2–10 years; **1999 Robert Mondavi Winery, Napa Valley** ★★ $$$ dry, medium-bodied, heavy tannin, medium acidity, drink in 1–8 years; **1998 Gallo of Sonoma, Sonoma County** ★★ $ dry, full-bodied, heavy tannin, high acidity, drink now–6 years; **1999 Estancia, California** ★ $$ dry, medium-bodied, medium tannin, medium acidity, drink now–5 years

recommended bordeaux blends

1998 Dalla Valle Vineyards Maya, Napa Valley　　★★★★ $$$$
dry, full-bodied, medium tannin, medium acidity　drink now–10 years
Despite the "difficult" vintage (per California standards), Dalla Valle turned out one of the year's best wines, with remarkably ripe fruit and finesse.

1999 Joseph Phelps Insignia, Napa Valley　　★★★★ $$$$
dry, full-bodied, heavy tannin, high acidity　drink in 2–12 years
What to get for the woman who has everything? A wine with everything.

1999 Rudd Jericho Canyon Vineyard, Napa Valley　★★★★ $$$$
dry, full-bodied, heavy tannin, medium acidity　drink in 2–12 years
A Bordeaux blend smoky with earth, herb, and tobacco notes, yet bursting with succulent fruit flavor.

1997 Beringer Howell Mountain Third Century Cabernet Franc, Napa Valley　　★★★ $$$$
dry, full-bodied, heavy tannin, high acidity　drink in 2–10 years
An imposing wine in an imposing bottle, this offers the typically intense flavor and tannin of Howell Mountain fruit—and more.

1998 Cain Five, Napa Valley　　★★★ $$$$
dry, full-bodied, heavy tannin, medium acidity　drink in 3–10 years
A steakhouse favorite, this will be even better after a few years, when the tannins soften and let the nutty blueberry flavors emerge.

1999 Colgin Cariad, Napa Valley　　★★★ $$$$
dry, full-bodied, heavy tannin, medium acidity　drink in 1–10 years
Another beautifully balanced, very limited production gem from Anne Colgin, with tons of peppery berry and herb flavors.

california **reds**

1999 Dominus Napanook, Napa Valley   ★ ★ ★ $$$$
dry, full-bodied, heavy tannin, medium acidity   drink in 2–10 years
Surprisingly earthy flavors give the second wine from the Bordelais-owned Dominus a compelling edge.

1999 Flora Springs Trilogy, Napa Valley   ★ ★ ★ $$$$
dry, full-bodied, medium tannin, high acidity   drink in 2–10 years
Elegant and mouthwateringly juicy, this is full of berry flavors infused with the scents of fresh cut cedar.

1998 Frog's Leap, Rutherford   ★ ★ ★ $$$$
dry, medium-bodied, medium tannin, high acidity   drink now–8 years
Frogs leap over vine; grapes ripen under sun; juicy berry flavors drip; great wine is certain.

1999 M. Consentino M. Coz Meritage, Napa Valley   ★ ★ ★ $$$$
dry, full-bodied, medium tannin, medium acidity   drink now–7 years
An almost viscous wave of black fruit flavor with herbal and floral notes that keep on coming.

1998 Geyser Peak Reserve Alexandre Meritage, Alexander Valley   ★ ★ ★ $$$
dry, full-bodied, full tannin, full acidity   drink in 2–12 years
Australian Daryl Groom, Geyser Peak's winemaker, makes a big and bold wine full of dark berry, violet, cedar, and mineral flavors.

1999 Justin Vineyards & Winery Isosceles, Paso Robles   ★ ★ ★ $$$
dry, full-bodied, heavy tannin, high acidity   drink in 1–8 years
A Bordeaux blend with a Pythagorean harmony of dark berry, chocolate, and toasted almond notes.

1998 Chateau St. Jean Cinq Cépages, Sonoma County   ★ ★ ★ $$
dry, full-bodied, heavy tannin, medium acidity   drink in 2–8 years
Cabernet supported by four other Bordeaux varieties creates a big, structured wine, full of mineral and berry flavors.

1999 Bedford Thompson Cabernet Franc, Santa Barbara County   ★ ★ $$
dry, medium-bodied, medium tannin, high acidity   drink now–5 years
Peppery herbal notes ride a lush, satiny wave of red cherry flavor. Terrific wine.

1999 Estancia Meritage, Alexander Valley   ★ ★ $$
dry, full-bodied, heavy tannin, high acidity   drink now–6 years
Consistently one of the better values in California Meritage, this takes a turn toward the exotic, with mulberry and sweet spice flavors.

**1999 Ironstone Vineyards Reserve Cabernet Franc,
Sierra Foothills** ★★ $$
dry, full-bodied, medium tannin, medium acidity   drink now–6 years
Good Cabernet Franc in the Bordeaux style, with smooth, peppery, berry flavors.

**2000 Kendall-Jackson Collage Cabernet Sauvignon-Merlot,
California** ★ $
dry, medium-bodied, medium tannin, medium acidity   drink now–2 years
Pleasant fruit flavors presented in a light, claretlike weight.

WINES WE WISH WE HAD MORE ROOM FOR

1999 Lail Vineyards J. Daniel Cuvée, Napa Valley ★★★★ $$$$ dry, full-bodied, medium tannin, medium acidity, drink in 1–10 years; **1999 Cardinale Napa County, Sonoma County** ★★★ $$$$ dry, full-bodied, heavy tannin, medium acidity, drink in 2–10 years; **1999 Chimney Rock Elevage Stags Leap District, Napa Valley** ★★★ $$$$ dry, full-bodied, heavy tannin, high acidity, drink in 2–10 years; **1999 Iron Horse Vineyards Benchmark T bar T, Alexander Valley** ★★★ $$$$ dry, full-bodied, medium tannin, medium acidity, drink in 1–10 years; **1998 Opus One, Napa Valley** ★★★ $$$$ dry, medium-bodied, full tannin, full acidity, drink in 1–12 years; **1998 St. Supéry Meritage, Napa Valley** ★★★ $$$ dry, medium-bodied, medium tannin, medium acidity, drink now–6 years; **1999 Decoy Migration, Napa Valley** ★★★ $$ dry, full-bodied, heavy tannin, high acidity, drink in 1–8 years; **1999 Geyser Peak Winemaker's Selection Petit Verdot, Alexander Valley** ★★★ $$ dry, full-bodied, medium tannin, high acidity, drink now–6 years; **1998 Beringer Alluvium, Knights Valley** ★★ $$$ dry, medium-bodied, medium tannin, high acidity, drink now–6 years; **1998 Lambert Bridge Crane Creek Cuvée, Dry Creek Valley** ★★ $$$ dry, full-bodied, heavy tannin, high acidity, drink in 1–10 years

MERLOT

Softer and more velvety than Cabernet Sauvignon, Merlot is extremely popular for its plummy, chocolaty, violet-scented profile. Winegrowers love Merlot because it ripens early, making it less susceptible to unpredictable autumn weather. Restaurateurs love it because it is usually easy to drink upon release, minimizing the need for costly storage facilities. Consumers love it because the bottle they pick up at the store is enjoyable at home that night, and there are so many styles that there's a Merlot for everything, from burgers to prime rib. Some people even like it with chocolate desserts. Today, it's hard to believe that twenty years ago Merlot was most commonly blended into Cabernet.

california **reds**

at the table
Velvety Merlot goes well with steaks and roasted game, but also with lighter meats such as pork and veal, especially if braised in red wine, or roasted with dark fruits like figs or prunes.

the bottom line A $10 Merlot can be perfectly decent, but cross the $20 mark to find excellence and $35 to near the realm of greatness. Prices range into the triple digits.

what to buy MERLOT

1998	1999	2000	2001
★★★	★★★	★★★	★★

recommended wines

1999 Shafer, Napa Valley　　　　　　　　　★★★★ $$$
dry, full-bodied, medium tannin, medium acidity　　drink now–10 years
A wine so delicious you almost won't want to swallow.

1999 Chappellet, Napa Valley　　　　　　　★★★★ $$
dry, full-bodied, medium tannin, medium acidity　　drink in 1–10 years
The red fruit and cedar flavors of this Merlot could move one to ecstasy.

1999 Cosentino Estate Oakville, Napa Valley　　★★★ $$$$
dry, medium-bodied, medium tannin, high acidity　　drink now–6 years
Generous fruit flavors have the hypnotic perfume of smoldering frankincense.

**1999 Nickel & Nickel Suscol Ranch,
Napa Valley**　　　　　　　　　　　　　　　★★★ $$$$
dry, full-bodied, medium tannin, high acidity　　drink in 2–10 years
Black fruit flavors with peppery bitter herb notes are unusual but delicious.

1999 Arrowood, Sonoma County　　　　　　★★★ $$$
dry, full-bodied, heavy tannin, medium acidity　　drink now–8 years
Muscled Merlot, with soft, dark plum flavors bulked up with tarry tannin and deep mineral notes.

1999 Duckhorn Vineyards, Napa Valley　　　★★★ $$$
dry, full-bodied, medium tannin, medium acidity　　drink now–10 years
As with all of Duckhorn's Merlots, their basic bottling is superbly made, with deep fruit flavors and complex structure.

1999 Kendall-Jackson Great Estates,
Sonoma County   ★★★ $$$
dry, full-bodied, heavy tannin, high acidity   **drink now–8 years**
Kendall-Jackson goes for the throat with big, blackberry flavors, lots of spice
and a brass-knuckled punch of minerality.

1999 Matanzas Creek Winery, Sonoma County   ★★★ $$$
dry, full-bodied, medium tannin, medium acidity   **drink now–10 years**
Smooth as velvet and provocatively flavored. Seduction in a bottle.

1999 Newton Unfiltered, Napa Valley   ★★★ $$$
dry, full-bodied, medium tannin, high acidity   **drink in 1–8 years**
Not for the faint-of-heart, this offers an abundance of blackberry flavors, with
appealing bitter chocolate and mineral notes.

1999 St. Clement, Napa Valley   ★★★ $$$
dry, full-bodied, medium tannin, medium acidity   **drink now–6 years**
Black cherry and spice flavors with impressive restraint.

1999 Stonestreet, Alexander Valley   ★★★ $$$
dry, full-bodied, heavy tannin, high acidity   **drink in 2–10 years**
Merlot with finesse, with flavors that range from blackberry to coffee to cedar
and spice.

1999 Clos du Val, Napa Valley   ★★★ $$
dry, medium-bodied, medium tannin, high acidity   **drink in 1–10 years**
No flash, just solid Merlot *à la bordelaise*.

1999 Lambert Bridge, Sonoma County   ★★★ $$
dry, full-bodied, heavy tannin, medium acidity   **drink in 2–10 years**
One of the best from Lambert Bridge in over a decade, with dark fruit and
spice flavors plus earthy mineral notes.

1999 Mietz Cellars, Sonoma County   ★★★ $$
dry, full-bodied, medium tannin, high acidity   **drink in 2–10 years**
A well-crafted Merlot whose berry flavors are joined by herbs, minerals, and a
bit of spice.

1999 Page Mill Winery, Napa Valley   ★★★ $$
dry, medium-bodied, medium tannin, high acidity   **drink now–8 years**
Beautiful, if not classic, this Merlot offers delicious and unusual flavors of
hazelnut, peach, and vanilla.

1998 Chalk Hill, Sonoma County   ★★ $$$$
dry, full-bodied, heavy tannin, medium acidity   **drink in 1–10 years**
A solid wine with tart fruit, lots of minerals and herb flavors.

47

california**reds**

1999 Beringer Appellation Collection, Napa Valley ★★ $$$
dry, medium-bodied, medium tannin, medium acidity   drink now–5 years
Beringer makes better Merlot, but this one can't be beat for good fruit flavors
and a bit of spice at the price.

1999 Robert Mondavi Winery, Napa Valley ★★ $$$
dry, medium-bodied, medium tannin, medium acidity   drink now–8 years
Give this time in the glass to show off its great berry, spice, and mineral flavors.

1998 Raymond Reserve, Napa Valley ★★ $$
dry, medium-bodied, medium tannin, medium acidity   drink now–6 years
Plum pudding in a bottle, with spicy, juicy black plum flavors kissed with vanilla.

1999 Rutherford Hill, Napa Valley ★★ $$
dry, full-bodied, medium tannin, medium acidity   drink now–8 years
Merlot provides smooth dark fruit flavors, with a touch of Cabernet Franc, Petit
Verdot, and oak to spice things up.

1999 Sterling Vineyards, Napa Valley ★★ $$
dry, full-bodied, medium tannin, medium acidity   drink now–8 years
Loads of berry flavors laden with spicy oak and a touch of coconut.

2000 Fetzer Vineyards Eagle Peak, California ★ $
dry, medium-bodied, medium tannin, medium acidity   drink now–2 years
Simple, easy-to-drink Merlot.

1999 Glass Mountain Quarry, California ★ $
dry, medium-bodied, medium tannin, high acidity   drink now–2 years
A fine, everyday wine, with soft, juicy flavors to complement anything from
BLTs to pasta and meat sauce.

WINES WE WISH WE HAD MORE ROOM FOR

1998 Markham Reserve, Napa Valley ★★★ $$$ dry, full-bodied,
medium tannin, medium acidity, drink now–7 years; **2000 Flora Springs
Estate, Napa Valley** ★★★ $$ dry, medium-bodied, medium tannin, high
acidity, drink now–6 years; **1999 Alexander Valley Vineyards Wetzel
Family Estate, Alexander Valley** ★★ $$ dry, medium-bodied, medium
tannin, medium acidity, drink now–4 years; **1998 Jepson, Mendocino
County** ★★ $$ dry, medium-bodied, medium tannin, medium acidity, drink
now–5 years; **1999 Rodney Strong, Sonoma County** ★★ $$ dry, full-
bodied, heavy tannin, medium acidity, drink now–5 years; **1999 Beringer
Founders Estate, California** ★ $ dry, medium-bodied, medium tannin,
medium acidity, drink now–2 years; **1999 Meridian Vineyards, California**
★ $ dry, medium-bodied, medium tannin, medium acidity, drink now–4
years; **1999 Talus, California** ★ $ dry, medium-bodied, medium tannin,
medium acidity, drink now

PINOT NOIR

There's an irony in the world of wine: grapes grown in the best, most fertile soils and warmer weather usually don't make very good wine. In California, this dictum is most true of the noble grape of Burgundy, Pinot Noir. The weather's just too good, and winemakers have been experimenting for ways to mitigate this "good" for the last few decades. In their struggles, a few things have become clear: One, that Pinot does best in cooler parts of the state like Santa Barbara, Sonoma's Russian River Valley, and Carneros. Two, that Pinot Noir in California will never be the same as it is in Burgundy; and three, that's all right, because California Pinots have their own appealing characteristics.

at the table

Pinot Noir offers a solution when everyone at the table has ordered something different. Light- to medium-bodied with firm but not chewy tannins, Pinot Noir pairs well with everything from salmon to lamb to roast duck. Vegetarian red wine lovers have no better friend.

the bottom line
Since Pinot Noir is fickle and difficult to grow, there isn't much bargain Pinot Noir. Plan to spend around $25, and up to $75 for the most exceptional examples.

what to buy PINOT NOIR

1997	1998	1999	2000	2001
★★★	★★	★★	★★★	★★★

recommended wines

2000 David Bruce Brosseau Vineyard, Chalone   ★★★★ $$$
dry, medium-bodied, medium tannin, medium acidity   drink now–10 years
Summer in a glass, with silky, fresh black cherry and raspberry flavors.

**1999 Flowers Vineyard & Winery Camp Meeting Ridge,
Sonoma Coast**   ★★★★ $$$
dry, full-bodied, medium tannin, medium acidity   drink now–10 years
Power and finesse culminate in satiny berry flavors with lovely floral vanilla notes and peppery tannin.

california**reds**

1999 Sanford Sanford & Benedict Vineyard,
Santa Barbara County ★ ★ ★ ★ $$$
dry, full-bodied, medium tannin, high acidity   **drink in 2–12 years**
If you love richly flavored Pinot with lots of finesse, this wine is for you.

2000 Au Bon Climat La Bauge Au-Dessus Bien Nacido Vineyard,
Santa Maria Valley ★ ★ ★ ★ $$
dry, medium-bodied, medium tannin, medium acidity   drink now–8 years
One of California's finest Pinot Noirs, with deep, beautifully balanced fruit, floral,
and herb flavors.

1999 Rutz Cellars Maison Grand Cru,
Russian River Valley ★ ★ ★ ★ $$
dry, medium-bodied, medium tannin, medium acidity   drink now–10 years
The time Keith Rutz spends in Burgundy as a *négociant* seems to have rubbed
off on this elegant California Pinot Noir.

2000 Gary Farrell Rochioli-Allen Vineyards,
Russian River Valley ★ ★ ★ $$$$
dry, medium-bodied, medium tannin, medium acidity   drink now–10 years
Fine, tart cherry flavors mingle with smoke in this fine wine from a great Pinot
Noir producer.

2000 Iron Horse Vineyards Thomas Road, Green Valley ★ ★ ★ $$$$
dry, medium-bodied, medium tannin, high acidity   drink now–10 years
Seductive, smooth cherry flavors are spiced up by black pepper notes.

1999 Saintsbury Reserve, Carneros ★ ★ ★ $$$$
dry, medium-bodied, medium tannin, medium acidity   drink now–10 years
Long a California Pinot leader, Saintsbury's Reserve lives up to its name with
delicious blackberry and dry orange peel flavors.

1999 Cambria Bench Break Vineyard, Santa Maria Valley ★ ★ ★ $$$
dry, medium-bodied, medium tannin, medium acidity   drink now–6 years
Salt and pepper notes provide a spicy balance for this berry-filled Pinot Noir.

2000 Chalone Vineyard, Chalone ★ ★ ★ $$$
dry, medium-bodied, medium tannin, high acidity   drink now–5 years
Chalone created an appellation with the quality of its Pinot Noir, impressively
balanced between fruit and mineral flavors.

2000 Foxen Vineyard Julia's Vineyard,
Santa Maria Valley ★ ★ ★ $$$
dry, full-bodied, medium tannin, high acidity   drink now–8 years
This earthy, fruity, herbal wine demonstrates what's possible from Santa
Barbara County's oldest Pinot Noir vineyard.

VINEYARD DESIGNATIONS

European winemakers have long been labeling their wines with vineyard names, recognizing that certain vineyards make wine of different or better quality than others in the same area. In the U.S., however, the idea was slow to catch on, until recently. Now, California winemakers seem to be slapping vineyard names on labels as quickly as they can. In theory, the concept is sound: grapes grown in different vineyards, with soils of different structure and mineral content and with slopes of varying degrees, exposure to sun, altitude, and temperature will logically taste different. But vineyard boundaries aren't always determined by geological or topographic concerns; sometimes zoning laws and real estate markets make the call. In addition, some famous vineyards, like Santa Barbara's Bien Nacido, cover hundreds of acres that encompass many microclimates and soil types. Given California's seismic instability, soil types can differ tremendously within a few feet. The lesson? Be open minded, but buyer beware.

1999 Landmark Grand Detour Van der Kamp Vineyards, Sonoma Mountain ★★★ $$$
dry, medium-bodied, medium tannin, high acidity   drink now–6 years
Aromatherapy in a glass, this is overflowing with floral scents and spicy baked cherry flavors.

1999 Robert Mondavi Winery, Carneros ★★★ $$$
dry, medium-bodied, medium tannin, medium acidity   drink now–8 years
Carneros's cool climate shows in the elegant red berry and smoky, roselike flavors of this Pinot Noir.

2000 Rochioli, Russian River Valley ★★★ $$$
dry, medium-bodied, medium tannin, medium acidity   drink now–10 years
With raspberry fruit flavors laden with minerals, Rochioli's Pinot Noir offers French finesse with robust California fruit.

1999 Thomas Fogarty Estate Reserve, Santa Cruz Mountains ★★★ $$$
dry, full-bodied, medium tannin, medium acidity   drink now–12 years
The strong cassis and dark cherry aromas may recall Cabernet, but one taste says Pinot Noir all over.

california**reds**

2000 Babcock Grand Cuvée, Santa Ynez Valley ★★★ $$
dry, full-bodied, medium tannin, medium acidity   drink now–10 years
Grand indeed, with juicy dark fruit coupled with smoke, herb, and mineral flavors.

1999 Foppiano Vineyards, Russian River Valley ★★★ $$
dry, medium-bodied, full tannin, medium acidity   drink now–12 years
Good fruit flavors, with smoky black tea and mineral notes and enough tannin
to take on braised lamb shanks.

2000 Handley, Anderson Valley ★★★ $$
dry, medium-bodied, medium tannin, high acidity   drink now–6 years
Lavender and rich plum flavors with spicy mineral notes from one of
California's best Pinot Noir regions.

**2000 Joseph Swan Vineyards Cuvée de Trois,
Russian River Valley** ★★★ $$
dry, medium-bodied, medium tannin, medium acidity   drink now–8 years
Seductive fruit flavors piqued with herbal, menthol qualities make this Pinot
impossible to resist.

2000 La Crema, Sonoma Coast ★★★ $$
dry, medium-bodied, medium tannin, high acidity   drink now–6 years
Cherry flavors and smoky, baconlike notes are balanced by high acidity.

**1999 Navarro Vineyards Méthode à l'Ancienne,
Anderson Valley** ★★★ $$
dry, medium-bodied, medium tannin, medium acidity   drink now–8 years
Tasty now, give this a little time for the bright cherry and walnutlike flavors to
really come into their own.

2000 Domaine Carneros, Carneros ★★ $$$
dry, medium-bodied, medium tannin, high acidity   drink now–5 years
Domaine Carneros's French heritage shows in the Burgundian restraint of this
Pinot, but not in its price.

1999 Robert Mondavi Winery, Napa Valley ★★ $$
dry, medium-bodied, medium tannin, high acidity   drink now–6 years
Classic California Pinot, finely balanced and true to type.

2000 Meridian Vineyards, Santa Barbara County ★★ $
dry, medium-bodied, medium tannin, high acidity   drink now–3 years
Good, fresh Pinot for a good price.

2000 Bouchaine B, California ★ $$
dry, medium-bodied, medium tannin, medium acidity   drink now–3 years
Fine Pinot flavor at a reasonable price.

**2000 Turning Leaf Coastal Reserve,
North Coast** ★ $
dry, medium-bodied, medium tannin, high acidity   drink now–2 years
Cherry and spice at a nice price.

2000 Acacia Carneros District, Napa Valley ★★ $$$ dry, medium-bodied, medium tannin, medium acidity, drink now–5 years; **2000 Byron, Santa Maria Valley** ★★ $$ dry, medium-bodied, medium tannin, medium acidity, drink now–5 years; **2000 Cuvaison, Carneros, Napa Valley,** ★★ $$ dry, medium-bodied, medium tannin, medium acidity, drink now–6 years; **2000 Hartford Family Wines, Sonoma Coast** ★★ $$ dry, full-bodied, medium tannin, high acidity, drink in 1–8 years; **2001 Camelot, California** ★★ $ dry, light-bodied, medium tannin, high acidity, drink now–3 years

ZINFANDEL

Zinfandel thrives in California, assuming as many guises as a Hollywood actor. It can be a rustic spaghetti red or a sophisticated claret; it can steal the stage as an intense, thick, high-alcohol bruiser, or charm as a second-rate starlet of a rosé known as White Zinfandel. As Zinfandel is one of the oldest vinifera grapes in the state, there's a fetish for wines made from vines that are as much as 100 years old. These "old-vine" Zins are purported to have a depth of character not achievable with younger vines. While many are indeed special, so are some younger ones.

at the table
Simple Zins, fruity yet high in acidity, are made for Italian-American favorites like pizza, stuffed peppers, and lasagna. More sophisticated wines are wonderful with lamb chops or braised veal shoulder, while the heartiest (i.e. highest alcohol) versions require more substantial fare like beef stew or a Moroccan lamb tagine.

the bottom line Enjoyable, simple Zinfandel can be had for under $15, while intensely concentrated, mostly old-vine Zinfandels start at $20 and can run to $40 or more.

what to buy ZINFANDEL

1997	1998	1999	2000	2001
★★★	★★	★★	★★	★★★

recommended wines

**1999 Chateau Potelle VGS Mt. Veeder Estate,
Napa Valley** ★★★★ $$$
dry, full-bodied, medium tannin, high acidity drink now–8 years
Blackberry, mineral, and herb flavors are as smooth as velvet.

2000 Ridge Lytton Springs, California ★★★★ $$$
dry, full-bodied, medium tannin, high acidity drink now–20 years
Seductive fruit and minerals sculpted by Zin master Paul Draper.

**1998 Joseph Swan Vineyards Lone Redwood Ranch,
Russian River Valley** ★★★★ $$
dry, medium-bodied, medium tannin, high acidity drink now–15 years
The smooth flavors of this wine come excitingly close to perfection.

**2000 Rosenblum Cellars Rockpile Road Vineyard,
Dry Creek Valley** ★★★★ $$
dry, full-bodied, medium tannin, high acidity drink now–12 years
Dried herb and Asian spice notes put an exotic spin on this mulberry-flavored Zin.

1999 Chouinard Old Vines Mohr-Fry Ranches, Lodi ★★★ $$
dry, full-bodied, medium tannin, high acidity drink now–8 years
A big wine, with smoky, peppery blackberry flavors and appealing minerality.

1999 Cline Ancient Vines, California ★★★ $$
dry, full-bodied, medium tannin, high acidity drink now–6 years
Like a berry patch in a eucalyptus grove next to a coal mine, this is terrifically fruity, herbal, and earthy all at once.

**1999 Foppiano Valera Vineyard Reserve,
Dry Creek Valley** ★★★ $$
dry, full-bodied, heavy tannin, high acidity drink in 1–8 years
A blockbuster Zinfandel, with bushels of berries, slabs of bacon, and wheelbarrows of peppery mineral flavors.

1999 Fritz Winery Old Vine, Dry Creek Valley ★★★ $$
dry, full-bodied, heavy tannin, high acidity drink now–8 years
If only all Zinfandels could be as good as this peppery, plummy, mineral-laden example.

1999 Lucas ZinStar Vineyard, Lodi ★★★ $$
dry, full-bodied, heavy tannin, high acidity drink now–4 years
A rustic wine full of berry and spice flavors, perfect for casual meals of barbecued brisket or short ribs.

1997 Mazzocco Vineyards Cuneo & Saini,
Dry Creek Valley ★★★ $$
dry, full-bodied, heavy tannin, high acidity   drink now–10 years
Mazzocco releases its Zinfandels a few years later than most wineries, allow-
ing glorious fruit, herb, and burnt sugar flavors to emerge. It's worth the wait.

2000 Robert Mondavi Winery, Napa Valley ★★★ $$
dry, medium-bodied, medium tannin, medium acidity   drink now–6 years
Expertly balanced between berry and mineral flavors, Mondavi's Zinfandel
does California's own "noble" grape proud.

2000 Sobon Estate ReZerve Zin,
Shenandoah Valley of California ★★★ $$
dry, full-bodied, heavy tannin, high acidity   drink now–5 years
If you love dry, Port-style Zins, here's a fine one to try.

1999 Ledson Old Vine, Russian River Valley ★★ $$$
dry, full-bodied, medium tannin, high acidity   drink now–8 years
Fifty-year-old vines give this wine intense flavors, with ripe, spicy berry fruit
weighted with minerals.

2000 Alderbrook OVOC, Dry Creek Valley ★★ $$
dry, medium-bodied, medium tannin, high acidity   drink now–4 years
A lighter style of Zinfandel, with bright berry flavors balanced by high acidity.

2000 Bonny Doon Vineyard Cardinal Zin Beastly Old Vines,
California ★★ $$
dry, medium-bodied, medium tannin, high acidity   drink now–4 years
Tart cherry flavors, palate-stimulating acidity, and a Ralph Steadman portrait
on the label to boot.

1999 Gallo of Sonoma Barrelli Creek Vineyard,
Alexander Valley ★★ $$
dry, full-bodied, medium tannin, high acidity   drink now–5 years
Mouthwatering Zinfandel, with smooth black cherry flavors seasoned with
dusty herb notes.

2000 Green & Red Vineyards Chiles Mill Vineyard,
Napa Valley ★★ $$
dry, medium-bodied, medium tannin, high acidity   drink now–6 years
Fresh green herbs and ripe red fruit play together in harmony.

2000 Ironstone Vineyards Old Vines Reserve, Lodi ★★ $$
dry, medium-bodied, medium tannin, medium acidity   drink now–5 years
Ironstone doesn't get much press, but the dark fruit and pinelike flavors of this
wine are worthy of attention.

california **reds**

1999 Kunde, Sonoma Valley ★★ $$
dry, medium-bodied, medium tannin, high acidity   drink now–4 years
Fine berry flavors lightly spiced—true spice addicts might want to try Kunde's
Shaw Vineyards 19th Century bottling instead.

1999 Sable Ridge Vineyards Old Vine Hensley-Lauchland Vineyard, Lodi ★★ $$
dry, full-bodied, medium tannin, medium acidity   drink now–5 years
Herbs, flowers, spice and lots of fruit make this a crowd-pleasing wine.

1999 Ravenswood, Amador County ★★ $
dry, full-bodied, medium tannin, high acidity   drink now–5 years
Minty, berry-laden flavors prove Ravenswood's reputation for Zinfandel.

2000 Shenandoah Vineyards of California Special Reserve, Amador County ★★ $
dry, medium-bodied, medium tannin, high acidity   drink now–3 years
This Gold Country wine doesn't strike the motherlode, but that's no reason not
to appreciate its riches.

2000 Dry Creek Vineyard Heritage Clone, Sonoma County ★ $$
dry, medium-bodied, medium tannin, high acidity   drink now–4 years
Any doubts of Zinfandel's southern Italian heritage will be erased with a taste
of this sunny, fruity, high-acid wine.

2000 Cline, California ★ $
dry, medium-bodied, medium tannin, high acidity   drink now–8 years
A reliable, everyday choice for spaghetti and meatballs or burgers.

2000 Rancho Zabaco Dancing Bull, California ★ $
dry, full-bodied, medium tannin, medium acidity   drink now–2 years
A good, simple Zin, nicely priced.

WINES WE WISH WE HAD MORE ROOM FOR

2000 Ridge Geyserville, California ★★★ $$$ dry, full-bodied, medium tannin, high acidity, drink now–20 years; **2000 Rosenblum Cellars Maggie's Reserve Samsel Vineyard, Sonoma Valley** ★★★ $$$ dry, full-bodied, heavy tannin, high acidity, drink now–8 years; **1999 Joseph Swan Vineyards Stellwagen Vineyard, Sonoma Valley** ★★★ $$ dry, medium-bodied, medium tannin, high acidity, drink now–12 years; **1999 Burgess, Napa Valley** ★★ $$ dry, medium-bodied, medium tannin, medium acidity, drink now–3 years; **2000 Gary Farrell, Dry Creek Valley** ★★ $$ dry, full-bodied, medium tannin, high acidity, drink now–5 years; **2000 Rancho Zabaco Sonoma Heritage Vines, Sonoma County** ★★ $$ dry, full-bodied, medium tannin, high acidity, drink now–5 years; **2000 Sobon Estate Cougar Hill, Shenandoah Valley of California** ★★ $$ dry, medium-bodied, medium tannin, high acidity, drink now–3 years; **2000 Kendall-Jackson Vintner's Reserve, California** ★ $ dry, medium-bodied, medium tannin, high acidity, drink now–3 years; **2000 Ravenswood, California** ★ $ dry, medium-bodied, medium tannin, high acidity, drink now–2 years; **2000 Robert Mondavi Coastal Private Selection, Central Coast** ★ $ dry, medium-bodied, medium tannin, high acidity, drink now–2 years

ITALIAN & RHÔNE VARIETALS

The similarity of climate between the Mediterranean and California didn't go unnoticed by early French and Italian immigrants, who brought vine cuttings from home to make wine, but it wasn't until the 1990s that interest was renewed in Italian varieties like Sangiovese, Barbera, and Nebbiolo. While the Cal-Itals tend to lack the refreshing acidity typical of the Italian versions, there are some excellent, full-bodied California examples.

French varieties like Petite Sirah, Mourvèdre, Syrah, Grenache, and Carignan (spelled Carignane in the U.S.) were revived in the 1980s by the "Rhône Rangers," a colorful band of winemakers who believed that since California's climate was close to that of the south of France, its best wines could be made from varieties indigenous to that part of the world. Their theory has been borne out by delicious wines that are often second to none in the state.

at the table

Simple Cal-Itals and juicy Rhônes belong with simple foods like grilled sausage and peppers or barbecued ribs; heartier versions are worthy of osso buco or wild mushroom pasta. Syrah has an herbal edge that matches wonderfully with roast lamb. Drink dense Petite Sirah with braised short ribs or lamb shanks.

the bottom line Simple but delicious Rhône blends start at $9 and run up to over $40 for some of the best. Single-varietal Barbera and Grenache are around $15 to $23, and Syrah reaches $40 or more. High-quality Sangiovese is $18 to $35.

what to buy SYRAH

1997	1998	1999	2000	2001
★★★	★★★	★★	★★★	★★★

57

recommended wines

1999 Alban Vineyards Reva Syrah, Edna Valley ★★★★ $$$
dry, full-bodied, medium tannin, high acidity   drink in 1–10 years
A beautifully smoky Syrah, this is dense with dark red berry flavors and hints of dried thyme.

2000 Dalla Valle Vineyards Pietre Rosso Sangiovese,
Napa Valley ★★★★ $$$
dry, full-bodied, medium tannin, high acidity   drink now–8 years
Beautiful dusty cherry, mineral, and spice flavors from one of the most exciting wineries in California.

1999 Elyse Syrah, Napa Valley ★★★★ $$$
dry, full-bodied, heavy tannin, medium acidity   drink in 2–10 years
Winemaker Ray Coursen adds a bit of white Viognier to his Syrah for a near-Côte Rôtie look-alike.

1999 Spring Mountain Vineyard Syrah,
Napa Valley ★★★★ $$$
dry, full-bodied, heavy tannin, high acidity   drink in 2–15 years
Some of France's best Syrah grows on steep hillsides; some of California's best comes from Spring Mountain, like this densely flavored wine.

1999 Tablas Creek Vineyard Reserve Cuvée,
Paso Robles ★★★★ $$$
dry, full-bodied, medium tannin, high acidity   drink now–12 years
Smooth as silk, spicy as a souk, and earthy as a coal mine, this is a great Rhône-style wine.

1998 Altamura Sangiovese, California ★★★ $$$
dry, medium-bodied, medium tannin, high acidity   drink now–8 years
Complex cherry and spice flavors evoke visions of Tuscany, especially next to a steak *fiorentino*.

1999 Bonny Doon Vineyard Le Cigare Volant,
California ★★★ $$$
dry, medium-bodied, medium tannin, high acidity drink now–10 years
Randall Grahm's homage to Châteauneuf-du-Pape continues to please earthlings from coast to coast.

1999 Ferrari-Carano Siena, Sonoma County ★★★ $$$
dry, medium-bodied, medium tannin, high acidity   drink now–5 years
A "Super Tuscan" by way of Sonoma, with rich cherry, herb, and leather flavors—at a surprisingly affordable price.

1999 Sable Ridge Vineyards Petite Sirah,
Russian River Valley   ★★★ $$$
dry, full-bodied, heavy tannin, high acidity   drink now–10 years
Big, but not brutish, like a linebacker who has studied years of ballet.
Impressive.

1999 Bedford Thompson Grenache, Santa Barbara County ★★★ $$
dry, full-bodied, heavy tannin, medium acidity   drink now–5 years
Groovy Grenache, bursting with berry, coconut, and Indian spice flavors.

1999 Bedford Thompson Mourvèdre, Santa Barbara County ★★★ $$
dry, full-bodied, heavy tannin, medium acidity   drink now–8 years
Big and black, yet full of finesse.

1999 Chameleon Cellars Sangiovese, North Coast   ★★★ $$
dry, medium-bodied, medium tannin, high acidity   drink now–6 years
One of the best "Cal-Itals," with appealing red cherry and mineral flavors
joined by lots of thirst-quenching acidity.

1999 Cline Ancient Vines Mourvèdre, Contra Costa County ★★★ $$
dry, full-bodied, medium tannin, high acidity   drink now–6 years
A marvelously minty, anise-laced, berry filled, and mineral-rich wine.

1999 Equus Mourvèdre, Paso Robles   ★★★ $$
dry, medium-bodied, medium tannin, high acidity   drink now–5 years
Absolutely luscious red cherry flavors balanced by high acidity. The Equus
Grenache is great, too.

1999 Girard Petite Sirah, Napa Valley   ★★★ $$
dry, full-bodied, heavy tannin, high acidity   drink now–10 years
Inky-dark wine, full of menthol and blackberry flavors, vanilla and spice.

1998 Markham Petite Sirah, Napa Valley   ★★★ $$
dry, full-bodied, heavy tannin, high acidity   drink in 1–8 years
A black-hearted beast, with blackberry, spicy oak, and tar flavors.

2000 Melville Syrah, Santa Rita Hills   ★★★ $$
dry, full-bodied, medium tannin, medium acidity   drink now–8 years
If Ahab ever got a taste of this spicy, smoky, berry-flavored wine, he might
have forgotten about that pesky white whale.

2000 Beckmen Vineyards Cuvée Le Bec,
Santa Barbara County   ★★★ $
dry, full-bodied, heavy tannin, medium acidity   drink in 2–10 years
An evocative pastiche of fruit, herb, and mineral flavors from a blend of four
Rhône grape varieties.

california reds

2000 Cartlidge & Browne Syrah, California ★ ★ $ $
dry, full-bodied, medium tannin, medium acidity   drink now–3 years
Generous berry flavors with telltale smoky Syrah notes for a low price.

2000 Chouinard Mohr-Fry Ranches Alicante Bouschet, Lodi ★ ★ $ $
dry, full-bodied, medium tannin, high acidity   drink now–4 years
The rarity of Alicante Bouschet bottled alone is reason enough to try this, but its smoky mulberry flavors are reason to try it again and again.

2000 Flora Springs Sangiovese, Napa Valley ★ ★ $ $
dry, medium-bodied, medium tannin, high acidity   drink now–6 years
Not classical Sangiovese, but delicious lavender-scented cherry and berry flavors.

2000 Geyser Peak Shiraz, Sonoma County ★ ★ $ $
dry, full-bodied, medium tannin, high acidity   drink now–3 years
An Australian spin on California Syrah, full of bold fruit flavors and good acidity.

1999 Joseph Phelps Le Mistral, California ★ ★ $ $
dry, full-bodied, heavy tannin, high acidity   drink now–3 years
One of the most consistent and easy-to-drink Rhône blends in the state.

2000 Shenandoah Vineyards ReZerve Barbera,
Shenandoah Valley of California ★ ★ $ $
dry, full-bodied, heavy tannin, high acidity   drink now–8 years
Beefy Barbera, with juicy blackberry flavors and burnt sugar notes.

2000 Zaca Mesa Syrah, Santa Ynez Valley ★ ★ $ $
dry, medium-bodied, medium tannin, medium acidity drink now–3 years
Smooth fruit, light spice, and a little smoke make for an easy quaff.

2000 Joseph Swan Vineyards Côtes du Rosa,
Russian River Valley ★ ★ $
dry, full-bodied, medium tannin, high acidity   drink now–3 years
Likc good French Crozes-Hermitage, with juicy fruit and earthy herbal flavors.

1998 Vigil Terra Vin, California ★ ★ $
dry, medium-bodied, medium tannin, high acidity   drink now–3 years
A juicy, inexpensive blend of Zinfandel and Carignane for casual meals.

1999 Camelot Syrah, California ★ $
dry, medium-bodied, medium tannin, medium acidity drink now–3 years
Juicy berry flavors, easy to drink. An everyday Syrah.

2000 Van Ruiten Taylor Cab-Shiraz, Lodi ★ $
dry, medium-bodied, medium tannin, high acidity   drink now–3 years
Thick strawberry jam flavors make this a good call for barbecue.

BEING AND NOTHINGNESS

It seems simple. Make a wine from a particular variety of grape, put its name on the label, and sell it. That's the convention in the U.S. and much of the world. But not so fast. The Bureau of Alcohol, Tobacco and Firearms (ATF) has to make sure that the grape you've made your wine from actually exists. Last year, Qupé winery released a wine made from Albariño, the famed grape of Spain's Rías Baixas and Portugal's Vinho Verde regions. Unfortunately, ATF bureaucrats hadn't decided if it was an "authentic grape." So, under the moniker of a winery they called "Verdad" ("truth" in Spanish), the vintners simply labeled it "White Wine." Well, in March 2002, the ATF finally did decide that Albariño actually exists (in its alternative spelling, Alvarinho, too), along with Fiano, an ancient grape indigenous to Italy's Campania region, and Black Corinth, which is mostly made into raisins. In May, these grapes joined the ranks of other approved varieties such as Burdin 4672, Gladwin 113, and Yuga.

WINES WE WISH WE HAD MORE ROOM FOR

2000 Babcock Syrah, Santa Barbara County ★★★ $$ dry, full-bodied, heavy tannin, medium acidity, drink in 1–8 years; **1998 Bonterra Vineyards Syrah, Mendocino County** ★★ $$ dry, medium-bodied, medium tannin, high acidity, drink now–4 years; **2000 Daniel Gehrs Syrah, Paso Robles** ★★ $$ dry, medium-bodied, medium tannin, medium acidity, drink now–4 years; **2000 Foppiano Vineyards Sangiovese, Alexander Valley** ★★ $$ dry, medium-bodied, heavy tannin, high acidity, drink now–5 years; **2000 Qupé Syrah, Central Coast** ★★ $$ dry, full-bodied, medium tannin, high acidity, drink now–5 years; **2000 Zaca Mesa Cuvée Z, Santa Barbara County** ★★ $$ dry, medium-bodied, medium tannin, high acidity, drink now–3 years; **1999 Glass Mountain Quarry Syrah, California** ★★ $ dry, medium-bodied, medium tannin, high acidity, drink now–2 years; **2000 Jade Mountain La Provençale, California** ★ $$ dry, full-bodied, heavy tannin, medium acidity, drink now–3 years; **2000 Ca' del Solo Big House Red, California** ★ $ dry, medium-bodied, medium tannin, medium acidity, drink now–2 years; **2000 Kendall-Jackson Collage Cabernet Sauvignon-Shiraz, California** ★ $ dry, medium-bodied, medium tannin, medium acidity, drink now–2 years

pacific
northwest

With a string of recent harvests that have been among the best in its winemaking history, the Pacific Northwest has been making headlines with its wines. Unlike California, where all sorts of varieties are grown, vintners in the Pacific Northwest tend to specialize. Oregon excels at Pinot Gris and Pinot Noir, while Washington focuses on Sauvignon Blanc, Chardonnay, Cabernet, Merlot, and increasingly, Syrah.

oregon

Oregon's cool temperatures and abundant rainfall are not ideal for most fine grape varieties, but, combined with the state's volcanic soils, they do wonders for finicky Pinot Noir, producing wines comparable to France's esteemed red Burgundies. The Willamette Valley is the state's most famous region; other important areas are the Umpqua and Rogue Valleys in the south, and the Columbia and Walla Walla Valleys (shared with Washington) in the central and eastern parts of the state.

on the label

As in California, most Oregon wines are identified by variety. However, if an Oregon wine specifies a grape, the wine must contain at least 90 percent of that grape, except for Cabernet Sauvignon, which must contain at least 75 percent. If the wine carries an appellation, 100 percent of the grapes must be from that area.

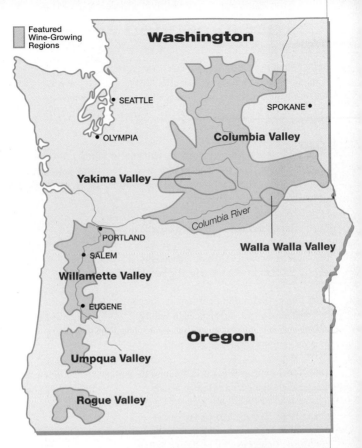

Featured Wine-Growing Regions

Washington

• SEATTLE

SPOKANE •

• OLYMPIA

Columbia Valley

Yakima Valley

Columbia River

PORTLAND

• SALEM

Walla Walla Valley

Willamette Valley

• EUGENE

Oregon

Umpqua Valley

Rogue Valley

white wines

While Pinot Gris does Oregon proud, Chardonnay can challenge it. The cooler climate makes for good Riesling, Gewürztraminer, and Pinot Blanc, too. Müller-Thurgau seems to produce better wines here than it does in its German homeland.

at the table

Try Gewürztraminer with spicy dishes. Drink Pinot Gris, Pinot Blanc, or Chardonnay with meaty fish like halibut, and the lighter Riesling with trout. Müller-Thurgau drinks best as an aperitif.

the bottom line All these wines can be found for $8 to $15, though Chardonnay can tip the scale at $40.

recommended wines

1999 Domaine Serene Clos du Soleil Vineyard
Dijon Clone Chardonnay, Willamette Valley ★ ★ ★ ★ $ $ $
dry, full-bodied, medium oak, high acidity drink now–10 years

One of America's great Chardonnays, with multiple levels of fruit, herb, and mineral flavors that end on sweet spice.

2000 Chehalem Reserve Pinot Gris, Willamette Valley ★ ★ ★ ★ $ $
dry, full-bodied, light oak, high acidity drink now–6 years

Dry yet dripping with buttery, apricot, and orange marmalade aromas, this is a white rich enough for duck or pork.

2000 Cristom Germaine Vineyard Chardonnay,
Willamette Valley ★ ★ ★ $ $
dry, medium-bodied, light oak, high acidity drink now–10 years

As juicy and flavorful as a yellow plum at the peak of ripeness.

1999 Domaine Drouhin Chardonnay, Oregon ★ ★ ★ $ $
dry, medium-bodied, light oak, high acidity drink now–8 years

Austere and rich simultaneously, with the freshness (and minerality) of an ocean breeze, and buttery elements, too.

2000 Sokol Blosser Pinot Gris, Willamette Valley ★ ★ ★ $ $
dry, medium-bodied, no oak, high acidity drink now–8 years

A powerful welterweight, with a knockout punch of orange, green apple, and almond flavors, yet ultimately light on its feet.

2000 Foris Gewürztraminer, Rogue Valley ★ ★ ★ $
dry, medium-bodied, no oak, high acidity drink now–3 years

Always look out for the quiet ones—like this floral, lemon-lime-flavored, and mineral-tinged seductress.

2000 Oak Knoll Pinot Gris, Willamette Valley ★ ★ ★ $
dry, full-bodied, no oak, high acidity drink now–4 years

This one pushes all the right Pinot Gris buttons: rich texture, blossom scents, and almond, orange, and berry flavors.

2000 Adelsheim Vineyard Pinot Blanc, Oregon ★ ★ $
dry, medium-bodied, no oak, medium acidity drink now–3 years

Wild strawberry and pear flavors get a small kick from acidity.

2000 Eyrie Vineyards Pinot Gris, Willamette Valley ★ ★ $
dry, medium-bodied, no oak, high acidity drink now–5 years

Fans of austere wines will love this fruit-light, mineral-heavy wine.

2000 Erath Vineyards Pinot Gris, Oregon ★ $
dry, medium-bodied, no oak, high acidity   drink now–2 years
Simple fruit salad flavors and zippy acidity make this a good choice for picnics.

2001 Bethel Heights Vineyard Pinot Gris, Oregon ★★★ $ dry, medium-bodied, no oak, high acidity, drink now–3 years; **NV Sokol Blosser Evolution Sixth Edition, American White Wine** ★★ $$ off-dry, light-bodied, no oak, high acidity, drink now; **2000 Adelsheim Vineyard Pinot Gris, Oregon** ★★ $ dry, medium-bodied, no oak, medium acidity, drink now–5 years; **2001 Chateau Benoit Müller-Thurgau, Willamette Valley** ★★ $ dry, medium-bodied, no oak, high acidity, drink now; **2000 Montinore Vineyards Gewürztraminer, Willamette Valley** ★★ $ off-dry, medium-bodied, no oak, high acidity, drink now–3 years

red wines

Merlot, Cabernet Franc, Cabernet Sauvignon, Syrah, and even some Zinfandel grow in the state (particularly in the warmer, southerly Rogue Valley), but Pinot Noir garners the most attention with complex, sophisticated wines.

at the table
Less "jammy" than California Pinot Noirs yet richer than Burgundian examples, Oregon Pinots are a natural compromise when there's both steak and fish on the table. They are also delicious with sliced duck breast with a huckleberry sauce. Pair the berry-rich, smooth Merlots and Cabernets with prime rib or a chunk of sharp Oregon cheddar.

the bottom line Pinot Noir is tricky to grow anywhere, and you'll pay for the trouble. A few bargains exist under $15, but you'll need over $20 for something really interesting. Cabernet and Merlot run $7 to $40.

what to buy PINOT NOIR

1997	1998	1999	2000	2001
★★	★★★	★★★★	★★★★	★★★

recommended wines

1999 Domaine Serene Grace Vineyard, Willamette Valley ★★★★ $$$$
dry, full-bodied, medium tannin, medium acidity   **drink now–12 years**
With profound pine aromas and wild berry, smoky, pine, and mineral flavors, this is a remarkable Pinot Noir.

1998 Sokol Blosser Watershed Block, Willamette Valley ★★★★ $$$$
dry, full-bodied, medium tannin, high acidity   **drink now–12 years**
Many Burgundian vintners would be pleased to take credit for this Pinot Noir, with ripe berry, spice, oak, and lots of mineral flavors.

2000 Beaux Frères The Beaux Frères Vineyard, Willamette Valley ★★★ $$$$
dry, medium-bodied, medium tannin, high acidity   **drink now–8 years**
The brothers-in-law are a rambunctious bunch, with bold and spicy fruit flavors, but they are well mannered, too, with fine balance.

1998 Domaine Drouhin Laurène, Oregon ★★★ $$$$
dry, full-bodied, medium tannin, high acidity   **drink now–10 years**
Made by Véronique Drouhin, daughter of the great Burgundy *négociant,* this is classic Pinot Noir, if richer than most Burgundies.

1999 Adelsheim Elizabeth's Reserve, Yamhill County ★★★ $$$
dry, medium-bodied, medium tannin, medium acidity   **drink now–5 years**
Light cherry flavors are balanced with a bit of herb and mineral notes and a seductive whisper of smoke.

1999 Argyle Reserve, Willamette Valley ★★★ $$$
dry, medium-bodied, medium tannin, medium acidity   **drink now–8 years**
Juicy, silky, raspberry, and orange spice flavors are made more luscious by their melting chocolate richness.

2000 Chehalem Rion Reserve, Willamette Valley ★★★ $$$
dry, medium-bodied, medium tannin, medium acidity   **drink now–8 years**
As smoky as a smokehouse and fruity as a bushel of berries, with spicy mineral flavors, too.

1998 Erath Vineyards Reserve, Willamette Valley ★★★ $$$
dry, medium-bodied, medium tannin, medium acidity   **drink now–10 years**
Tasty as a blackberry betty, with juicy fruit and homey melting brown sugar flavors.

APPELLATION CONTRÔLÉE ULAN BAATAR?

About two decades ago, a nascent Washington wine industry came up with a curious ad campaign. It suggested that since the state is at the same latitude as Bordeaux, its wines would naturally be as fine. In fact, if that were true, Maine, Nova Scotia, and Mongolia would be full of up-and-coming vintners. Now that no one disputes Washington's ability to produce world-class wines, such comparisons are a thing of the past. Until, of course, the Mongolians decide to get into the picture.

2000 Panther Creek Freedom Hill Vineyard,
Willamette Valley ★★★ $$$
dry, full-bodied, heavy tannin, high acidity drink in 1–8 years
Powerful Pinot, with black fruit and a quarry's worth of mineral flavors, this could use some cellar time to relax.

2000 Bethel Heights Vineyard, Willamette Valley ★★★ $$
dry, medium-bodied, medium tannin, medium acidity drink now–6 years
A sip of this recalls a field full of lavender and blackberries. Wonderfully balanced by acidity and mineral flavors.

2000 Eyrie Vineyards, Willamette Valley ★★ $$
dry, light-bodied, medium tannin, high acidity drink now–6 years
Eyrie takes a Burgundian approach to Pinot Noir, offering one lighter in weight than other Oregonian examples, but with bewitching berry and herb flavors.

2000 Duck Pond Cellars, Oregon ★★ $
dry, medium-bodied, medium tannin, high acidity drink now–3 years
The exception to the rule that Pinot is always expensive, this offers raspberry and orange flavors with finesse at an affordable price.

WINES WE WISH WE HAD MORE ROOM FOR
2000 Cristom Reserve, Willamette Valley ★★★★ $$$ dry, medium-bodied, medium tannin, medium acidity, drink now–8 years; **2000 Domaine Serene Yamhill Cuvée, Willamette Valley** ★★★ $$$ dry, full-bodied, medium tannin, medium acidity, drink now–8 years; **2000 Cristom Mt. Jefferson Cuvée, Willamette Valley** ★★★ $$ dry, medium-bodied, medium tannin, medium acidity, drink now–5 years; **2000 Belles Soeurs Shea Vineyard, Willamette Valley** ★★ $$$ dry, medium-bodied, medium tannin, high acidity, drink now–3 years; **1999 Montinore Vineyards, Willamette Valley** ★★ $ dry, medium-bodied, medium tannin, high acidity, drink now–8 years

washington state

Washington might be just north of Oregon, but it's worlds away in terms of climate and viticulture. Whereas Oregon's largest wine regions are in the cool and damp western part of the state, Washington's lie in the arid desert valleys east of the Cascade Range. The area's dry, hot summers and bitterly cold winters are as good for grapes as they are for apples. The state has become famous for Chardonnay, and it produces arguably the finest Merlot in the country.

on the label

As in Oregon, labeling by grape variety is most common.

white wines

With fresh fruit flavors and refreshing acidity, Washington's Chardonnays offer relief for those weary of too much butter and oak. Oak is used but often with a light touch. Though Semillon and Sauvignon Blanc are traditionally paired in Bordeaux, they often go it alone in Washington, where Semillon generally attains enough acidity to carry its satiny, honeyed orange flavors forward for some of the state's most appealing white wines, and Sauvignon Blanc offers tart acidity and immediately appealng grassy, lemon zest flavors.

at the table

Lean-bodied with mineral flavors and high acidity, Washington Chardonnays do well with light dishes like baked snapper or cornmeal-crusted trout. More full-bodied versions can stand up to grilled salmon or acorn squash risotto.

Light, zesty Sauvignon Blanc matches mild fish like sole, or raw oysters. Semillon has a bit more body and does well with crab or smoked trout. Blends of the two work well with richer dishes like chicken in a cream sauce or seared tuna.

the bottom line Despite their high quality, Washington State whites continue to offer good value. Fine Sauvignon Blanc and Semillon, straight or blended, shouldn't set you back more than $15. Even Chardonnay rarely costs more than $25 a bottle.

recommended wines

2000 Desert Wind Vineyard Semillon, Wahluke Slope, Columbia Valley ★★★ $$
dry, full-bodied, light oak, medium acidity   drink now–5 years
A luscious display of pear, peach, and nutty flavors, balanced by good acidity.

2000 L'Ecole Nº 41 Chardonnay, Columbia Valley ★★★ $$
dry, medium-bodied, light oak, high acidity   drink now–6 years
How good can Washington State Chardonnay be? Check out this creamy, citrus, and mineral-flavored wine to see.

2000 Di Stefano Sauvignon Blanc, Columbia Valley ★★★ $
dry, medium-bodied, no oak, high acidity   drink now–2 years
There's an abundance of peach and citrus flavors and floral hints, but it's the minerals that take over. Think steamed shellfish.

2000 L'Ecole Nº 41 Barrel Fermented Semillon, Columbia Valley ★★★ $
dry, full-bodied, medium oak, medium acidity   drink now–6 years
One of the best Semillons in America, full of creamy fig, honey, and lemon flavors. L'Ecole's Seven Hills Semillon is even better, if harder to find.

2000 Covey Run Fumé Blanc, Washington State ★★ $
dry, medium-bodied, no oak, high acidity   drink now–2 years
Tasty wine, full of juicy pear, grassy herb, and mineral notes.

2000 Hogue Fumé Blanc, Columbia Valley ★★ $
dry, medium-bodied, light oak, medium acidity   drink now–2 years
More than just another lemony Sauvignon, with a touch of oak that brings out appealing tropical flavors matched by a refreshing grassiness.

2000 Snoqualmie Vineyards Chardonnay, Columbia Valley ★★ $
dry, medium-bodied, light oak, high acidity   drink now–3 years
Good, everyday Chardonnay with mild apple, lemon, and spice flavors, and a peck of oak.

washington **reds**

**2000 Chateau Ste. Michelle Sauvignon Blanc,
Columbia Valley**   ★ $
dry, light-bodied, light oak, high acidity   drink now–1 year
The light, lemony flavors are easy to enjoy without a thought; hints of oak and
mineral notes might give you other ideas.

1999 Covey Run Barrel Select Chardonnay, Yakima Valley   ★ $
dry, medium-bodied, light oak, high acidity   drink now–2 years
Pleasant citrus and light vanilla flavors for a fair price.

red wines

MERLOT, CABERNET SAUVIGNON & CABERNET FRANC

Washington excels in Bordeaux grape varieties, particularly
Merlot, but also Cabernet Franc and Cabernet Sauvignon.
Although full-bodied, these wines tend to have less power than
some from California, but more balance, with higher acidity and
more earth tones.

at the table

These reds require hearty foods. Try Merlot with leg of lamb or
roast pork, and the more tannic Cabernet Sauvignon with
braised brisket, lamb shanks, or grilled beef tenderloin.
Cabernet Franc shines with steak *au poivre*. Vegetarians will
want to try grilled or smoked tofu.

the bottom line The big three (Columbia Crest
Winery, Chateau Ste. Michelle, and Hogue Cellars, which control
nearly 50 percent of the state's production) offer a reasonable
selection of Washington wines under $15, but for the best quality,
you'll spend $18 to $30. A few bottles reach up to $95

what to buy MERLOT & CABERNET SAUVIGNON

1997	1998	1999	2000	2001
★★★	★★★	★★★	★★★	★★★

recommended wines

1999 Andrew Will Champoux Vineyard Cabernet Sauvignon,
Washington State   ★★★★ $$$
dry, full-bodied, medium tannin, medium acidity   drink in 1–10 years
Andrew Will's penchant for super-ripe fruit shows in the explosive berry and
spice flavors. Try his Sorella Bordeaux blend, too.

1999 Chateau Ste. Michelle Reserve Merlot,
Columbia Valley   ★★★ $$$
dry, full-bodied, heavy tannin, medium acidity   drink in 2–10 years
Washington's wine behemoth puts out a big wine, full of cassis, mineral, and
lavender flavors, and heavy tannin. Give it time.

1997 Columbia Winery Red Willow Vineyard Milestone Merlot,
Yakima Valley   ★★★ $$$
dry, medium-bodied, medium tannin, high acidity   drink now–5 years
An elegant, Bordeaux-like wine, with lovely fruit and light floral flavors, a hint
of spice and appetite-encouraging acidity.

1999 Hogue Genesis Merlot, Columbia Valley   ★★★ $$
dry, full-bodied, heavy tannin, medium acidity   drink now–8 years
Big and beautiful blackberry flavors show from first pour, but it would be even
better after a few years in the cellar to soften the tannin.

2000 Hedges CMS, Columbia Valley   ★★★ $
dry, full-bodied, medium tannin, medium acidity   drink now–5 years
This blend of Cabernets, Merlot, and Syrah offers concentrated berry, brown
sugar, and pungent herb flavors at a great price.

1997 Desert Wind Vineyard Ruah, Wahluke Slope,
Columbia Valley   ★★ $$$$
dry, full-bodied, heavy tannin, medium acidity   drink now–10 years
Lovers of bittersweet chocolate will love the chocolaty, blackberry flavors
made savory with minerals and bitter herbs.

1999 Canoe Ridge Vineyard Merlot,
Columbia Valley   ★★ $$
dry, full-bodied, heavy tannin, medium acidity   drink now–6 years
Long a favorite, Canoe Ridge's Merlot consistently pleases with substantial
berry flavors and a piquant mintiness.

1998 Kiona Merlot, Columbia Valley   ★★ $$
dry, full-bodied, heavy tannin, medium acidity   drink now–5 years
Smoky Merlot with dark plum and earthy, spicy flavors.

washington **reds**

2000 Sagelands Four Corners Merlot, Columbia Valley ★★ $
dry, full-bodied, medium tannin, medium acidity   **drink now–5 years**
They weren't kidding when they named this winery: sage scents flow from the glass, joined by dark berry and mineral flavors.

1998 Snoqualmie Vineyards Merlot, Columbia Valley ★★ $
dry, medium-bodied, medium tannin, medium acidity   **drink now–3 years**
Smooth, with refined berry and floral flavors.

WINES WE WISH WE HAD MORE ROOM FOR

1999 Di Stefano Sogno, Columbia Valley ★★★★ $$$ dry, medium-bodied, medium tannin, medium acidity, drink now–10 years; **1999 Chateau Ste. Michelle Cold Creek Vineyard Cabernet Sauvignon, Columbia Valley** ★★★ $$$ dry, full-bodied, heavy tannin, medium acidity, drink in 1–12 years; **2000 L'Ecole Nº 41 Seven Hills Vineyard Merlot, Walla Walla Valley** ★★★ $$$ dry, full-bodied, medium tannin, medium acidity, drink now–10 years; **1999 Columbia Crest Grand Estates Merlot, Columbia Valley** ★★ $ dry, full-bodied, medium tannin, medium acidity, drink now–5 years; **1999 Covey Run Cabernet Sauvignon, Columbia Valley** ★★ $ dry, medium-bodied, medium tannin, medium acidity, drink now–4 years

OTHER RED WINES

Syrah is quickly catching up to the quality of Washington's Bordeaux-style wines. Lemberger, a fruity, peppery import from Austria (where it's known as Blaufränkisch), is a local specialty.

at the table

Washington Syrahs require big food, such as braised oxtails or mushroom Stroganoff. Simple Lembergers are great for barbecues, though more serious versions are great with roast duck.

the bottom line Washington Syrah is a deal at $15 to $30 a bottle; Lemberger runs $8 to $15.

recommended wines

1998 Columbia Winery Red Willow Vineyard Syrah, Yakima Valley ★★★ $$$
dry, full-bodied, medium tannin, high acidity   **drink now–8 years**
One of Washington's best Syrahs, this is bursting with peppery berry and smoke flavors and lashes of vanilla-scented oak.

**1999 Columbia Winery Red Willow Vineyard Sangiovese,
Yakima Valley** ★★★ $$
dry, medium-bodied, heavy tannin, medium acidity   drink now–4 years
A "Wash-Ital," as in "wash it all" down with this bright cherry and spice gem.

2001 Glen Fiona Bacchus Vineyard Syrah, Columbia Valley ★★★ $$
dry, full-bodied, medium tannin, medium acidity   drink now–8 years
Open this now and dive into a punch bowl of fruit flavors; age for a year to let
the smoked pepper flavors have their turn.

**1998 Hogue Genesis Blue Franc-Lemberger,
Columbia Valley** ★★★ $
dry, full-bodied, medium tannin, high acidity   drink now–5 years
With excellent blackberry and charcoal-like flavors, this super-duper Blue
Franc goes well beyond other limp-bodied Lembergers.

1998 Kiona Syrah, Red Mountain ★★ $$
dry, full-bodied, medium tannin, medium acidity   drink now–5 years
Syrah is typically smoky; this is as smoky as a lit cigar, but also as fruity as a
basket of plums.

2000 Chateau Ste. Michelle Syrah, Columbia Valley ★★ $
dry, full-bodied, heavy tannin, medium acidity   drink in 1–6 years
There's nothing subtle about this Syrah, full of black berry and tar flavors, plus
copious amounts of toasted oak. Age it.

2000 Kiona Lemberger, Washington State ★★ $
dry, medium-bodied, medium tannin, high acidity   drink now–3 years
Washington's equivalent to California's Zinfandel shows appealing, fresh berry
flavors with a lightly spicy and smoky end.

2000 Snoqualmie Syrah, Columbia Valley ★★ $
dry, full-bodied, medium tannin, medium acidity   drink now–5 years
A few minutes in the glass brings complex herb and smoke notes out of this
very berry wine.

GREAT VINTAGES NORTHWEST

Northwest vintners were very happy with their wines in
1998, amazed in 1999, and dazzled by 2000. What about
2001? Let's just say few of them are feeling the effects of
global warming. But with wines from all four vintages on
the market today, it's easy to see not only how good the
region's wines can be, but also how well they age.

new york state

With all the attention paid to West Coast wines, even New Yorkers are surprised to learn that their state is the country's second largest wine producer. Long Island gets the most attention for its excellent Merlot, Cabernet Sauvignon, and Cabernet Franc, but don't forget the Finger Lakes region, the source of some of the country's finest Riesling and Pinot Noir.

BUFFALO
Lake
Erie
Lake Erie

on the label

New York follows the American standard of labeling by grape variety. A few winemakers use proprietary names for blends.

white & rosé wines

In New York, Chardonnay rules, with zippy acidity and mineral flavors that recall France more than California, though the state's Pinot Blanc is getting better and better and may one day challenge Chardonnay's predominance. Hybrids like Seyval Blanc or Vidal Blanc tend to make simple, fruity wines, as does Gewürztraminer, which can be especially aromatic. Rieslings from the Finger Lakes, whether bone dry or dessert-sweet, are the finest in the U.S. New York State rosés are usually dry with tasteful fruit and mineral flavors.

at the table

Dry New York Rieslings are a natural for freshwater fish like pike, though they're also perfect for crab cakes, or better yet, clam bakes. Pair light Long Island Chardonnays with seared tuna or grilled swordfish; oakier ones with lobster or scallops. Chill Seyval or Vidal Blanc for simple, interesting aperitifs. A dry rosé goes well with poached salmon.

the bottom line New York whites are a bargain. Top-quality dry Rieslings run no more than $15, though some dessert-style versions run as high as $30. Gewürztraminers and hybrids run $15 or less. Chardonnays hover around $12 to $16, though a few might climb to $25. Fine rosés cost $8 to $12

what to buy WHITE & ROSÉ WINES

1999	2000	2001
★★★	★★★	★★★★

recommended wines

1999 Hermann J. Wiemer Chardonnay, Finger Lakes ☆ ★ ★ ★ ★ $
dry, medium-bodied, medium oak, high acidity   drink now–6 years
Hermann Wiemer, one of America's great Riesling masters, also makes one of its finest Chardonnays, with a great balance of citrus, mineral, and lightly spicy oak flavors.

2001 Dr. Konstantin Frank Reserve Johannisberg Riesling, Finger Lakes ☆ ★ ★ $$
dry, medium-bodied, no oak, high acidity   drink now–8 years
This mineral-laden, citrus- and light pineapple-flavored wine is so Germanic it is as if the Mosel flowed into the Finger Lakes.

2001 Dr. Konstantin Frank Rkatsiteli, Finger Lakes ☆ ★ ★ ★ $$
dry, medium-bodied, no oak, high acidity   drink now–5 years
What's pungent as Sauvignon Blanc, aromatic as Riesling, and profound as Loire Valley Chenin? Rkatsiteli, said to be the worlds' fourth most planted white wine grape.

2000 Lieb Pinot Blanc, North Fork ☆ ★ ★ ★ $$
dry, medium-bodied, no oak, high acidity   drink now–5 years
Pinot Blanc's a rarity on Long Island, but the compelling candied orange and pear flavors of this wine might move a rapidly evolving industry in its direction.

1999 Millbrook Proprietor's Special Reserve Chardonnay, Hudson River Region ☆ ★ ★ ★ $$
dry, full-bodied, medium oak, medium acidity   drink now–8 years
The winery that puts the Hudson Valley on the wine map balances fruit flavors with mineral and crème caramel notes.

1999 Schneider Chardonnay, North Fork ☆ ★ ★ ★ $$
dry, medium-bodied, medium oak, medium acidity   drink now–5 years
Here's a wine that has the finesse of an Old World Chardonnay, but the creamy fruitiness favored in New World examples.

2001 Hermann J. Wiemer Dry Johannisberg Riesling, Finger Lakes ☆ ★ ★ ★ $
dry, medium-bodied, no oak, high acidity   drink now–8 years
For Riesling lovers only, this is mineral-laden and herb-rich with pinelike scents and citrus flavors lurking in the background.

2001 Macari Sauvignon Blanc, North Fork ☆ ★ ★ ★ $
dry, medium-bodied, no oak, high acidity   drink now–2 years
New York's best Sauvignon Blanc, with citrus, mineral, and grassy flavors.

O CANADA/VIVA MEXICO

Canada is too cold to make good wine and Mexico, too hot, right? Wrong. Both countries have places where the weather is less extreme than in the rest of the country. The best Canadian wines are dessert wines, especially—surprise—ice wine, though they make dry whites like Riesling and Pinot Blanc and good reds from Cabernet Franc, Pinot Noir, and Baco Noir. Mexico produces Chardonnay, Sauvignon Blanc, and Chenin Blanc, but its best wines are reds from Syrah, Tempranillo, Cabernet Sauvignon, Nebbiolo, and Zinfandel. Wines from both countries are slowly but steadily entering the U.S. market. Some wineries to look for:

Canada Burrowing Owl Vineyard, Cave Spring Cellars, Henry of Pelham, Inniskillin, La Frenz, Pelee Island Winery, Quail's Gate Estate Winery

Mexico Château Camou, L.A. Cetto, Monte Xanic

2000 Palmer Vineyards Gewürztraminer, North Fork ⚲   ★★★ $
dry, medium-bodied, no oak, high acidity   drink now–5 years
Spice, spice, spice, suspended in tropical fruit and earth flavors. Fascinating.

2001 Paumanok Semi-Dry Riesling, North Fork ⚲   ★★★ $
off-dry, medium-bodied, no oak, high acidity   drink now–5 years
Just the slightest bit off-dry, this fragrant Riesling would be perfect with seared, pepper-crusted tuna.

2000 Peconic Bay Winery Riesling, North Fork ⚲   ★★★ $
dry, medium-bodied, no oak, high acidity   drink now–5 years
Plenty of appealing fruit and a light floral quality make this easy to enjoy, yet the mineral flavors add a serious note, too.

2001 Wölffer Rosé, The Hamptons ⚲   ★★★ $
dry, medium-bodied, high acidity   drink now–2 years
One of the best rosé wines from America, this offers dry floral, slight berry, and citrus flavors encased in minerals.

2000 Fox Run Vineyards Gewürztraminer, Finger Lakes ⚲   ★★ $$
dry, medium-bodied, no oak, high acidity   drink now–4 years
Smoky Gewürz, with an abundance of bitter mineral, some dried citrus peel, and dry rose flavors.

**2000 Channing Daughters Scuttlehole Chardonnay,
The Hamptons** ▼ ★★ $
dry, medium-bodied, no oak, high acidity   drink now–3 years
The opposite of California Chardonnay, heavily mineral and lightly fruity.

**2001 Clinton Vineyards Tribute Seyval Blanc,
Hudson River Region** ▼ ★★ $
dry, medium-bodied, no oak, medium acidity   drink now–3 years
A fascinating wine from a French-American hybrid, this gives light citrus and
melon flavors when young, and more caramel and nutty notes with a bit of age.

2001 Martha Clara Vineyards Semillon, North Fork ▼ ★★ $
dry, medium-bodied, no oak, high acidity   drink now–3 years
Semillon has a small presence on Long Island, but the maple and lemon flavors of Martha Clara's might change this.

2001 Millbrook Tocai Friulano, Hudson River Region ▼ ★★ $
dry, light-bodied, no oak, high acidity   drink now–3 years
Rare anywhere in the U.S., this northern Italian grape assimilates nicely in the
Hudson Valley, offering nutty apple and melon flavors.

1999 Peconic Bay Winery Rosé of Merlot, North Fork ▼ ★ $$
dry, medium-bodied, high acidity   drink now–1 years
Spice and minerals keep the exuberant fruit in check.

2001 Paumanok Chenin Blanc, North Fork ▼ ★ $
dry, light-bodied, no oak, high acidity   drink now
Light, lively, and lemony, with hints of apple blossom and pear.

2001 Salmon Run Johannisberg Riesling, New York ▼ ★ $
dry, light-bodied, no oak, high acidity   drink now–2 years
Dr. Konstantin Frank's second-label Riesling doesn't have the depth of the
winery's first, but it is full of peach and citrus flavors balanced by crisp acidity.

WINES WE WISH WE HAD MORE ROOM FOR
2001 Hermann J. Wiemer Gewürztraminer, Finger Lakes ★★★ $$ off-dry,
medium-bodied, no oak, high acidity, drink now–8 years; **2000 Paumanok
Barrel Fermented Chardonnay, North Fork** ★★★ $$ dry, medium-bodied,
medium oak, high acidity, drink now–5 years; **2001 Dr. Konstantin Frank
Gewürztraminer, Finger Lakes** ★★ $$ dry, medium-bodied, no oak, high
acidity, drink now–5 years; **2001 Channing Perrine Mudd Vineyard
Sauvignon Blanc, North Fork** ★★ $ dry, medium-bodied, no oak, high acidity,
drink now–2 years; **2001 Fox Run Vineyards Riesling, Finger Lakes** ★★ $
dry, medium-bodied, no oak, high acidity, drink now–5 years; **2000 Palmer
Vineyards Chardonnay, North Fork** ★★ $ dry, medium-bodied, no oak, high
acidity, drink now–3 years

red wines

The Finger Lakes region produces fine Pinot Noirs with smoky cherry and mineral flavors. Some from the Hudson Valley are good, too. But the state's top reds are from Long Island, where the Gulf Stream allows a growing season three weeks longer than in other parts of the state, a necessity for varieties such as Merlot and Cabernet Sauvignon. Cabernet Franc is the star, though, making medium-bodied wines full of peppery red currant flavors like those that are grown in France's Loire Valley.

at the table
For Long Island's best reds: New York strip, of course, or venison from the Hudson Valley's Millbrook Farms (available nationwide). Pinot Noir is perfect with duck or cassoulet.

the bottom line
Expect to pay $16 to $20 for most Long Island wines, though proprietary blends can cost as much as $35. Few Finger Lakes Pinot Noirs run more than $16.

what to buy RED WINES

1997	1998	1999	2000	2001
★★★	★★★★	★★	★★	★★★★

recommended wines

1999 Dr. Konstantin Frank Reserve Cabernet Sauvignon, Finger Lakes ★★★ $$$
dry, medium-bodied, medium tannin, high acidity   drink now–6 years
Black raspberry, plum, vanilla, and spice, superbly balanced. Delicious.

1999 Fox Run Vineyards Meritage, Finger Lakes ★★★ $$$
dry, full-bodied, medium tannin, high acidity   drink now–8 years
A Bordeaux blend that most Californians would be proud to have made.

2000 Paumanok Grand Vintage Cabernet Sauvignon, North Fork ★★★ $$$
dry, full-bodied, medium tannin, high acidity   drink in 2–10 years
Black as night and juicy as blackberries at the height of summer ripeness.

VANITY FAIR?

In the last three years, between $30 to $40 million have been invested in the Long Island wine industry, mostly by deep-pocket investors who have made their fortunes in the worlds of finance or mass-media. Some recent entrants into the scene include Vincent Galluccio, former managing director of Metromedia Fiber Network, at Gristina; investment banker Paul Lowerre, at Peconic Bay; and Michael Lynne, president of New Line Cinema, at Bedell-Corey Creek. Given that northern Long Island has become the playground of Manhattan's rich, some suspect these wineries are just vanity projects. But as long-time Long Island winemakers point out, anything that raises the profile of the region and drives quality upward benefits everyone. And after all, what tycoon would want his name on a mediocre bottle of wine?

2001 Hermann J. Wiemer Pinot Noir, Finger Lakes ★★★ $$
dry, medium-bodied, medium tannin, high acidity   drink now–5 years
The focus here is on the sultry, smoky, herbal qualities of Pinot Noir.

1998 Macari Cabernet Franc, North Fork ★★★ $$
dry, full-bodied, medium tannin, medium acidity   drink now–8 years
This fine Cabernet Franc has no inhibitions about its piquant pepperiness, nor its indulgence in ripe cassis and black cherry flavors.

2000 Palmer Vineyards Proprietor's Reserve Cabernet Franc, North Fork ★★★ $$
dry, full-bodied, medium tannin, high acidity   drink in 1–8 years
Long Island wine promoters often point to the region's climatic similarity to Bordeaux, but they could just point to this wine, Bordeaux-like in every way except for the price.

2000 Schneider Cabernet Franc, North Fork ★★★ $$
dry, medium-bodied, medium tannin, medium acidity   drink now–8 years
From a business school project to one of Long Island's best wineries, Schneider gets straight A's with wines like this Cabernet Franc, full of ripe berry, sweet spice, and peppery flavors.

1999 Dr. Konstantin Frank Pinot Noir, Finger Lakes ★★ $$
dry, medium-bodied, medium tannin, medium acidity   drink now–6 years
Mineral flavors with dusty tannin against a red cherry background testify to the Finger Lakes' ability with Pinot Noir.

1999 Lieb Merlot, North Fork   ★★ $$
dry, medium-bodied, medium tannin, high acidity   drink now–4 years
Herbal, with tart red berry and tobacco flavors and a spicy tannin edge.

2000 Millbrook Cabernet Franc, New York State   ★★ $$
dry, medium-bodied, medium tannin, medium acidity   drink now–5 years
Berry- and cherry-rich, with pinches of vanilla and spice.

WINES WE WISH WE HAD MORE ROOM FOR
2000 Palmer Vineyards Reserve Merlot, North Fork ★★★ $$$ dry, full-bod-
ied, heavy tannin, high acidity, drink in 2–8 years; **1999 Peconic Bay Winery
Cabernet Franc, North Fork** ★★★ $$ dry, medium-bodied, medium tannin,
high acidity, drink now–5 years; **1999 Wölffer Cabernet Franc, The Hamptons**
★★ $$$ dry, medium-bodied, medium tannin, high acidity, drink now–5 years;
2001 Channing Daughters Fresh Red Merlot, The Hamptons ★★ $ dry,
medium-bodied, medium tannin, medium acidity, drink now; **NV Dr. Konstantin
Frank Fleur de Pinot Noir, Finger Lakes** ★ $ dry, light-bodied, light tannin,
medium acidity, drink now–1 year

OTHER STATES

California, New York, Washington, and Oregon might get
all the credit for the U.S. wine industry, but all fifty states
make wine. Some of it is made from fruits other than
grapes, but there is a lot of top quality grape wine, too.
Some wineries to look for:

Connecticut Chamard Winery

Idaho Ste. Chapelle Winery

Maryland Elk Run

Michigan Chateau Grand Traverse, L. Mawby

Missouri Mount Pleasant Winery, St. James Winery,
          and Stone Hill Winery

New Jersey Tomasello

New Mexico Gruet Winery

North Carolina Westbend Vineyards

Pennsylvania Chaddsford Winery

Rhode Island Sakonnet Vineyards

Texas Cap*Rock Winery, Lllano Estacado

Virginia Barboursville Vineyards, Chrysalis Vineyards,
          Horton Cellars, Linden Vineyards

france

The French didn't invent wine, but for winemakers and connoisseurs everywhere, France is the ultimate inspiration. The classic wines from Bordeaux, Burgundy, Champagne, and the Rhône are the models on which others around the world are based. And though some copies come close to (and may even surpass) the originals, they never achieve the *je ne sais quoi* that sets apart French wine. Bacchus truly has no better home.

grapes & styles

France offers nearly every style of wine, from the light, racy whites of Muscadet to the dark monsters of Cahors. Different regions have different winemaking traditions and techniques that have been judged, over time, to make the best wines in that region.

French winegrowers tend to place much emphasis on *terroir*, a key concept in France. It loosely translates as "earth," but the term goes beyond the mineral content of the soil to encompass the climate, the vineyard's exposure to the sun, the wind, even the scents of aromatic plants growing nearby. A wine's *terroir* reflects those elements that indicate the place from which it came. It's no accident that many Parisian bistros list wines by regions rather than by vintages or producers. Customers expect a wine from a specific region to taste a certain way, regardless of who made it and when.

on the label

Perhaps following the notion of *terroir,* French labels traditionally mention the region in which the wine was grown rather than the grapes used to make it. The wines of Alsace are an exception, and occasionally, for international marketing reasons, vintners in other regions mention grape varieties as well.

Featured Wine-Growing Regions

REIMS • Champagne
PARIS •
STRASBOURG •
Alsace
ORLEANS •
NANTES • Loire Valley
DIJON •
Burgundy
Atlantic Ocean
LIMOGES •
LYON •
BORDEAUX •
Bordeaux
Rhône Valley
Southwest
AVIGNON • NICE •
NIMES • Provence
MARSEILLE
Languedoc-
Roussillon   Mediterranean Sea

To ensure consistency and a level of quality in traditional winegrowing regions, the French established standards to codify the grapes and techniques permitted in each area. This system of standards is called *Appellation d'Origine Contrôlée* (AOC or AC). The hierarchy of AOC standards, from highest to lowest, is as follows:

AOC wines must be made in accordance to strict rules concerning geography, grape varieties, harvest size, vinification techniques, and the amount of alcohol in the wine. These standards vary from region to region, and there may be subregions within an appellation (or "named" region) where even stricter standards apply. For example, the requirements for a wine labeled Pommard, a subregion of Côte de Beaune, are higher than those labeled Côte de Beaune, itself a subregion of Bourgogne, which is yet more permissive. Generally speaking, the more specific the appellation, the higher the quality of wine. Most French wine imported into the U.S. bears an AOC label.

Vin Délimité de Qualité Supérieure wines come under similar regulations as AOC wines, but the standards are slightly less stringent. VDQS wines make up less than 1 percent of total French wine production.

Vin de Pays wines carry a regional designation and must meet certain standards for quality. Though many Vins de Pays are undistinguished, some vintners use the designation to experiment with grapes and vinification techniques that are prohibited under AOC regulations, producing some superlative wines.

Vin de Table wines can come from anywhere in the country, and do not have to meet any requirements, except that they cannot carry the name of a grape or region on their label. Vins de Table are generally of a quality befitting their lowly distinction, but a handful of iconoclastic winemakers use the freedom of the designation to produce some exceptional wines.

alsace

Alsace occupies a unique place in France, sharing its border as well as much of its cultural identity with Germany. (After all, it was part of Germany twice in the last century). The similarity is notable not only in the Germanic names of people and places, but also in the predominance of German grapes like Riesling, Gewürztraminer, and Sylvaner. Nevertheless, Alsatian wine is distinctly French, with fragrant aromas, ripe but dry fruit flavors, and racy acidity.

grapes & styles

Alsace grows grape varieties rarely seen elsewhere in France. Riesling, Gewürztraminer, and Sylvaner have obvious German roots. Others, like Pinot Gris and Pinot Blanc, are French, but seldom appear in other regions. There is also some Muscat. The few reds are made mostly from Pinot Noir. There is also a sparkling wine, Crémant d'Alsace, but it is for sweet wines that the region is justly famous. There are two categories: *Vendange Tardive* ("late harvest") and the sweeter, rarer *Sélection de Grains Nobles*. See page 284 for sweet wine recommendations. Dry or sweet, many Alsatian wines can age for a decade or longer.

on the label

Wines from Alsace tend to be labeled by grape variety, and when they are, the law decrees that they must contain 100 percent of that grape. Some labels bear the designation Grand Cru, indicating that they have been made from Gewürztraminer, Muscat, Pinot Gris, or Riesling grown in one of the fifty vineyards that have been officially designated as superior. However, since there are controversies regarding Grand Cru status, some firms prefer to drop the term from the vineyard designation, and some use a proprietary name to indicate a superior cuvée instead. Terms like Réserve Personnelle or Cuvée Particulière have no legal meaning but they are generally applied to wines of especially good quality.

what to buy ALSACE

1996	1997	1998	1999	2000	2001
★★★	★★★	★★	★★★	★★★	★★★

PINOT BLANC & PINOT GRIS

Alsatian Pinot Blancs are generally light-bodied with nutty and lemony flavors, charming and enjoyable to drink young. Alsatian Pinot Gris, on the other hand, tends to be relatively full-bodied, with nutty, smoky flavors and hints of apricot and dried orange—quite a difference in style from Italy's Pinot Grigio, though it's the same grape. Tokay-Pinot Gris and Tokay d'Alsace are other names for the grape.

at the table

Simple Pinot Blanc matches well with simple foods like baked snapper or a summer spaghetti topped with chopped ripe tomatoes, basil, and a dash of olive oil. Pour Pinot Gris with Alsatian specialities such as *choucroute garnie*, or rich meats like roast goose.

the bottom line Fine examples of Pinot Blanc can be found for next to nothing—$10. There's less Pinot Gris produced in Alsace, so prices are higher, with solid values starting around $16 and heading to $60.

recommended wines

**2000 Domaine Weinbach Cuvée Laurence Tokay
Pinot Gris** ★★★★ $$$$
off-dry, full-bodied, no oak, high acidity drink now–15 years
A seductive display of peachy flavors from one of France's few female vintners, Laurence Faller.

2000 Domaine Agathe Bursin Pinot Blanc ★★★★ $$
dry, medium-bodied, no oak, high acidity drink now–8 years
Bursin takes Pinot Blanc to another plane, offering a wine with intensely aromatic pear and floral flavors.

2000 Domaine Marcel Deiss Belbenheim Pinot Gris ★★★ $$$
dry, medium-bodied, no oak, medium acidity drink now–10 years
Unexpected spice, strawberry, and smoky mineral notes give this fragrant, ripe wine a pleasant twist.

2000 Domaine Zind-Humbrecht Vieilles Vignes Pinot Gris ★★★ $$$
off-dry, full-bodied, no oak, high acidity drink now–13 years
Zind-Humbrecht wines are some of Alsace's most luxurious and pricey, but this luscious, butterscotch- and mango-filled example is relatively affordable.

2000 Josmeyer Le Fromenteau Tokay Pinot Gris ★★★ $$$
dry, medium-bodied, no oak, high acidity drink now–10 years
Lovely smoke, fruit, and mineral flavors mingle pleasureably now, but they'll only get better with age.

2000 Josmeyer Mise du Printemps Pinot Blanc ★★★ $$$
dry, medium-bodied, no oak, high acidity drink now–5 years
Crisp lemon and apple flavors go down easy, but savor it for the almond and mineral flavors that emerge with a little air.

1999 Trimbach Réserve Personnelle Pinot Gris ★★★ $$$
dry, full-bodied, no oak, high acidity drink now–12 years
Butter-rich yet fresh, this is filled with tropical fruit and cinnamon-like flavors.

1999 Domaine Mittnacht-Klack Tokay Pinot Gris ★★★ $$
dry, full-bodied, no oak, high acidity drink now–10 years
Berry, wildflower, and mushroom notes remind of a walk in the forest.

1999 Domaines Schlumberger Les Princes Abbés Pinot Gris ★★★ $$
off-dry, full-bodied, no oak, high acidity drink now–10 years
Luxuriously ripe apricot flavors make this almost rich enough for dessert, yet it remains on the dry side. A bit of botrytis adds fascinating depth.

CHALLENGES TO THE
APPELLATION CONTRÔLÉE SYSTEM

France's Appellation Contrôlée system, regarded as a model for wine regions worldwide, is being challenged. Noting that chemical fertilizers, pesticides, commercial yeasts, and temperature-controlled fermentation blur many of the attributes that differentiate one region's wines from another (undermining the original notion of the appellation system), many vintners throughout France have signed a Charter of Quality that champions sustainable agriculture practices and sets a hierarchy of standards ranging from viticultural to vinicultural practices. Another association, Terra Vitis, requires members use sustainable agricultural practices, such as extremely limited pesticide use. In contrast, AOC rules only limit the types and quantity of grapes produced within a specific area. While the appellation system and the private initiatives are not mutually exclusive, the possibility of a multitiered system within, but not controlled by, AOC boards might create regional stratification. To head off this possibility, the Champagne growers' association is working to impose sustainable agriculture standards on every Champagne vintner. More information on the Charter of Quality is available on www.coulee-de-serrant.com/chartequaliteang.htm.

1999 Léon Beyer Tokay Pinot Gris ★★ $$
dry, medium-bodied, no oak, medium acidity   drink now–6 years
Glazed citrus peel flavors combine with nuts and berries.

2000 Hugel et Fils Cuvée Les Amours Pinot Blanc ★★ $
dry, light-bodied, no oak, medium acidity   drink now
Lovely, lemony, and lively, this is excellent to have around the house.

2000 Domaine Auther Pinot Blanc-Auxerrois ★★ $
dry, medium-bodied, no oak, medium acidity   drink now–3 years
Fine summer sipping with enough fruity oomph to take it into the post-season.

2000 Léon Beyer Pinot Blanc ★★ $
dry, medium-bodied, no oak, high acidity   drink now–2 years
Charming wine, with delightful pear and almond flavors.

2000 Domaine Eugene Meyer, Pinot Blanc ★ $
dry, light-bodied, no oak, high acidity   drink now–2 years
A little air brings out the floral notes in this lemony, mineral-laden wine.

2000 Domaine Paul Blanck Pinot Blanc d'Alsace ★ $
dry, light-bodied, no oak, high acidity   drink now
Green apple crisp, with palate-pleasing mineral notes.

GEWÜRZTRAMINER & RIESLING

Some find Gewürztraminer too heady; others appreciate its piquant bouquet of rose, gardenia, honeysuckle, orange blossom, and clove. Gewürztraminer styles range from medium- to full-bodied; the best Gewürz ("spice" in German) also offer stonelike, smoky flavors.

Whereas Gewürztraminer shows its cards up front, Riesling is the straight flush played with the perfect poker face. Unlike most German Rieslings, which are often slightly sweet and low in alcohol, those from Alsace are stone dry, medium-bodied, but powerful wines full of citrus zest, ripe peach, and mineral flavors. The classic petrol flavors of Riesling emerge with age. This may sound strange, but it can be delicious.

at the table

Gewürztraminer can stand up to full-flavored, pungent, or spicy foods. A ripe Alsatian Munster cheese sprinkled with cumin is a classic accompaniment, though spicy Indian foods like tandoori chicken work well, too. Or, play its floral flavors off a delicate fish fillet.

Alsatian Riesling is one of the world's most flexible wines. It's delicate enough for light fish, yet powerful enough for veal; it has the acidity to cut through cream sauces and the flavors to stand up to spicy curries. Sweet late-harvest styles are brilliant with foie gras, especially when accompanied by sautéed fruit. See page 284 for sweet wine recommendations.

the bottom line It's hard to find a better value than Alsatian Riesling. Those for $12 are very good; for $25, glorious; above that, heavenly. Basic Gewürztraminer starts around $13, though wines for $18 to $23 can offer a tremendous jump in quality. Gewürz at $30 and up can be sublime.

recommended wines

2000 Domaine Weinbach Cuvée Ste-Catherine L'Inédit
Grand Cru Schlossberg Riesling ★★★★ $$$$
off-dry, full-bodied, high acidity, no oak   drink now–20 years
This *inédit* or "novel," wine, made in only exceptional years, is silky, lush, and almost sweet, but so well balanced it begs for lobster, scallops, or foie gras.

1997 Comtes d'Eguisheim Gewurztraminer ★★★★ $$$
off-dry, full-bodied, no oak, high acidity   drink now–10 years
All of Gewürztraminer's qualities—rose, stone, lime, and spice—are here in perfect balance.

2000 Domaine Ostertag Muenchberg
Grand Cru Riesling ★★★★ $$$
dry, full-bodied, no oak, high acidity   drink now–12 years
A tropical paradise, with loads of pineapple, kiwi, and mango flavors accented by wispy smoke notes.

2000 Domaine Zind-Humbrecht Heimbourg
Riesling ★★★★ $$$
dry, full-bodied, no oak, high acidity   drink in 2–15 years
This muscular wine bulges with sweet and savory orange and almond flavors and powerful minerality.

2000 Hugel et Fils Jubilee Riesling ★★★★ $$$
dry, medium-bodied, no oak, high acidity   drink now–12 years
An Alsace great, with peach, mineral, and floral flavors so tightly wound they could explode at any moment.

1998 Trimbach Cuvée des Seigneurs de Ribeaupierre
Gewurztraminer ★★★★ $$$
dry, full-bodied, no oak, medium acidity   drink now–20 years
As with all Trimbach wines, this shows its noble lineage with floral, smoke, spice, and grapefruitlike flavors, as concentrated as they are graceful and elegant.

2000 Albert Mann Grand Cru Furstentum
Gewurztraminer ★★★ $$
medium-sweet, full-bodied, no oak, medium acidity   drink now–15 years
Stony flavors wind through fragrant rose and orange blossom flavors.

2000 Albert Mann Grand Cru Schlossburg Riesling ★★★ $$
dry, medium-bodied, no oak, high acidity   drink now–10 years
Break through the shell of mineral flavors and a prize of ripe pineapple, herb, and compelling petrol notes awaits.

1999 Domaine Auther Winzenberg Grand Cru Riesling   ★ ★ ★ $$
dry, medium-bodied, no oak, medium acidity   drink now–8 years
Ripe fruit, herbal, almost dill-like flavors and loads of minerals say Grand Cru,
though thc low pricc says *vin* for every table.

2000 Domaine Schoffit Alexandre Gewurztraminer   ★ ★ ★ $$
off-dry, full-bodied, no oak, high acidity   drink now–15 years
Typical of this small producer, this super wine is loaded with floral and fruit flavors as well as profound mineral notes.

1998 Trimbach Réserve Riesling   ★ ★ ★ $$
dry, full-bodied, no oak, high acidity   drink now–10 years
An abundance of nut, citrus, and mineral flavors crafted in the classic
Trimbach style: dry, intense, and with sharp acidity.

2000 Kuentz-Bas Tradition Gewurztraminer   ★ ★ $$
dry, full-bodied, no oak, medium acidity   drink now–5 years
A smoky, spicy, floral sampling of a New Zealander making wine in Alsace.
Look for his Grand Cru wlnes, too.

2000 Château d'Orschwihr Bollenberg Riesling   ★ ★ $
dry, medium-bodied, no oak, high acidity   drink now–8 years
Need more minerals in your diet? Drink this smoky, flinty wine: it goes down
easily with peachlike flavor.

2000 Preiss-Henny Riesling   ★ ★ $
dry, medium-bodied, no oak, high acidity   drink now–4 years
Fans of austere, mineral-heavy Riesling should add this to their cellars.

2000 Domaines Schlumberger Fleur Gewurztraminer   ★ $$
off-dry, full-bodied, no oak, high acidity   drink now–5 years
As the name intimates, this peach and mineral-laden wine packs in the floral
flavors.

OTHER ALSATIAN WHITES

Alsace makes some excellent wines from Muscat, with abundant
honeysuckle and citrus flavors. Chasselas is usually light and sim-
ple; Sylvaner a little fuller with higher acidity. Neither command
very high prices, and they are often blended together for simple,
affordable wines. Pinot Auxerrois, widely planted in Alsace, also
usually appears in blends, or in undistinguished bottles labeled
(legally) Pinot Blanc. Look for Pinot Auxerrois that are actually
labeled as such; the best can offer terrific nutty and smoky flavors.

recommended wines

1998 Domaine Marcel Deiss Burg Bergheim ★★★★ $$$
dry, full-bodied, no oak, medium acidity   **drink now–15 years**
Riesling, Pinot Gris, and Gewurztraminer create a wild white loaded with mineral flavors joined by tangerine, grapefruit, and floral notes.

2000 Domaine Zind-Humbrecht Herrenweg de Turckheim
Muscat ★★★★ $$$
dry, full-bodied, no oak, high acidity   **drink now–7 years**
This superb Muscat from a landmark vineyard is powerfully aromatic with nuances of honey and minerals.

2000 Domaine Ostertag Barrique Pinot Gris ★★★ $$$
dry, medium-bodied, medium oak, high acidity   **drink now–8 years**
Maverick winemaker André Ostertag breaks Alsatian tradition by aging his wines in small oak barrels, giving the quince and citrus flavors of Pinot Gris a rich, spicy edge.

2000 Domaine Zind-Humbrecht Pinot d'Alsace ★★★ $$$
dry, medium-bodied, light oak, high acidity   **drink now–6 years**
Olivier Humbrecht juggles Pinots Blanc, Auxerrois, and Chardonnay (botanically, a type of Pinot) to make one excellent wine, full of spicy, cured lemon notes and deep minerality.

2000 Domaine Agathe Bursin Eminence Sylvaner ★★★ $$
off-dry, medium-bodied, no oak, medium acidity   **drink now–5 years**
Though Sylvaner isn't considered noble enough to be labeled Grand Cru, this impressively floral, limey, mineral-filled wine shows the nobility of the highly rated Zinnkoepflé vineyard.

2000 Josmeyer L'Isabelle ★★★ $$
dry, medium-bodied, no oak, high acidity   **drink now–10 years**
Alluring floral notes, fine minerality, and spice make this one of this year's great pleasures.

2000 Dopff & Irion Crustacés ★ $
dry, light-bodied, no oak, high acidity   **drink now**
Light lemon and herb flavors are just the thing to go with—what else?—shellfish.

2000 Hugel et Fils Gentil ★ $
dry, light-bodied, no oak, high acidity   **drink now**
Breezy floral and citrus flavors, plus a low price, make this a wonderful wine for casual drinking.

bordeaux

Many wine lovers consider Bordeaux the quintessential French wine. It is elegant, but has substance. It is perfumed, but not overly so. It can be elitist, but gives few airs. And although Bordeaux at the top end is infamous for the prices it reaches, with nearly 700 million bottles produced a year, there's a lot that can be found for, if not a pittance, at least significantly less than a king's ransom.

lay of the land

Bordeaux is conventionally divided into three parts: the Left Bank, on the west side of the Gironde Estuary and the Garonne River; the Right Bank, on the east side of the estuary and the Dordogne River; and Entre-Deux-Mers ("between two seas"), a white wine region that lies between the two rivers. The northern part of the Left Bank is known as the Médoc, the most prestigious part of which is the Haut-Médoc. Within Haut-Médoc are several famous villages or communes, such as St-Julien, St-Estèphe, Margaux, and Pauillac. Graves, on the left bank but farther south, contains the prestigious subregion Pessac-Léognan. Farther south still is Sauternes, known for its luxurious sweet whites. The Right Bank is famous for the red wine appellations of Pomerol and St-Émilion, where Merlot tends to play a greater part in the wines, making for more lush, generous wines.

on the label

The most basic red and white wines are labeled simply Bordeaux or Bordeaux Supérieur, indicating that they are made from grapes grown in any of the appellations of the entire region. A step up is Cru Bourgeois, applied to wines grown within any of the appellations of the Médoc.

On the Left Bank, wines may also carry a Cru Classé designation, indicating that the vineyard and property were officially designated as superior sites according to a "classified growth" system invented in 1855 for the wines of the Médoc and Sauternes. The highest rank in this classification scheme is First Growth (Premier Cru) and continues down the line to Fifth Growth. The specific ranking is rarely seen on wine labels, however, as most châteaux prefer to use only Grand Cru Classé or

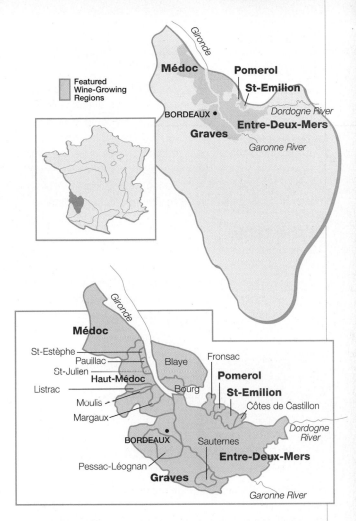

Featured
Wine-Growing
Regions

Médoc

Pomerol

St-Emilion

BORDEAUX •

Dordogne River

Graves

Entre-Deux-Mers

Garonne River

Gironde

Médoc

St-Estèphe

Pauillac

St-Julien

Haut-Médoc

Listrac

Moulis

Margaux

BORDEAUX •

Pessac-Léognan

Graves

Blaye

Bourg

Fronsac

Pomerol

St-Emilion

Côtes de Castillon

Sauternes

Dordogne River

Entre-Deux-Mers

Garonne River

Cru Classé. While a First Growth rank remains a guarantee of a superlative wine, approach the rest of the rankings with deliberation, as some wineries outperform their designation, while the quality of others has declined.

On the Right Bank, the wines of St-Émilion are classified according to their own system, devised in 1955 and revised every ten years. Here, the highest rank is Premier Grand Cru, followed by Grand Cru Classé. As with the Left Bank classifications, the rankings can be useful but discrepancies warrant caution. The wines of Pomerol remain unclassified.

white wines

grapes & styles

White wine may come in second in Bordeaux, but it is diverse and much beloved. Styles range from the simple, refreshing wines of Entre-Deux-Mers to the sophisticated dry wines of Graves that can be aged for years to take on impressive richness and complexity. And the long-lived wines of Sauternes and Barsac are among the most treasured dessert wines on earth. Whatever the style, AOC-sanctioned white Bordeaux wines are made with Sauvignon Blanc, Sémillon, and/or Muscadelle.

at the table

Just remember *Entre deux huitres, Entre-Deux-Mers* ("Between two oysters, between two seas") when it comes to pairing Entre-Deux-Mers with food: these light, lemony, high-acidity white wines are wonderful with raw shellfish. The richer whites of Graves or Médoc demand heavier fare, like lobster, salmon, or rabbit with a creamy sauce.

the bottom line Good Entre-Deux-Mers can cost $10 or less. Most white Graves run between $10 and $22, though wines from top producers can fetch over $50.

recommended wines

**2000 Château Carbonnieux Grand Cru Classé,
Pessac-Léognan** ★★★ $$$
dry, medium-bodied, light oak, high acidity   drink now–10 years
White Graves typified, with level after level of stone and peach flavors that please and challenge the palate.

2000 Les Arums de Lagrange, Bordeaux ★★★ $$
dry, full-bodied, medium oak, high acidity   drink now–10 years
Few Bordeaux producers put as much effort into white wine as Lagrange. The efforts show in this buttery peach cobbler of a white, balanced by firm acidity.

1999 Château La Louvière, Pessac-Léognan ★★ $$
dry, medium-bodied, light oak, medium acidity   drink now–6 years
A tropical paradise, with tropical fruit flavors suffused with a light stoniness.

1999 Château La Tour Léognan, Pessac-Léognan ★★ $$
dry, medium-bodied, medium oak, high acidity drink now–3 years
Château Carbonnieux's second-tier wine offers many of the same ripe fruit and stony qualities as its famed parent, for half the price.

2000 Baron de Rothschild Légende R, Bordeaux ★★ $
dry, medium-bodied, light oak, high acidity drink now–4 years
Surprisingly rich, this is full of candied violet scents and buttery marmalade flavors of orange and spice.

2001 Château Bonnet, Entre-Deux-Mers ★★ $
dry, medium-bodied, no oak, high acidity drink now
Lively peach flavors with a grassy freshness make for pure pleasure before dinner or with a first course of fish.

2000 Château d'Hourcat, Pessac-Léognan ★★ $
dry, medium-bodied, light oak, high acidity drink now–4 years
There are peaches among Pessac's gravel in this fruity, floral, and fine wine.

2001 Château Haut Rian, Bordeaux ★ $
dry, light-bodied, no oak, high acidity drink now
Light and citrusy flavors against a backdrop of tart mineral notes make for good summer sipping.

2001 Marquis de Chasse Réserve Sauvignon Blanc-Sémillon, Bordeaux ★ $
dry, medium-bodied, no oak, high acidity drink now–1 year
Apple and citrus flavors with mouthwatering acidity make a great match for a big bowl of *moules marinières*.

red wines

grapes & styles

Almost three-quarters of Bordeaux's wine is red, made from one or more of six varieties: Merlot, Cabernet Sauvignon, Cabernet Franc, Malbec, Petit Verdot, and Carmenère (listed in order of importance). Merlot is the most common grape, especially on the Right Bank, where it contributes to the plummy, violet-scented wines of Pomerol and St-Émilion. Cabernets tend to dominate on the Left Bank, where they make more tannic wines with black currant flavors and scents that recall pencil lead. While there are some lighter "claret" styles, many of these wines require long cellaring.

at the table

With its strong tannin, and acidity, red Bordeaux cries out for steak or roast rack of lamb. Vegetarians might find smoked and grilled tofu to work, or anything with Roquefort or Stilton.

the bottom line Bordeaux is dear, both to the hearts and pocketbooks of wine lovers. Top-ranked wines start at $150 upon release, and prices typically escalate with time. With the heralded 1999 and 2000 vintages—which have particular cachet among collectors wanting wines from the end of the 20th and beginning of the 21st centuries in their cellars—prices are not coming down soon. But there is some relief. Because of intense interest in the 2000 vintage, many stocks of 1998 and 1999 wines have remained unsold, and there may be impressive discounts to come. Look, too, to some of the wineries that outperform their rank with wines that can challenge their more illustrious—and much more expensive—kin. More reasonably priced yet are wines from less famous appellations such as Moulis, Listrac, and the Côtes de Fronsac, Castillon, and Bourg.

what to buy BORDEAUX RIGHT BANK

1991	1992	1993	1994	1995	1996
no stars	★	★★	★★★	★★★	★★★★

1997	1998	1999	2000	2001
★★	★★★★	★★★	★★★★	★★★

what to buy BORDEAUX LEFT BANK, EXCLUDING GRAVES

1991	1992	1993	1994	1995	1996
★	★	★★	★★★	★★★★	★★★★

1997	1998	1999	2000	2001
★★	★★★	★★★	★★★★	★★★

what to buy RED GRAVES

1991	1992	1993	1994	1995	1996
★	★	★★★	★★★	★★★	★★★

1997	1998	1999	2000	2001
★★★	★★	★★	★★★★	★★★

FIRST-RATE SECOND LABELS

Grand Cru Bordeaux is often exceptional, but it comes at a price, up to several hundred dollars a bottle. But many wineries release "second-label" wines, which might be second-tier compared to their hallmark wines, are by no means second-rate. And they cost a whole lot less. Here are a few to look for:

Alter Ego de Palmer (Château Palmer)

Carruades de Lafite (Château Lafite-Rothschild)

Château Bahans-Haut Brion (Château Haut-Brion)

Château Haut-Bages Avérous (Château Lynch Bages)

Clos du Marquis (Château Léoville-Las Cases)

Lady Langoa (Château Langoa-Barton)

Les Fiefs de Lagrange (Château Lagrange)

Les Forts de Latour (Château Latour)

Les Pensées de Lafleur (Château Lafleur)

Les Tourelles de Longueville (Château Pichon-Longueville)

Pavillon Rouge du Château Margaux (Château Margaux)

Sarget de Gruaud-Larose (Château Gruaud-Larose)

recommended wines

1999 Château Gazin, Pomerol　　　　　　　★★★★ $$$$
dry, full-bodied, medium tannin, medium acidity　　drink in 2–15 years
Absolutely luscious, with flavors as pronounced as a ripe, firm black cherry covered with excellent bittersweet chocolate.

1999 Clos Fourtet Premier Grand Cru Classé, St-Émilion　　　　　　　★★★ $$$
dry, full-bodied, medium tannin, high acidity　　drink in 2–12 years
Archetypal St-Émilion, with berry flavors balanced beautifully with mocha and smoky mineral notes.

1999 Château Haut-Bailly, Pessac-Léognan　　　　　　　★★★ $$$
dry, full-bodied, heavy tannin, high acidity　　drink in 1–12 years
Graves moderne, full of salt and pepper, mineral and spice, but also rich in ripe cherry and cedar flavors.

france **bordeaux**

1999 Château Léoville-Barton, St-Julien ★★★ $$$
dry, full-bodied, heavy tannin, medium acidity   drink in 3–20 years
With black currant, black mineral, and black licorice flavors, this wine consistently outperforms its second-growth standing, at a fraction of first-growth price.

1999 Château Pontet Canet, Pauillac ★★★ $$$
dry, medium-bodied, medium tannin, medium acidity drink in 2–12 years
In the battle between black fruit and spicy oak, fruit has gained the upper hand, but wait a few years for the armistice to be signed.

1999 Château Bouscaut, Pessac-Léognan ★★★ $$
dry, full-bodied, heavy tannin, medium acidity   drink in 3–12 years
Swirl the glass to conjure visions of a fire in the fireplace, autumn leaves, leather, and raspberries. The region's gravelly soils add deep mineral flavors.

1998 Château de Lamarque, Haut-Médoc ★★★ $$
dry, full-bodied, heavy tannin, medium acidity   drink in 2–12 years
This wine offers all that a more prestigious winemaker could only hope to achieve: smooth black fruit, bitter chocolate, tobacco, and herb flavors.

1999 Château Grand-Puy-Ducasse, Pauillac ★★★ $$
dry, full-bodied, heavy tannin, medium acidity   drink in 3–15 years
Low-cost Pauillac power, tannin-peppered and full of dark fruit and truffle flavors.

1999 Château La Croix de Gay, Pomerol ★★★ $$
dry, medium-bodied, medium tannin, medium acidity drink in 3–15 years
Terrific Pomerol at a terrific price, with concentrated red berry and fresh-roasted coffee aromas and flavors.

1999 Château Lafon-Rochet, St-Estèphe ★★★ $$
dry, full-bodied, heavy tannin, medium acidity   drink in 2–15 years
This exemplifies the "grand" in Grand Cru, with full fruit and earthy flavors like licorice, minerals, and toasty tobacco. Buy a case to enjoy over a decade.

1999 Château Rauzan-Gassies, Margaux ★★★ $$
dry, medium-bodied, medium tannin, medium acidity drink in 3–12 years
The typhoon of roasted fruit, floral, and coffee flavors makes for rough seas right now, but time promises smooth sailing.

1999 Château La Fleur Peyrabon Cru Bourgeois, Pauillac ★★ $$$
dry, full-bodied, medium tannin, high acidity   drink in 2–12 years
Pauillac defined, with heavy black fruit, vanilla, and mineral flavors.

1998 Château Moulin du Cadet, St-Émilion ★★ $$$
dry, full-bodied, medium tannin, high acidity   drink now–6 years
This has St-Émilion's soft, plummy flavors plus an intriguing gamey note.

1998 Château Canon, Canon-Fronsac ★★ $$
dry, medium-bodied, medium tannin, high acidity   drink now–5 years
Claret defined, with its vibrant red fruit flavors, a bit of spice, and its palate-tickling acidity.

1999 Château Cap de Faugères, Côtes de Castillon ★★ $$
dry, medium-bodied, medium tannin, medium acidity   drink now–5 years
Good everyday Bordeaux, with soft cherry flavors joined by smoke and a slight herbal note. Excellent value.

1999 Château Haut-Beauséjour, St-Estèphe ★★ $$
dry, full-bodied, heavy tannin, high acidity   drink in 2–8 years
A ready pleasure, with full flavors of blackberry, pepper, and some herbs.

1999 Château La Couronne Grand Cru, St-Émilion ★★ $$
dry, medium-bodied, heavy tannin, medium acidity   drink in 1–8 years
A medley of reds: brick red in color, bright red in cherry flavor, and rusty red in its earthy minerality.

**1999 Château La Tour Carnet Grand Cru Classé,
Haut-Médoc** ★★ $$
dry, medium-bodied, medium tannin, medium acidity   drink in 1–8 years
A strumpet of a wine with tawdry cherry and plum flavors and a tart mouth.

1999 Les Fiefs de Lagrange, St-Julien ★★ $$
dry, full-bodied, heavy tannin, medium acidity   drink in 1–10 years
Château Lagrange's "second" wine is anything but second-rate. Revel in its luxurious berry, floral, and smoke flavors.

1999 Château Fonréaud Cru Bourgeois, Listrac-Médoc ★★ $
dry, medium-bodied, heavy tannin, medium acidity   drink in 2–8 years
Red fruit flavors hide behind a scrim of smoke, but time will clear the air.

1999 Château Tournefeuille, Lalande de Pomerol ★★ $
dry, medium-bodied, medium tannin, medium acidity   drink now–8 years
Plum, blackberry, and mineral flavors graced with Pomerol's elegance, but not its normally high price.

1999 Château Labégorce, Margaux ★ $$
dry, medium-bodied, medium tannin, high acidity   drink now–5 years
Nutty fruit flavors provide substance, while Margaux's *terroir* infuses it with its florid charm.

1998 Baron de Rothschild Légende R, Bordeaux ★ $
dry, medium-bodied, medium tannin, high acidity   drink now–5 years
Easy to drink, with light, peppery, cranberry flavors and fine tannin.

1999 Château Greysac Cru Bourgeois, Médoc   ★ $
dry, medium-bodied, medium tannin, medium acidity   drink now–3 years
Classic claret for everyday drinking.

2000 Château La Croix Sainte-Anne, Bordeaux Supérieur   ★ $
dry, medium-bodied, medium tannin, high acidity   drink now–4 years
A lovely garnet hue leads to peppery plum and berry flavors. Let it breathe.

WINES WE WISH WE HAD MORE ROOM FOR
1999 Château Clarke, Listrac-Médoc ★★ $$$ dry, medium-bodied,
heavy tannin, medium acidity, drink now–6 years; **1999 Château Coufran
Cru Bourgeois, Haut-Médoc** ★★ $$ dry, full-bodied, medium tannin,
medium acidity, drink now–6 years; **2000 Château Clos Beauséjour,
Côtes de Castillon** ★★ $ dry, full-bodied, medium tannin, high acidity,
drink in 1–6 years; **1998 Château des Mille Anges, Premières Côtes
de Bordeaux** ★ $ dry, medium-bodied, medium tannin, high acidity, drink
now–4 years

burgundy

Burgundy, the wine of kings and court, represents, in some
ways, the heart of France: grand and noble in pedigree, but
often frustrating in reality. At best, Burgundies reflect a perfect
balance between sun-ripened fruit, minerals from the soil, and
an ethereal smokiness. At their worst, they are pallid reflections
of the ideal. In between, they are the ultimate tease, offering
inklings of ecstasy but holding out with promises for the future.

lay of the land
Burgundy is divided into five distinct districts, from north to
south: Chablis, the Côte d'Or (itself divided into the Côte de
Nuits and the Côte de Beaune), the Côte Chalonnaise, Mâcon,
and Beaujolais.

grapes & styles
Almost all white Burgundy is made from Chardonnay, though
some is made from Aligoté (and labeled as such), and one AOC
is devoted to Sauvignon Blanc, Sauvignon de St-Bris.
Chardonnay styles range from simple, crisp Mâcons to richer,
barrel-fermented Premier and Grand Cru wines. All tend to have
citrus and mineral notes and high acidity.

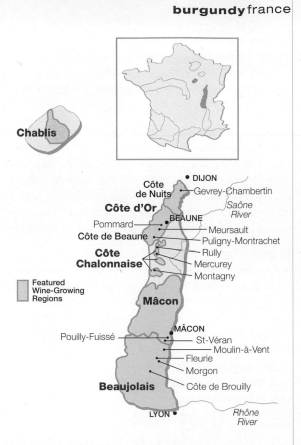

For red Burgundy, Pinot Noir is responsible for the wines everywhere except in Beaujolais, where Gamay makes cherry-juicy reds. The Pinot Noirs tend to be light- to medium-bodied, with smoky berry and mineral flavors and medium tannin. Though they may not be dark and heavy, red Burgundy can age excellently, taking on seductive, earthy complexity.

on the label

Burgundy wines are labeled by region. Broadly speaking, the more specific the regional designation, the more complex the wine. The most basic wines are labeled simply *Bourgogne* (French for "Burgundy"), which indicates only that the wine was produced in Burgundy from designated grape varieties. (Sometimes the grape variety will also appear on the label, such as Bourgogne-Pinot Noir.) A description of the higher levels follows on the next page.

District Wine produced from designated grapes grown in one of the named districts—Chablis, for instance. If the label includes the term "Villages," like Chablis-Villages, the wines come from an even more specific area, and thus tend to have more character.

Village Wines made from grapes grown within the boundaries of a particular village, such as Chambolle-Musigny. The designation is helpful since the soil type and climate are frequently more consistent within village boundaries than within an entire district, and so the wines tend to demonstrate a particular *terroir.* However, since village boundaries are drawn for reasons other than geology, there are limits to assertions of specific character.

Premier Cru Wines made from grapes grown within one of the fewer than 600 Burgundy vineyards that have been designated as superior, or Premier Cru, can mention the name of the vineyard along with the designation Premier Cru, for example, Les Combettes Premier Cru in Puligny-Montrachet. The term can also be used by wineries that have blended grapes from different Premier Cru vineyards within a single village, such as Chassagne-Montrachet Premier Cru. Note that Premier Cru is secondary to Grand Cru in Burgundy, unlike in Bordeaux, where Premier Cru is superior.

Grand Cru Of the 4,500 vineyards in Burgundy, only thirty-three are entitled to the lofty title Grand Cru. These vineyards usually produce the finest, most concentrated and complex wines in the region, requiring several years of aging for their potential to emerge. They often go by only their vineyard name: for example, Montrachet, Chambertin, or Le Musigny. And, frequently, their reputation is so great that the words Grand Cru won't even appear on the label. If the names don't ring Grand Cru in your ears, the prices certainly will.

A note of caution, however: Burgundy is confusing, a bureaucratic puzzle that contains logic, but not necessarily reason. Vineyards ranked for the quality of the fruit they produce can be owned by dozens of different people, some of whom have only a few rows of vines. The grapegrowers can then use the grapes to make their own wine, or they can sell them to a different winemaker. Some growers make wine only to sell it to other companies that blend, bottle, and label it under their own name. In addition, a few vineyards traverse the borders of more than one village, each of which is so eager to draw on the vineyard's fame that they have changed their names to include that of the famed site. So, while the wines of Aloxe-Corton are often excellent, they aren't Corton.

at the table

Chablis' lean, chalky mineral flavors match the briny qualities of oysters. A simple Mâcon white is right for grilled chicken. Premier or Grand Cru whites are richer, more substantial wines powerful enough for salmon or pork loin, especially if they've been aged.

Red Burgundy is one of the most versatile wines, with examples light enough for fish and rich enough for venison. With their soft but substantial tannin and delicacy of flavor, Burgundies can be an excellent choice when everyone at the table has ordered something different.

the bottom line Mâcons begin at $10; Bourgogne Blancs and a few village wines are under $20. Premier and Grand Cru wines start at $35 and skyrocket from there.

Red Burgundy is expensive, though often less expensive than Bordeaux despite its reputation and the fact that the region produces one-tenth as much as Bordeaux. Good, basic Bourgogne-appellation wines can be found for $16, but Premier and Grand Cru reds start at $40 and climb steeply from there.

chablis

Chablis produces some of the best Chardonnay on earth. The region's cool climate keeps acidity levels high and the lemon and pear flavors dry, while its chalky, limestone soil often adds a steely edge. Most basic Chablis are free of the flavors of oak, though some vintners employ new oak barrels for modern styles and richer Premier Cru and Grand Cru wines meant to age.

what to buy CHABLIS

1997	1998	1999	2000	2001
★★★	★★★	★★★	★★	★★

recommended wines

2000 Christian Moreau Père et Fils Grand Cru Les Clos ★ ★ ★ ★ $$$$
dry, medium-bodied, light oak, medium acidity   **drink in 2–12 years**
Give this time to build on its already impressive base of citrus, nuts, smoke, and mineral flavors.

1999 Domaine William Fèvre Grand Cru Les Preuses   ★ ★ ★ $$$$
dry, medium-bodied, medium oak, high acidity   **drink now–12 years**
Plenty of smoky oak combines with fat fruit and minty flavors for a great wine.

2000 Domaine Laroche Les Vaudevey Premier Cru   ★ ★ ★ $$$
dry, medium-bodied, no oak, high acidity   **drink in 1–10 years**
Hold this for a year: its light, crisp mineral flavors will blossom.

2000 Jean-Marc Brocard Premier Cru Vaucoupin   ★ ★ ★ $$
dry, medium-bodied, no oak, high acidity   **drink now–8 years**
Kumquat and tangerine flavors meld with almonds and peaches in this classic, lightly mineral wine.

1998 La Chablisienne Premier Cru Les Fourchaumes   ★ ★ ★ $$
dry, medium-bodied, light oak, high acidity   **drink now–12 years**
From one of the finest wine co-ops worldwide, a Chablis of concentrated orange, dry honey, and deep mineral flavors, beautifully balanced.

2000 Christian Moreau Père et Fils   ★ ★ $$
dry, medium-bodied, no oak, medium acidity   **drink now–4 years**
Clean, clear Chardonnay made smoky with minerals, not oak.

2000 Domaine Laroche St-Martin   ★ ★ $$
dry, medium-bodied, no oak, medium acidity   **drink now–4 years**
Chablis, easy and enjoyable with mineral notes and plenty of ripe fruit.

2000 William Fèvre Champs Royaux   ★ ★ $$
dry, medium-bodied, no oak, high acidity   **drink now–2 years**
Light minerality makes room for a bevy of grapefruit and green apple flavors.

2000 Alain Geoffroy Cuvée Vieilles Vignes   ★ ★ $
dry, medium-bodied, light oak, high acidity   **drink now–3 years**
Bargains from Burgundy are hard to find, but this floral, orange-flavored, and distinctively mineral wine fits the bill.

2000 Domaine Hamelin, Petit Chablis   ★ ★ $
dry, light-bodied, no oak, high acidity   **drink now–2 years**
Not at all *petit,* but rich as salted hazelnuts and tangy as a grapefruit.

côte d'or

Named the "Golden Slope," the Côte d'Or produces the world's finest Chardonnays and Pinot Noirs. The region is divided into the Côte de Nuits in the north, best known for its smoky, cherry-scented reds from famous villages such as Gevrey-Chambertin, Morey-St-Denis, Vosne-Romanée, and Vougeot; and the Côte de Beaune in the south, heralded for its medium-bodied white wines that explode with ripe citrus and tropical flavors when given a little time in the cellar and glass. Revered villages include Chassagne-Montrachet, Meursault, and Puligny-Montrachet. The Côte de Beaune also boasts red wines such as the powerful Pommard and the silky Volnay, as well as the lighter Aloxe-Corton and Beaune. In both the Côte de Nuits and the Côte de Beaune, the finest wines are labeled simply with their vineyards, such as Montrachet or Romanée-Conti.

what to buy COTE D'OR WHITE WINES

1998	1999	2000	2001
★★★	★★★	★★★	★★★

what to buy COTE D'OR RED WINES

1998	1999	2000	2001
★★★	★★★	★	★★

recommended white wines

2000 Domaine Amiot Guy & Fils Premier Cru Les Demoiselles, Puligny-Montrachet ★★★★ $$$$
dry, full-bodied, medium oak, high acidity — drink in 1–12 years
Surrounded by Grand Cru vineyards, Les Demoiselles achieves a class rarely displayed by other Premier Cru vineyards. The smoky fruit and nut flavors are as intense as they are sublime.

2000 Michel Coutoux Grand Cru, Montrachet ★★★★ $$$$
dry, full-bodied, medium oak, high acidity — drink now–12 years
Grand Cru? *Mais oui!* Aromas of fruit and almond take on an almost custardy richness in flavor.

france **burgundy**

1998 Domaine Jobard-Morey Premier Cru Les Charmes, Meursault ★★★★ $$$
dry, full-bodied, medium oak, high acidity   drink now–12 years
Not your average Meursault, aromatic and full of nutty, spicy flavor. Great.

2000 Domaine Fernand & Laurent Pillot Premier Cru Vide Bourse, Chassagne-Montrachet ★★★ $$$
dry, medium-bodied, medium oak, high acidity   drink now–10 years
Oak aromas hit first, but they dissolve into harmonious lemony, smoky bliss.

1999 Leroy, Meursault ★★★ $$$
dry, medium-bodied, medium oak, high acidity   drink now–8 years
Meursault is as Meursault does, with dry lemon-lime flavors and lashes of matchstick oak flavors.

1999 Domaine Joseph Drouhin, St-Aubin ★★★ $$
dry, medium-bodied, no oak, high acidity   drink now–4 years
Spicy strawberry, apricot, and herb flavors pleasantly surprise in this light white.

2000 Olivier Leflaive Les Sétilles, Bourgogne ★★★ $
dry, medium-bodied, light oak, medium acidity   drink now–2 years
Olivier Leflaive makes top-level Burgundy, but even his low-priced basic Bourgogne wins for its floral, lemon-lime flavors.

2000 Bouchard Père & Fils, Puligny-Montrachet ★★ $$$
dry, medium-bodied, light oak, high acidity   drink now–6 years
Classic Puligny with the mineral and citrus flavors that make the village famous.

1999 Domaine Michel Picard Château de Chassagne-Montrachet En Pimont, Chassagne-Montrachet ★★ $$$
dry, medium-bodied, medium oak, high acidity   drink now–8 years
Beyond the toasty oak, there's plenty of orange and spice flavor.

2000 Labouré-Roi, Puligny-Montrachet ★★ $$$
dry, medium-bodied, light oak, high acidity   drink now–6 years
Textbook Puligny-Montrachet, full of mineral and concentrated citrus flavors balanced by a light, smoky oak.

1999 Louis Jadot Clos de Malte, Santenay ★★ $$$
dry, medium-bodied, heavy oak, high acidity   drink in 2–8 years
Time will sand the oak's influence to smooth harmony with the citrus and spice flavors.

2000 Michel Coutoux Les Narvaux, Meursault ★★ $$$
dry, medium-bodied, medium oak, medium acidity   drink now–7 years
Classic Meursault with rich citrus, caramel, oak, and mineral flavors.

1999 Alex Gambal Cuvée Préstige, Bourgogne ★★ $$
dry, medium-bodied, no oak, high acidity   drink now–3 years

American-born *négociant* Gambal has been assembling some of the most interesting and fairly priced Burgundies available, like this herbal, floral, citrus-flavored example.

1999 Maison Champy, Bourgogne Blanc ★★ $$
dry, medium-bodied, no oak, high acidity   drink now–3 years

Pure enjoyment, with ripe, true citrus flavors from first to last.

1999 Henri Clerc Les Riaux Chardonnay, Bourgogne ★★ $
dry, medium-bodied, no oak, high acidity   drink now–2 years

Smoke and lemon flavors are made more indulgent by a creamy texture; a super value from an excellent producer.

recommended red wines

2000 Domaine Dujac Grand Cru, Echezeaux ★★★★ $$$$
dry, full-bodied, medium tannin, high acidity   drink in 2–12 years

Wow. Black cherry, deep minerals, smoky tobacco, and more. Wines like this are why people get so excited about Burgundy.

1999 Labouré-Roi Grand Cru, Clos de Vougeot ★★★★ $$$$
dry, full-bodied, heavy tannin, high acidity   drink in 2–15 years

Power, complexity, and balance.

**2000 Domaine Maume Premier Cru,
Gevrey-Chambertin** ★★★ $$$$
dry, medium-bodied, medium tannin, medium acidity   drink in 1–8 years

Two Premier Cru vineyards are blended to produce a captivating mélange of wild berry, spice, and gamey flavor.

**2000 Domaine Méo-Camuzet Premier Cru Les Chaumes,
Vosne-Romanée** ★★★ $$$$
dry, medium-bodied, medium tannin, medium acidity   drink now–10 years

This might be almost California-like in its ripe berry flavors, but it has classic Burgundy structure.

**1999 Vincent Girardin Premier Cru Les Damodes,
Nuits-St-Georges** ★★★ $$$$
dry, full-bodied, medium tannin, high acidity   drink in 1–12 years

A Nuits-St-Georges that packs bushels of blackberry, pecks of pepper, and mines of mineral flavors.

BURGUNDY BLUES

With names like Romanée-Conti, Montrachet, Chambertin, and Corton-Charlemagne within its boundaries, Burgundy is revered by wine lovers around the world. But all is not well outside of these hallmark regions. As *Wine Spectator* reported in July 2002, *vignerons* from Mâcon and the Côte Chalonnaise, angry over the large quantities of unsold 2000 and 2001 vintage wines, are protesting that regional officials aren't doing enough to promote their products. Regional officials claim that the problems are overproduction of mediocre wines and competition from good quality New World wines. Wine lovers disappointed by more than one bottle of sub-par Burgundy can only agree.

1999 Domaine Joseph Drouhin, Chambolle-Musigny ★★★ $$$
dry, full-bodied, medium tannin, medium acidity drink now–8 years
A real pleasure, with spicy raspberry flavors and a sprinkle of minerals.

1999 Jean-Claude Belland Grand Cru Clos de la Vigne au Saint, Corton ★★★ $$$
dry, full-bodied, medium tannin, medium acidity drink now–8 years
Corton's dark fruit and mineral depth, plus toasted nut flavors, without its usual heart-stopping price.

2000 Nicolas Potel Vieilles Vignes, Volnay ★★★ $$$
dry, medium-bodied, heavy tannin, medium acidity drink in 2–12 years
A bruiser with a soft side, with deep black fruit and mineral flavors graced by hints of lavender.

2000 Domaine Les Champs de l'Abbaye, Bourgogne ★★★ $$
dry, full-bodied, medium tannin, medium acidity drink now–5 years
This may not be classical, but the big, tart raspberry flavors infused by exotic spices sure are delicious.

2000 Domaine Sylvain Cathiard, Bourgogne ★★★ $$
dry, medium-bodied, medium tannin, medium acidity, drink now–6 years
All one hopes for in a Burgundy: bright berry, mineral flavors, a decent price.

1999 Edmond Monnot Premier Cru Clos de la Boutière, Maranges ★★★ $$
dry, full-bodied, heavy tannin, medium acidity drink now–10 years
Nuts, berries, and spice. An excellent wine to grace holiday tables.

**1999 Domaine Bruno Clair Premier Cru La Dominode,
Savigny-Les-Beaune** ★★ $$$$
dry, full-bodied, heavy tannin, medium acidity **drink now–8 years**
Berry, spicy mineral, and smoky flavors are made extra appealing with their velvety texture.

1999 Bouchard Père & Fils, Gevrey-Chambertin ★★ $$$
dry, medium-bodied, medium tannin, high acidity **drink now–5 years**
Tart cherry, light vanilla, and smoky mineral flavors from a reliable producer.

**1998 Château de Monthelie Premier Cru Sur La Velle,
Monthelie** ★★ $$$
dry, medium-bodied, medium tannin, high acidity **drink now–6 years**
Full of acidity, spicy berry, animal, and bitter herb flavors, this would be great with roast pork loin.

2000 Domaine Chevrot, Maranges Sur Le Chêne ★★ $$
dry, medium-bodied, medium tannin, medium acidity **drink now–4 years**
Mineral notes jump out from this light, spicy, raspberry-flavored wine.

2000 Domaine Vincent Prunier, Auxey-Duresses ★★ $$
dry, medium-bodied, medium tannin, medium acidity **drink now–6 years**
If "barnyard" applied to Burgundy brings a smile to your face, you'll love this earthy example.

1999 Louis Jadot, Fixin ★★ $$
dry, light-bodied, medium tannin, high acidity **drink now–5 years**
Sleek yet fleshy with cherry flavors and slightly bitter herbal notes, this shows off Fixin's charm.

côte chalonnaise

The Côte Chalonnaise may be less famous than the Côte d'Or to the north, but its winemakers make a lot of very good wine, both red and white. The region's lack of stardom means that its prices are gentler than those of the Côte d'Or. Look for Pinot Noirs from Givry, Mercurey, and Rully; Chardonnays from Montagny and Rully. And don't forget Aligoté, a lesser-known white grape that makes crisp, mineral-laden wines. Some of the best are from Bouzeron, an appellation dedicated solely to the grape where it tends to take on more weight and spice than usual.

recommended white wines

1999 Faiveley Clos Rochette, Mercurey ★★★ $$$
dry, medium-bodied, medium oak, medium acidity **drink in 1–10 years**
Give this a little time for the peach, raspberry, smoke, and stone flavors to meld, and it will reward.

2000 Olivier Leflaive Premier Cru, Rully ★★★ $$
dry, medium-bodied, light oak, high acidity **drink now–4 years**
This Rully combines a surprising earthiness with orange, herb, and mineral flavors.

2000 Château Génot-Boulanger Les Bacs, Mercurey ★★ $$
dry, medium-bodied, light oak, medium acidity **drink now–4 years**
An earthy wine whose orange and lemon flavors are underlaid by a palate-pleasing stoniness.

1999 Domaine Michel Picard Premier Cru Château de Davenay, Montagny ★★ $$
dry, medium-bodied, light oak, high acidity **drink now–6 years**
Appealing candied lemon flavors are balanced by savory almond notes and lots of minerality.

1999 Domaine Michel Picard Domaine Champs Perdrix, Bourgogne Côte Chalonnaise ★ $
dry, medium-bodied, no oak, high acidity **drink now–3 years**
Its palate-cleansing lemon and mineral flavors make this an excellent match for oysters.

recommended red wines

1999 Domaine Michel Juillot Premier Cru Clos des Barraults, Mercurey ★★★ $$$
dry, medium-bodied, medium tannin, medium acidity **drink in 1–8 years**
A tight, powerful wine that needs time and air to let loose its meaty cherry flavors.

1999 Chofflet-Valdenaire, Givry ★★ $$
dry, medium-bodied, medium tannin, high acidity **drink now–4 years**
Feisty fruit and spice flavors buck on an earthy base.

1999 Domaine du Bourgneuf, Mercurey ★★ $$
dry, medium-bodied, medium tannin, high acidity **drink now–5 years**
Simple and enjoyable, a circus of spicy black raspberry flavors.

mâcon

Not so long ago, Mâcon wines were regarded as wines for quaffing, rarely suitable for a fine repast. Things have changed. Winemakers from other parts of Burgundy have flocked here to take advantage of the region's potential, putting the emphasis back on quality, not quantity. The great majority of Mâcon wine is white, always dry, with good acidity and mineral flavors. Pouilly-Fuissé is its most well-known appellation and, accordingly, the most expensive, though the wines of St-Véran often are just as good and cost less. Look for wines that append "Villages" or the name of a village to Mâcon for some of the best values. Mâcon-Viré or Mâcon-Lugny are particularly good.

what to buy MACON

1998	1999	2000	2001
★★★	★★★★	★★	★★★

recommended wines

2000 Château Fuissé Tête de Cru, Pouilly-Fuissé ★★★ $$$
dry, medium-bodied, light oak, high acidity · drink now–6 years
Hard as a green apple in early fall, a bit of air loosens up and enriches the austere, mineral-flecked flavors.

2000 Domaine des Deux Roches, Mâcon Davayé ★★★ $$
dry, medium-bodied, light oak, high acidity · drink now–5 years
Intensely aromatic, full of spicy tropical fruit, herbs, and minerals.

**2000 J.J. Vincent Propriété Marie-Antoinette Vincent,
Pouilly-Fuissé** ★★★ $$
dry, medium-bodied, medium oak, medium acidity · drink now–3 years
With rich citrus and some buttery, briochelike aromas, this wine might have saved a queen her head.

2000 Domaine Thomas, St-Véran ★★ $$
dry, medium-bodied, light oak, high acidity · drink now–3 years
Lusciously seductive, with nutty citrus and tropical fruit flavors, this could compete with Chardonnays at twice the price.

2000 Louis Jadot, Pouilly Fuissé ★★ $$
dry, medium-bodied, light oak, high acidity   drink now–6 years
Flavorful as slow-cooked quince butter, refreshing as strawberry lemonade. Fine wine.

2000 Olivier Merlin, Mâcon la Roche Vineuse Blanc ★★ $$
dry, light-bodied, no oak, high acidity   drink now–3 years
This offers deep mineral and ripe citrus flavors that even more esteemed Burgundy regions would be proud to claim.

2000 Domaine des Valanges, St-Véran ★★ $
dry, medium-bodied, no oak, medium acidity   drink now–3 years
Playing to St-Véran's strengths, this offers some ripe fruit flavors, but the game's really in the minerals.

**2000 Labouré-Roi St-Armand,
Mâcon-Villages** ★★ $
dry, medium-bodied, no oak, high acidity   drink now–2 years
Apple, pear, and citrus flavors make this a real crowd pleaser; its low price allows you to actually serve it to a crowd.

2000 Joseph Drouhin, Mâcon-Villages ★ $
dry, light-bodied, no oak, medium acidity   drink now
Good, easy-priced Mâcon with refreshing citrus, apple, and light spice flavors.

2000 Régnard Chardonnay, Mâcon-Lugny ★ $
dry, light-bodied, no oak, high acidity   drink now–3 years
Buttery flavors add richness without weight to this mineraly, fruity wine.

beaujolais

Most wine made in Beaujolais is red, though there are a few excellent Chardonnays produced. But unlike the rest of Burgundy, where red wine is made from Pinot Noir, red Beaujolais is made from Gamay grapes. Though it's commonly thought of as a simple, fruity, light-bodied quaff for uncomplicated occasions, Beaujolais can be complex, with wonderful cherry and berry flavors, and enough body and tannin to stand up to a hearty meal—or even age. To find such an example, however, you'll have to look beyond Beaujolais Nouveau, the simplest type. There are four levels of Beaujolais produced:

Beaujolais Nouveau Made directly after harvest and released on the third Thursday of November, just in time for Thanksgiving, Beaujolais Nouveau is as simple as wine gets—and it is always inexpensive.

Beaujolais While these wines tend to have more body than most Beaujolais Nouveau, they often lack their fresh charm.

Beaujolais-Villages Made from grapes grown within the borders of thirty-nine select villages in the region, and with more care than simple Beaujolais, many village wines offer some complexity and depth in their flavors, a reflection of the granite-laced soil from which they come.

Cru Beaujolais Grown within one of the region's ten best hillside villages, these can be serious wines, their dark red color holding bold berry flavors and noticeable tannin. Since they usually don't carry Beaujolais on the label, look for the village name: Brouilly, Chénas, Chiroubles, Côte de Brouilly, Fleurie, Juliénas, Morgon, Moulin-à-Vent, Régnié, and St-Amour.

at the table
Put a light chill on the simplest bottles of Beaujolais and quaff on a hot day with hamburgers or picnic foods. More complex examples are built for bistro foods: sausages, lamb stew, *boeuf bourguignon*, or roast chicken and *frîtes* would be perfect pairings for these wines.

the bottom line The simplest Beaujolais is cheap: $6; superior Beaujolais runs up to $25.

recommended wines

1999 Louis Jadot Château des Jacques La Roche, Moulin-à-Vent ★★★★ $$
dry, medium-bodied, medium tannin, medium acidity   drink now–10 years
Quartz-rich soils give this wine's cherry and stone flavors a thrilling tension.

2001 Domaine Chignard Les Moriers, Fleurie ★★★ $$
dry, medium-bodied, medium tannin, high acidity   drink now–10 years
Fleurie is called *"la cru des dames,"* but this is a gender-bender, with rustic maple and buckwheat aromas, dark mineral and flowery, wild strawberry flavors.

113

2000 Domaine Laurent Dumas et Fils Vieilles Vignes, Fleurie ★★★ $$
dry, medium-bodied, medium tannin, medium acidity drink now–6 years
There's a delicious strawberry sweetness balanced by rhubarb tartness in this seductively smoky Gamay.

2000 Louis-Claude Desvignes Côte du Py, Morgon ★★★ $$
dry, medium-bodied, medium tannin, high acidity drink now–6 years
From one of Beaujolais's beacons comes this excellent wine full of earthy flavors like anise and tar, blackberry, and wild herbs.

2001 Nicole Chanrion, Côte de Brouilly ★★★ $$
dry, medium-bodied, medium tannin, high acidity drink now–8 years
Startling pure black cherry flavors gain a deep minerality from the blue granite-rich soils of Côte de Brouilly.

2000 Potel-Aviron Vieilles Vignes, Fleurie ★★★ $$
dry, medium-bodied, medium tannin, medium acidity drink now–7 years
As the appellation suggests, floral elements meld with fruit and mineral flavors so concentrated they could only come from old vines.

2001 Château Thivin, Brouilly ★★ $$
dry, medium-bodied, medium tannin, high acidity drink now–4 years
Archetypal Beaujolais, albeit at a very high level, with wonderful strawberry and tart cherry flavors. Thivin's Côte de Brouilly is even better.

2000 Domaine Berrod, Beaujolais Villages ★★ $
dry, medium-bodied, medium tannin, medium acidity drink now–2 years
Berrod gives a lot of wine for the money, with deep blackberry, cocoa, and mineral flavors.

2000 Jean-Paul Brun Terres Dorées L'Ancien Vieilles Vignes, Beaujolais ★★ $
dry, medium-bodied, medium tannin, medium acidity drink now–4 years
It may be classified as simple "Beaujolais," but there's nothing ordinary about this wine, with all its spicy fruit and mineral flavors.

2001 Georges Duboeuf, Régnié ★ $
dry, medium-bodied, medium tannin, medium acidity drink now–3 years
Slight spice, light smoke, and delicate fruit flavors contrast pleasantly with a roasted, meaty character.

2000 Joseph Drouhin, Beaujolais Villages ★ $
dry, light-bodied, light tannin, high acidity drink now
While the rest of the world reaches for Beaujolais Nouveau, reach for this, with fresh berry flavors and lots of acidity.

loire valley

If not the largest wine region in volume, the Loire Valley is certainly France's longest, following the Loire River some 250 miles from France's center to the Atlantic Ocean. This distance brings a diversity of microclimates and soil types, with a matching diversity of wines. But with the exception of Sancerre and Pouilly-Fumé, Loire wines are underappreciated in the U.S., even though Loire vignerons make some of the best, most diverse wines in France, at any price. Lucky for wine lovers, those prices are low.

grapes & styles

From only three white wine grapes—Chenin Blanc, Melon de Bourgogne, and Sauvignon Blanc—the Loire produces white wines that range from tart, fresh Muscadets to unctuous, sweet, tropical-scented Bonnezeaux. Rosés and reds range from the light, cherry-scented Pinot Noirs grown in the east to the smoky, peppery Cabernet Francs of Chinon and Bourgeuil.

Featured
Wine-Growing
Regions

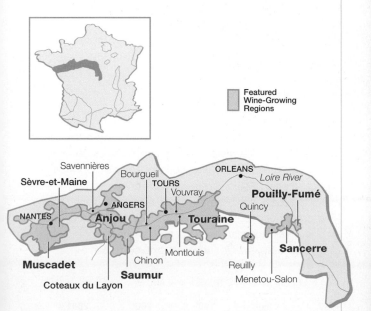

Savennières

Sèvre-et-Maine

Bourgueil

ORLEANS

Loire River

Pouilly-Fumé

NANTES

ANGERS

TOURS

Vouvray

Quincy

Anjou

Touraine

Montlouis

Sancerre

Muscadet

Chinon

Reuilly

Menetou-Salon

Coteaux du Layon

Saumur

on the label

Loire wines are labeled by appellation, even though most of them contain only one type of grape. Like Burgundy, traditions are so well established that the place indicates what's in the bottle.

white wines

at the table

The Loire Valley is arguably France's gastronomic heart, famous for its oysters, game, cheese, salmon, eel, and pork. And as you might guess, there's a wine for each of these. Muscadet is unparalleled for oysters; grassy Sancerre was made for chalky *chèvre*. Try Pouilly-Fumé with freshwater fish or crayfish. Chenin from the Anjou has enough presence to match a pork roast or rich fish like salmon. Dry Vouvray is a natural with fried bream. Sweeter versions are good with Chinese food.

the bottom line Quality Muscadet can be found for less than $10, and outstanding Savennières sells for $14 to $19. Good Vouvray starts around $15 and runs into the mid-$20s. Wines from neighboring Montlouis start at $9. Wines priced outside these ranges are usually exceptional.

CHENIN BLANC

Chenin Blanc reaches its apex in the center of the Loire Valley. Vouvray is its most famous appellation, with wines that range from *sec* (dry) to *demi-sec* (off-dry) and *moelleux* (medium to very sweet), as well as creamy sparklers. But it's most thrilling in Savennières and Anjou, where it makes dry wines with intense lime zest, apricot, and honey flavors deepened with mineral notes. Most can be enjoyed young, though some are meant for aging. Nicolas Joly's legendary versions even come with instructions. Chenin Blanc also makes luxuriously textured dessert wines.

what to buy DRY CHENIN BLANC

1997	1998	1999	2000	2001
★★★	★★★	★★	★★	★★

116

HOWLING AT THE MOON

Biodynamics (*biodynamie* in French), organic agriculture with profound, alchemist, and homeopathic twists, is sweeping France as an antidote to the ills of modern, chemical-dependent agronomy. More than simply eschewing chemical fertilizers, herbicides, and pesticides, practitioners of biodynamics view the earth as an organism, living in symbiosis with the air and cosmos. Since humans affect the earth, they consider it their responsibility to see that it is continuously nurtured. Moreover, the positions of the moon, sun, and stars at any given time are believed to affect different aspects of plant growth at that particular time. Biodynamic farmers schedule their activities in accordance to the positions of the cosmos, the season, and the time of day. Skeptical? Well, you may want to try the wines of Nicolas Joly, the owner of Savennières' Coulée de Serrant, or Burgundy's Domaine Leflaive, Alsace's Domaines Zind-Humbrecht, Kreydenweiss and Ostertag, the Rhône's M. Chapoutier, California's Robert Sinskey, Joseph Phelps and Topolos, or wines from any number of other wineries that have gone biodynamic.

recommended wines

1999 Nicolas Joly Coulée de Serrant, Savennières   ★ ★ ★ ★ $ $ $ $
dry, full-bodied, medium oak, medium acidity   drink in 2–20 years
An ambrosial combination of dry yet honeyed nut, apricot, and mineral flavors from one of the world's most compelling vintners. Joly's Becherelle is an excellent lower-priced option.

2000 Domaine Huet Clos du Bourg Sec, Vouvray   ★ ★ ★ ★ $ $
dry, medium-bodied, no oak, high acidity   drink now–15 years
Everything that Vouvray can be, with light floral notes gracing dense mineral, citrus, and smoke flavors.

2000 Domaine des Baumard Trie Spéciale, Savennières ★ ★ ★ $ $ $
dry, full-bodied, no oak, high acidity   drink now–12 years
Luscious as a baked pear pulled from the oven and glazed with spiced orange marmalade. Age will make it sublime.

1999 Château de Chamboureau Cuvée d'Avant, Savennières ★★★ $$
dry, medium-bodied, light oak, high acidity   drink now–10 years
All the mineral you'd expect from Savennières, plus lots of lime and nutty flavors.

2000 Château d'Epiré Cuvée Spéciale, Savennières ★★★ $$
dry, full-bodied, no oak, high acidity   drink now–10 years
A study in citrus, with flavors like tangerine, Meyer lemon, and starfruit. Give it time: those flavors will deepen and become more complex.

2000 François Chidaine Les Tuffeaux Demi-Sec, Montlouis ★★★ $$
off-dry, full-bodied, no oak, high acidity   drink now–10 years
A Montlouis that rivals great Vouvray, with phantomlike truffle flavors partnered with minerals and pineapple.

1999 Champalou Le Clos du Portail, Vouvray ★★ $$
off-dry, full-bodied, medium oak, high acidity   drink now–15 years
Like biting into a ripe apricot dusted with spice, this barrel-aged Vouvray might not be traditional, but it may start a tradition.

2000 Domaine Deletang Les Batisses, Montlouis ★★ $$
dry, light-bodied, no oak, high acidity   drink now–2 years
Refreshing as fresh limeade, with sweet spice, pear, and citrus flavors.

2000 Domaine Le Peu de la Moriette, Vouvray ★★ $$
dry, light-bodied, no oak, high acidity   drink now–6 years
Tropical flavors of pineapple and guava are enriched with an earthy minerality.

2001 Vincent Raimbault Sec, Vouvray ★★ $$
dry, medium-bodied, no oak, medium acidity   drink now–4 years
A palate perker, with loads of lime and mineral flavors.

2000 Château de la Guimonière, Anjou ★★ $
dry, medium-bodied, light oak, medium acidity   drink now–5 years
Chenin as interpreted in Anjou, with creamy flavors lined with lime and a slightly nutty oxidization.

2000 Marquis de Goulaine, Vouvray ★★ $
dry, medium-bodied, no oak, high acidity   drink now–4 years
Vouvray with verve, full of citrus and mineral flavors with a pinch of sweet spice.

2000 Michel Picard, Vouvray ★ $
off-dry, full-bodied, no oak, high acidity   drink now–4 years
The perfect wine with Chinese take-out; a touch sweet, a tad spicy, readily available, and inexpensive.

MELON DE BOURGOGNE

Melon is the grape responsible for Muscadet. Dry, high in acid, and often slightly yeasty, Muscadet is made for shellfish, especially the oysters that come from the cold waters of the estuary to the Atlantic, near where the wine is grown. Look for Muscadets labeled *sur lie* (on lees), which means the wine stayed in contact with the yeasty sediment left after fermentation. These wines tend to develop more complex flavor. A slight *pétillance*, or sparkle, is typical. Muscadet from Sèvre-et-Maine tends to be the best.

recommended wines

2000 Château de la Ragotière Muscadet sur Lie, Sèvre-et-Maine ★★★ $
dry, medium-bodied, no oak, high acidity   drink now–2 years
With tart lemon flavors, a bit of fat and an ocean of mineral flavors, this screams for a platter of oysters.

2001 Domaine de la Pépière Clos de Briords Muscadet sur Lie, Sèvre-et-Maine ★★★ $
dry, medium-bodied, no oak, high acidity   drink now–3 years
A mine's worth of minerals, a Mojito's worth of lime; in no way another throwaway Muscadet.

2001 Domaine Les Hautes Noëlles Muscadet sur Lie, Côtes de Grandlieu ★★★ $
dry, light-bodied, no oak, high acidity   drink now–1 year
Wonderful, with juicy pear and tart lime flavors framed by Muscadet's unmistakable seashell-like minerality.

2000 Claude Branger La Versaine des Hallay Muscadet sur Lie, Sèvre-et-Maine ★★ $
dry, medium-bodied, no oak, high acidity   drink now–1 year
Bigger than most Muscadet, with room for more lime and mineral flavors, this has the heft for fat, sautéed scallops.

2000 Marquis de Goulaine Muscadet sur Lie, Sèvre-et-Maine ★★ $
dry, medium-bodied, no oak, high acidity   drink now–1 year
Give this a chill and bring home a couple dozen oysters: the crisp lemon and mineral flavors are a perfect match.

SAUVIGNON BLANC

Sancerre and Pouilly-Fumé in the eastern Loire Valley express some of the best Sauvignon Blanc qualities, with grassy, lemon, and gooseberry flavors and refreshing acidity. Pouilly-Fumé is a bit heavier than Sancerre, with more mineral flavors. Its name comes as much from the frequent fog in its vineyards as the supposedly smoky qualities the wine acquires from the flinty soil.

recommended wines

2000 Pascal Jolivet La Grande Cuvée, Pouilly-Fumé ★★★★ $$$
dry, full-bodied, no oak, medium acidity   drink now–8 years
Among the finest Pouilly-Fumés, with a universe of flavors ranging from floral to smoke to juicy citrus.

2000 Domaine Mardon Vieilles Vignes, Quincy ★★★ $$
dry, medium-bodied, no oak, medium acidity   drink now–3 years
Quincy is often overlooked for more famous Loire regions, but excellent fruit-laden wines like Mardon's could change that.

2000 Michel Redde La Moynerie, Pouilly-Fumé ★★★ $$
dry, medium-bodied, no oak, high acidity   drink now–5 years
Smoked almond and floral flavors offer luxury amidst austere minerality.

2001 Philippe Raimbault Apud Sariacum, Sancerre ★★★ $$
dry, medium-bodied, no oak, high acidity   drink now–3 years
Zingy kiwi flavors provide the cover for an army of mineral flavors. Very good.

2000 Domaine Dominique Guyot, Pouilly-Fumé ★★ $$
dry, medium-bodied, no oak, medium acidity   drink now–4 years
Fuméd Fumé, with dry berry flavors and extra-smoky mineral notes.

2000 Fournier Père & Fils Les Belles Vignes, Sancerre ★★ $$
dry, medium-bodied, no oak, high acidity   drink now–3 years
A classic portfolio of ripe citrus, herb, and earthy mineral flavors.

2000 Jean-Claude Chatelain, Pouilly-Fumé ★★ $$
dry, medium-bodied, no oak, high acidity   drink now–4 years
Frisky grapefruit, grass, and green pepper flavors jump out of the glass.

2000 Patient Cottat Vieilles Vignes, Sancerre ★★ $$
dry, medium-bodied, no oak, high acidity   drink now–3 years
Very fine, straight-ahead Sancerre, with peppery herb, lime, and mineral flavors.

red wines

Except perhaps for Bordeaux's famous Château Cheval Blanc, the Loire Valley's Cabernet Francs are the best in the country. Here in the coolness of the center Loire Valley, Cabernet Franc produces dry, light- to medium-bodied red wines with subtle flavors of tart cherries, raspberries, earth, and herbs with moderate tannin. There is also some Pinot Noir grown to the east in Sancerre. Sancerre rouge tends to be light-bodied with cherry flavors and good acidity, but it rarely goes beyond basic Burgundy in quality.

at the table

With high acidity and medium body, Loire reds complement rather than overwhelm. Cabernet Franc's foresty fruit and peppery, earthy notes make it a perfect match for the region's abundant game as well as its charcuterie, especially pork *rillettes*. Red Sancerre is simpler but does equally well with pork, and it's light enough for salmon.

the bottom line The world's ignorance is your gain: the best Loire reds rarely sell for more than $30; most stay within $16 to $23.

what to buy CABERNET FRANC

1997	1998	1999	2000	2001
★★★	★★★	★★	★★	★★★

recommended wines

2000 Bernard Baudry Les Grézeaux, Chinon ★★★★ $$$
dry, full-bodied, heavy tannin, medium acidity drink now–12 years
Rubens *sur la Loire:* a fleshy, well-structured Cabernet Franc painted in blackberry, vanilla, and mineral tones. Destined to grow wild with age.

1999 Catherine et Pierre Breton Les Perrières, Bourgueil ★★★ $$$
dry, full-bodied, medium tannin, high acidity drink in 1–10 years
This version of a Paris bistro standard, with dark berry, Bourbon, and hard stony flavors, would have most Parisians asking "*Qu'est-ce que c'est que ça?*"

2000 Charles Joguet Les Petites Roches, Chinon   ★★★ $$
dry, medium-bodied, heavy tannin, high acidity   drink now–4 years
Called *Jeunes Vignes* ("young vines") until the vines turned thirty this year, this
lives up to its name change with fine mineral (and blackberry) flavors.

1999 Domaine de Chatenoy, Menetou-Salon   ★★ $$
dry, medium-bodied, medium tannin, high acidity   drink now–3 years
Good Pinot Noir for relatively little money, with meaty, tart cherry flavors,
smoke, and lots of minerals.

**1999 Fournier Père & Fils Les Belles Vignes,
Sancerre**   ★★ $$
dry, medium-bodied, heavy tannin, high acidity   drink now–3 years
Pinot Noir flavors of roasted cherry, nuts, leather, and spice at a lower-than-
normal Pinot Noir price.

1999 Thierry Nérrison, Bourgueil   ★★ $$
dry, medium-bodied, heavy tannin, high acidity   drink now–5 years
Nérrison, one of France's best sommeliers and most dedicated winemakers,
shows Cabernet Franc in all its peppery glory.

2000 Château de Fesles Vieilles Vignes, Anjou   ★★ $
dry, medium-bodied, medium tannin, medium acidity   drink now–4 years
Old vines suck all the smoky mineral flavors they can out of the soil, giving the
cassislike fruit flavors unusual depth.

**2000 Domaine Filliatreau Château Fouquet,
Saumur**   ★★ $
dry, medium-bodied, medium tannin, medium acidity   drink now–5 years
The earth is talking in this biodynamically-produced Cabernet Franc, full of
peppery herb, mineral, and berry flavors.

2000 Domaine Ogereau, Anjou-Villages   ★★ $
dry, medium-bodied, heavy tannin, high acidity   drink now–4 years
A deal among deals: rich in fruit, mineral and herbal flavors, this Cabernet
Franc offers a lot for little.

2001 Domaine du Pavillon, Côte Roannaise   ★ $
dry, medium-bodied, light tannin, high acidity   drink now–1 year
A ringer for good, bistro Beaujolais, made from Gamay in a region closer to
Beaujolais than it is to most Loire regions.

2000 Domaine Ricard Le Vilain Petit Rouge, Touraine   ★ $
dry, medium-bodied, medium tannin, high acidity   drink now–2 years
A simple, earthy Cabernet Franc that can wash down whatever happens to be
offered for dinner, from salmon steaks to duck confit.

the midi

French wine was born in the south of France, back when Roman settlers planted vines. Since the 19th century, enormous quantities of wine have been produced here—most of it, frankly, bad. That changed in the 1970s, when vintners began employing better vinification techniques and planting higher quality grapes. Today, the region produces some of the most interesting wines in the country.

lay of the land

Three distinct regions that border the Mediterranean make up the Midi: Provence, in the east, which extends from about Cannes to Arles; Languedoc, from about Arles to nearly the Pyrenees, where it runs into Roussillon, a rugged region with a Catalan flavor hard against the mountains. Languedoc and Roussillon are typically hyphenated into one region.

languedoc-roussillon

The Languedoc is the most anarchic region in France today. Encouraged by the government to improve the quality of the region's wine, local vintners have used the Vin de Pays appellation to its best effect for the leeway it gives in experimenting with grape varieties and wine techniques. Now, though most of its wines bear the lowly Vin de Pays designation, some of these are the country's most exciting wines.

grapes & styles

Most Languedoc wine is red, but there are some whites from international grapes like Sauvignon Blanc and Chardonnay, as well as local varieties like Grenache Blanc, Maccabéo, Muscat, Picpoul, and Viognier. Carignan is the most popular red wine grape; when treated well, it can produce spicy, berry-flavored wines with good body. Those of Corbières are among the best. Deep, dark Mourvèdre and smoky Syrah are sometimes added for more full-bodied wines in other areas such as Minervois.

123

Grenache makes up a percentage of the Rhône-style wines in Costières de Nîmes, as well as the hearty Spanish-inflected wines of Collioure, near the Spanish border. The Languedoc is also famed for its Vins Doux Naturels (VDNs), sweet wines such as the Grenache-based, Port-like wines of Collioure called Banyuls, and the Muscats of Frontignan and Rivesaltes.

on the label

The most common designation in Languedoc-Roussillon is Vin de Pays d'Oc, which means that the wine can be made from grapes grown anywhere within the region. Most Vin de Pays d'Oc wines are inexpensive and list the grape used to make the wine on the label. Vins de Pays wines appended by the name of a place, such as Vins de Pays de l'Hérault, come from specific areas within the Languedoc and are subject to more restrictions of grape varieties and production levels than a Vin de Pays wine. There are also numerous VDQS and AOC wines in the Languedoc that are subject to yet more stringent laws regarding grapes allowed and viticultural and vinification standards. In general, the more specific the place name, the higher the standards, and so wines from the smallest appellations, like Montpeyroux, Pic St-Loup, Faugères, and La Clape often offer the most *terroir,* or regional character.

at the table

Hearty reds like Collioure, Cabernet-based wines, and some Minervois, need hearty foods like grilled rosemary-and-garlic-marinated meats, lamb stew, or cassoulet. Softer reds like Corbières are perfect for grilled chicken or charcuterie. Drink whites with sea bass or other saltwater fish.

the bottom line Wonderful Languedoc wines can still be found for $9 or so. Wines from more specific appellations can run into the $20s or higher, especially if they are fashionable, like Collioure or Pic St-Loup. Mas de Daumas Gassac used to be the costliest Languedoc wine (and one of the best) at $30, but the Rothschilds' new release, Baron'arques, sells for $40.

what to buy LANGUEDOC-ROUSSILLON

1998	1999	2000	2001
★★★★	★★★★	★★★	★★★

recommended white & rosé wines

2001 Mas de Daumas Gassac, Vin de Pays de l'Hérault ★★★ $$$
dry, medium-bodied, light oak, high acidity **drink now–8 years**
This is consistently one of the most interesting white wines made anywhere, very dry but nowhere near austere, with wonderfully intense fruit, almond, and herbal flavors.

2000 Trisser Chardonnay, Limoux ★★★ $$$
dry, medium-bodied, medium oak, high acidity **drink now–8 years**
The best still French Chardonnay outside of Burgundy, full of mineral, citrus, and toasty oak flavors.

2000 Domaine La Combe Blanche Le Blanc, Vin de Pays des Côtes du Brian ★★ $$
dry, full-bodied, light oak, high acidity **drink now–4 years**
Mouthwatering as fresh quince jam on brioche toast, but in liquid form. A delicious wine.

2000 Château de Jau, Côtes du Roussillon ★★ $
dry, medium-bodied, no oak, medium acidity **drink now–2 years**
This unique, trans-Mediterranean trio of grape varieties offers a juicy mélange of peach melba and herbal flavors.

2000 Château Miquel Rosé, St-Chinian ★★ $
dry, light-bodied, light tannin, high acidity **drink now**
Refreshing, but not frivolous, this light and smoky wine offers tart cherry flavor but also palate-cleansing minerals.

2000 Michel Laroche Chardonnay, South of France ★★ $
dry, medium-bodied, no oak, high acidity **drink now–3 years**
You won't confuse this with Laroche's Chablis wines, but it offers appealing tropical flavors balanced by fresh acidity.

2001 Vichon Sieur d'Arques Viognier, Vin de Pays d'Oc ★★ $
dry, medium-bodied, no oak, medium acidity **drink now–2 years**
A simple delight, with fresh summertime fruit flavors like peach and yellow plum.

2001 Vignerons Jonquières St-Vincent Rosé Tradition, Costières de Nîmes ★★ $
dry, light-bodied, medium acidity **drink now**
Sangria-like in flavors, but dry and well balanced by mineral and herbs. Very good indeed.

recommended red wines

**2000 Le Domaine Magellan Les Murelles,
Vin de Pays de Côtes de Thongue** ★★★★ $$
dry, medium-bodied, heavy tannin, medium acidity   drink now–6 years
Grenache and Carignan tango to a sultry tune of deep blackberry, herb, and
mineral flavors. Superb.

2000 Mas de Daumas Gassac, Vin de Pays de l'Hérault ★★★ $$$
dry, medium-bodied, medium tannin, medium acidity drink in 2–12 years
The winery that proved Languedoc can offer elegance provides another
graceful wine, full of herbal, mineral, and fruit flavors. Age will soften the oak.

2000 La Cuvée Mythique, Vin de Pays d'Oc ★★★ $$
dry, full-bodied, medium tannin, medium acidity   drink now–5 years
A blend of local varieties gives a dark, mysterious wine full of fruit, herb, and
mineral oil flavors.

1999 Château Bousquette, St-Chinian ★★★ $
dry, full-bodied, heavy tannin, medium acidity   drink in 2–10 years
A sophisticated taste of the south, with juicy dark fruit and leather flavors
embedded in a fine minerality.

2000 Domaine du Mas Cremat, Côtes du Roussillon ★★★ $
dry, full-bodied, medium tannin, high acidity   drink now–8 years
A wild herb- and lavender-scented wine, full of berry and charred mineral flavors.

**1999 Château Camplazens Syrah-Grenache,
Coteaux du Languedoc La Clape** ★★ $$
dry, medium-bodied, heavy tannin, medium acidity drink now–6 years
Spice, fruit, and cocoa flavors come together with charmingly gruff elegance.

2000 Dupéré Barrera Paradoxides, Coteaux du Languedoc ★★ $$
dry, medium-bodied, medium tannin, medium acidity drink now–4 years
It's worth buying a bottle of this for the small green salamander on the label,
but the wild herb, berry, and leather flavors make it worth buying a second.

2000 Château La Baronne Montagne d'Alaric, Corbières ★★ $
dry, full-bodied, medium tannin, high acidity   drink now–6 years
A stand-out Corbières, with velvety smooth fruit and mineral flavors.

2000 Col des Vents, Corbières ★★ $
dry, medium-bodied, medium acidity, medium tannin drink now–3 years
As the name suggests, this is reminiscent of Mediterranean winds sweeping
through the rough hillsides of Corbières, with rustic, herbal, sun-kissed flavors.

1999 Domaine de la Casa Blanca, Collioure ★★ $
dry, full-bodied, medium tannin, medium acidity   drink now–5 years
Smoky as a brush fire raging across herb-covered hillsides, this wine deserves nothing less than spit-roasted lamb.

**2000 Fortant de France Cabernet Sauvignon,
Vin de Pays d'Oc** ★★ $
dry, medium-bodied, heavy tannin, medium acidity   drink now–3 years
A relief from over-priced Cabernet, Fortant offer spicy, herbal, berry flavor for less than $10.

1998 Les Clos de Paulilles, Collioure ★★ $
dry, full-bodied, heavy tannin, medium acidity   drink now–5 years
Open this an hour or so before serving, so it's possible to chew through the meaty berry and mineral-laden flavors.

1999 Mas des Capitelles, Faugères ★★ $
dry, medium-bodied, medium tannin, high acidity   drink now–3 years
Fresh Faugères, this is full of fragrant fruit, fennel, and floral flavors from first to final sip.

**2000 Moulin de Gassac Terrasses de Guilhem,
Vin de Pays de l'Hérault** ★★ $
dry, medium-bodied, medium tannin, medium acidity   drink now–2 years
This juicy, smoky, cherry-filled wine offers exceptional everyday drinking. Keep a few bottles on hand for impromptu get-togethers.

1999 Domaine de la Boissière, Costières de Nîmes ★ $$
dry, medium-bodied, medium tannin, medium acidity   drink now–4 years
Languedoc's outlet to the Rhône Valley brings forth a cherry- and vanilla-scented wine infused with balsam flavors.

**2000 Le Jaja de Jau Syrah-Grenache,
Côtes du Roussillon** ★ $
dry, medium-bodied, medium tannin, medium acidity   drink now–2 years
Pull the cork on this spicy, earthy, and fruity *"jaja"* (Paris slang for simple bistro wine), and enjoy.

WINES WE WISH WE HAD MORE ROOM FOR
2000 Château d'Oupia, Minervois ★★★ $ dry, medium-bodied, medium tannin, medium acidity, drink now–4 years; **1999 Les Deux Rives, Corbières** ★★ $ dry, medium-bodied, medium tannin, high acidity, drink now–4 years; **2000 Barton & Guestier Cabernet Sauvingon, Vin de Pays d'Oc** ★ $ dry, medium-bodied, medium tannin, medium acidity, drink now–2 years; **2001 Vichon Sieur d'Arques Merlot, Vin de Pays d'Oc** ★ $ dry, medium-bodied, medium tannin, medium acidity, drink now–3 years

provence

Once a land of rough reds drunk by peasants and flighty rosés drunk by jet-setters along the Riviera, Provence is now home to powerful, elegant reds and intelligent rosés redolent of the wonderful aromas of the region's wild, herb-covered hills.

grapes & styles

Provence's most famous white wine is Cassis, which despite the name, has nothing to do with black currants. It's a light-bodied wine made from regional grapes like Bourboulenc, Clairette, Marsanne, Sauvignon Blanc, and Ugni Blanc. The region is more famed for its rosés, however, which are nearly always dry, with wonderful strawberry, fennel, and herbal flavors. With rare exceptions, Provence whites and rosés should be enjoyed young.

Provence's red wines tend to be blends of local varieties such as Carignan, Cinsault, Grenache, Mourvèdre, and Syrah, though Cabernet Sauvignon is becoming more popular, too. Examples from Les Baux de Provence and Coteaux d'Aix-en-Provence tend to be full-bodied with generous soft cherry and cassis flavors. Bandol, the only region in France where Mourvèdre dominates, produces big and bold wines with flavors of leather, truffles, blackberries, and herbs, and tannin that allow these wines to age ten years or more.

at the table

If you see "Provençal" on a menu, or dishes with rosemary, garlic, tomatoes, and olives, you'll do well with a Provence wine. Young Provence whites can be refreshing on their own, as well as complement a simple, grilled snapper or mullet. The region's rosés are excellent with a lightly salty, creamy *brandade de morue* or an aromatic, tomatoey seafood stew, while the reds are ideal for leg of lamb or suckling pig roasted over rosemary.

the bottom line Whites that have escaped the tourists can be found in shops for around $10. Rosés start around $10, though some sought-after labels run $35-plus. Good reds from Les Baux run $14 to $30, Cabernet blends to $45. Powerful Bandol reds start at $18 and reach $45 for some of the best wines in France.

what to buy PROVENCE RED WINES

1997	1998	1999	2000	2001
★★★	★★★★	★★★	★★★	★★★

recommended white & rosé wines

2000 Domaine Tempier Rosé, Bandol ♀   ★★★★ $$
dry, medium-bodied, high acidity   drink now–12 years
With a bouquet garni of herb and mineral notes in the berry flavors, this rosé reaches a higher plane than most.

**2000 Domaines Ott Clos Mireille Blanc de Blancs,
Côtes de Provence** ♀   ★★★ $$$
dry, medium-bodied, no oak, high acidity   drink now–5 years
This citrusy, floral, mineral-laden wine is anything but a simple summer fling.

2001 Domaine du Gros'Noré, Bandol ♀   ★★★ $$
dry, light-bodied, no oak, high acidity   drink now–3 years
This white wine's delightful apple, lime, and mineral flavors may be light, but they leave a lasting mark.

**2000 Ott Sélection Les Domaniers Rosé,
Côtes de Provence** ♀   ★★★ $
dry, light-bodied, high acidity   drink now
Domaines Ott may make some of the world's most profound (and pricey) rosés, but they make a darn good light-hearted, affordable version, too.

2001 Château Routas Rouvière Rosé, Coteaux Varois ♀   ★★ $
dry, medium-bodied, high acidity   drink now
With light strawberry and orange flavors, keep a bottle of this chilled at all times for easy sipping.

2000 Château Routas Wild Boar White, Coteaux Varois ♀   ★★ $
dry, medium-bodied, no oak, medium acidity   drink now–1 year
The grapes the wild boars didn't eat went into this marvelous, mineral-laden, citrus-flavored wine.

**2001 Jean-Luc Colombo Côte Bleue Pioche et Cabanon Rosé,
Aix-en-Provence** ♀   ★★ $
off-dry, medium-bodied, medium acidity   drink now
A soft rosé with berry and orange zest flavors.

2001 Les Vignerons de Grimaud Rosé Cuvée du Golfe St-Tropez, Côtes de Provence ♀ ★★ $
dry, light-bodied, medium acidity drink now
Can't get to St-Tropez this year? A sip of this will put you in the yachting set.

2001 Château de Roquefort Corail Rosé, Côtes de Provence ♀ ★ $
dry, light-bodied, medium acidity drink now
Light and zippy, this is perfect for summer sipping.

recommended red wines

1999 Domaine du Gros'Noré, Bandol ★★★★ $$$
dry, full-bodied, heavy tannin, medium acidity drink in 2–10 years
Great Bandol, black, earthy, and refined.

2000 Domaine Tempier, Bandol ★★★ $$$
dry, full-bodied, heavy tannin, medium acidity drink in 2–10 years
Tempier seduces with lavender, animal, and black berry flavors, evocative of the rustic yet sophisticated charms of Provence.

1999 Jean-Luc Colombo Les Pins Couchés Côte Bleue, Aix-en-Provence ★★★ $$
dry, full-bodied, heavy tannin, medium acidity drink in 2–10 years
Rhône Syrah master Colombo returns to his Provençal roots with a deeply cherry-flavored wine from Syrah and local Mourvèdre.

2000 Château de Roquefort Pourpre, Côtes de Provence ★★ $$
dry, full-bodied, medium tannin, high acidity drink in 1–8 years
Profound mineral flavors reflect the power of old vines; deep blackberry flavors prove the power of the sun. Smoky oak knits everything together.

1998 Château Romanin, Les Baux de Provence ★★ $$
dry, full-bodied, medium tannin, high acidity drink now–4 years
Provence in a bottle, with wild herb and sun-fattened berry flavors.

1999 Domaine Le Galantin, Bandol ★★ $$
dry, full-bodied, heavy tannin, medium acidity drink in 2–10 years
Hard, black, and delicious, this is full of dark berry, stone, tobacco, and licorice flavors; a Bandol to age.

2000 Château de Roquefort Les Mûres, Côtes de Provence ★★ $
dry, full-bodied, medium tannin, medium acidity drink now–5 years
"Les mûres" (blackberries) are in evidence, but that's not all, with spice and the haunting perfumes of wild herbs.

rhône valley

From the sharp, rocky slopes in the temperate north and the vast plains and low, rolling hills of the warm, sunny south, the Rhône Valley could almost be considered two separate wine regions, each with its own grapes and *terroir,* if it weren't for the Rhône River that ties them together.

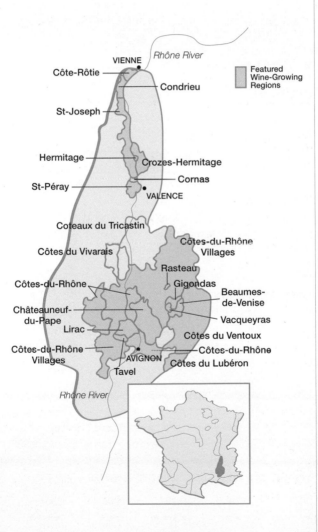

VIENNE
Rhône River
Côte-Rôtie
Condrieu

Featured Wine-Growing Regions

St-Joseph

Hermitage
Crozes-Hermitage
Cornas
St-Péray
VALENCE

Coteaux du Tricastin

Côtes-du-Rhône Villages

Côtes du Vivarais

Rasteau

Côtes-du-Rhône
Gigondas

Beaumes-de-Venise

Châteauneuf-du-Pape
Vacqueyras

Lirac
Côtes du Ventoux

Côtes-du-Rhône Villages
Côtes-du-Rhône
AVIGNON
Côtes du Lubéron
Tavel

Rhône River

northern rhône

The steep, granite hillsides alongside the Rhône are home to some of the region's finest wines. The difficult terrain of Hermitage and Cornas yields some of the Rhône's most intense wines, while the terraced, schist-soiled hills of Côte Rôtie produce equally fine but more elegant wines. All three benefit from some age, so look for wines from the more gently sloped St-Joseph and Crozes-Hermitage for softer wines to drink tonight.

white wines

grapes & styles

Except in Condrieu, Rhône white wines are made from Marsanne, Roussanne, and/or Viognier, which give dry, full-bodied whites that range from simple Crozes-Hermitage to sophisticated Hermitage and St-Joseph, which require age. Condrieu, the northernmost appellation, is dedicated entirely to Viognier, producing both dry and sweet versions. Château-Grillet is a tiny appellation of a single estate in Condrieu that produces Viognier of unique character.

at the table

The white wines of the northern Rhône tend to be rich and sophisticated, fitting for special-occasion meals of roast goose, shad roe, or roasted sturgeon. Sweet Condrieu is a classic match with seared foie gras.

the bottom line High demand and relatively small supply bring high prices for the best northern Rhône wines. Simple St-Joseph whites start at $26 and Condrieu at $25, though fine, ageworthy examples of each range upward of $35.

what to buy NORTHERN RHONE WHITES

1997	1998	1999	2000	2001
★★	★★★	★★★★	★★★	★★★★

recommended wines

1999 Domaine J.L. Chave, Hermitage   ★★★★ $$$$
dry, full-bodied, light oak, medium acidity   drink now–12 years
What all white Rhône wines hope to be, with lush fruit elegantly balanced with spice and mineral flavors, and many years of life ahead.

2000 Domaine Yves Cuilleron Les Chaillets, Condrieu   ★★★ $$$$
dry, full-bodied, medium oak, high acidity   drink in 2–12 years
A master of northern Rhône whites shows he is also a master of Condrieu with a wine of rich tropical flavors, a touch of oak, and abundant minerals.

2000 Jean-Luc Colombo La Belle de Mai, St-Péray   ★★★ $$$
dry, full-bodied, medium oak, high acidity   drink now–6 years
Eighty-year-old Roussanne vines provide impressively flavorful ripe peach and apple flavors spiced with smoky oak and mineral.

1999 M. Chapoutier Les Meysonniers, Crozes-Hermitage   ★★★ $$$
dry, medium-bodied, light oak, medium acidity   drink now–5 years
This Marsanne is as granitelike as any mason could wish for, with confected orange and spice flavors providing a little padding.

2000 Domaine Gilles-Robin Cuvée Alberic Bouvet, Crozes-Hermitage   ★★ $$
dry, medium-bodied, light oak, high acidity   drink now–4 years
This may be as herbal and aromatic as a Loire Sancerre, yet its fat, smoky texture places it squarely in the northern Rhône.

red wines

grapes & styles

Syrah dominates in the northern Rhône. The Syrahs of St-Joseph tend to be the lightest and least tannic, with up to 10 percent of Marsanne and Roussanne allowed to be blended in, but just south, in Cornas, comes a tannic monster made exclusively from Syrah. Traditional Cornas, such as those made by Auguste Clape, require fifteen years to tame; modern examples, such as those from Jean-Luc Colombo, who destems grapes before fermenting to reduce tannin and ages a percentage of the wine in new oak barrels, are more accessible when young. North of St-Joseph, the terraced vineyards of Côte Rôtie give long-lived Syrahs with roasted fruit flavors and a fragrant hint of Viognier, which can make up 20 percent of the wine.

Across the river, the steep, sun-soaked granite hillsides of Hermitage were once considered the source of the greatest wines in France. Fashions have changed, but the quality of the wines has only improved. The appellation's wines are based on Syrah with up to 15 percent Roussanne and Marsanne allowed, and good examples require a decade or more to tame their smoky, tannic edges into cassis, plum, and roasted meat flavors. The same varieties are grown in the vineyards that sprawl around Hermitage for the wines of Crozes-Hermitage, but the results are worlds apart. Even the best examples will have much less tannin, smoky flavor, and complexity, though they can be enormously enjoyable for their juicy plum flavors.

at the table

Tannic northern Rhône reds demand hearty food. Drink Hermitage and Cornas with venison or a hunter's stew of game and wild mushrooms. A softer Côte Rôtie combines well with lamb or roasted game birds.

the bottom line The high prices the best northern Rhône wines command seem reasonable considering their quality. Red St-Joseph and Crozes-Hermitage can be had for $18 to $40. Hermitage and Cornas start at about $35, Côte Rôtie at $40, and reach into the $100s for sought-after bottlings.

what to buy NORTHERN RHONE REDS

1997	1998	1999	2000	2001
★★★	★★★	★★★★	★★★	★★★

recommended wines

1999 A. Clape, Cornas   ★★★★ $$$$
dry, full-bodied, heavy tannin, high acidity   drink in 3–30 years
One for the ages, by one of the world's great winemakers. If you like them black and tannic, you can do no better.

1999 Domaine J.L. Chave, Hermitage   ★ ★ ★ ★ $$$$
dry, full-bodied, heavy tannin, high acidity   drink in 2–20 years

A Gene Kelly of a wine: powerful yet full of finesse, with ripe fruit, minerals, and acidity dancing in perfect step.

1999 Alain Voge Vieilles Vignes, Cornas   ★ ★ ★ ★ $$$
dry, full-bodied, heavy tannin, medium acidity   drink in 3–15 years

Classic Cornas from a classic Cornas producer: big, bold, and black. Give this air and time.

1999 E. Guigal Brune et Blonde de Guigal, Côte-Rôtie   ★ ★ ★ ★ $$$
dry, full-bodied, heavy tannin, medium acidity   drink in 3–20 years

Côte-Rôtie runs in Guigal's blood, and this one's nearly as thick, with dark fruit that seems to ooze smoke from its pores.

1999 Pascal Jamet Côte Sud, St-Joseph   ★ ★ ★ $$
dry, medium-bodied, medium tannin, medium acidity   drink now–8 years

Don't miss the wines of this young producer, whose berry-laden Côte Sud captures the essence of St-Joseph, with smoke, spice, and herb notes.

1999 Paul Jaboulet-Aîné Domaine de Thalabert, Crozes-Hermitage   ★ ★ ★ $$
dry, full-bodied, medium tannin, high acidity   drink in 2–10 years

One of the Rhône greats, full of smoky, meaty flavors impressively combined with berry, leather, and pepper.

1999 Delas Frères Les Launes, Crozes-Hermitage   ★ ★ $$
dry, medium-bodied, medium tannin, high acidity   drink now–4 years

It may be simple, but it has all the fundamentals down right: smoke, earth, and ripe berry flavors.

1999 Domaine Les Chênes Verts, Crozes-Hermitage   ★ ★ $$
dry, medium-bodied, medium tannin, medium acidity   drink now–4 years

Fruity but not frivolous, this Crozes gets a dusting of mineral and spice that makes it seem more serious. Good value.

2000 M. Chapoutier Petite Ruche, Crozes-Hermitage   ★ ★ $$
dry, medium-bodied, medium tannin, medium acidity   drink now–5 years

Chapoutier's "young vines" Crozes isn't ready to sit at the big table, but with smoky cherry and a peppery meatiness, it shows a lot of promise.

2000 Pascal Jamet, Vin de Pays   ★ ★ $
dry, medium-bodied, medium tannin, medium acidity   drink now–3 years

When Jamet becomes more famous you'll be proud to say, "I was drinking this back when…" Terrific spicy, smoky Syrah for a terrific price.

1999 Domaine René Rostaing, Côte-Rôtie ★★★★ $$$$ dry, full-bodied, heavy tannin, medium acidity, drink in 3–20 years; **2000 J.L. Selection Offerus, St-Joseph** ★★★ $$$ dry, full-bodied, medium tannin, high acidity, drink now–8 years; **1999 Jean-Luc Colombo Le Prieuré, St-Joseph** ★★★ $$ dry, full-bodied, medium tannin, high acidity, drink now–8 years; **2000 Stephen Cornu, Crozes-Hermitage** ★★ $$ dry, medium-bodied, medium tannin, medium acidity, drink now–5 years

southern rhône

The climate becomes distinctly more Mediterranean in the southern Rhône Valley. Here, with more sun, warmth, and less steep slopes, vines produce more abundantly, supplying up to 95 percent of the entire region's wines. Second only to Bordeaux in the volume of wines given an Appellation Contrôlée, the southern Rhône is a great place to look for quality at a good price.

grapes & styles

Grenache prevails, but many different grapes are grown in the south. The region's most famous appellation, Châteauneuf-du-Pape, allows up to thirteen varieties—both red and white—in its wines. Among these are Mourvèdre, Syrah, Cinsault, Grenache, Roussanne, and Bourboulenc. Other AOC regions like Gigondas and Vacqueyras have similar allowances, but differences in *terroir* and blending formulas make for quite different wines. Dry, strong, Grenache-based rosés are made in Tavel.

on the label

Rhône wines are labeled by region. The most basic designation, Côtes-du-Rhône, can be applied to wines from anywhere in the Rhône Valley, though most of the wines come from the south. Wines that append "Villages" to the label must be from one of sixty-four villages and satisfy requirements concerning crop yields (low) and alcohol levels (high). Of these, sixteen are permitted to add the village name to the label: for example, Côtes-du-Rhône Villages Rasteau. The best villages, such as Châteauneuf-du-Pape, Gigondas, and Vacqueyras, are allowed to use the village name on its own.

On the periphery of Côtes-du-Rhône are several lesser-known regions that produce similarly styled wines, such as Côtes du Lubéron, Coteaux du Tricastin, and Côtes du Ventoux.

at the table

The light flavor yet rich texture of Rhône whites make them a natural match for Marseille's signature dish, bouillabaisse. Rosés from Tavel are dry and strong enough to stand up to pork, veal, or roasted chicken. The spicy raspberry flavors of Grenache-based reds can stand up to a simple charred steak or the intricate spice of a Moroccan tagine. Châteauneuf-du-Pape, Gigondas, and Vacqueyras have the body for garlic-studded leg of lamb.

the bottom line Basic Côtes-du-Rhône wines—whites, rosés, and reds—start at $9, but spend a few more dollars for a village-designated bottle, like Rasteau at $13, or Vacqueyras from $15 to $20. Gigondas used to be a cheaper alternative to Châteauneuf du Pape, but word got out and it now starts at about $18. That's still inexpensive compared to some exceptional Châteauneuf-du-Pape that can exceed $100.

what to buy SOUTHERN RHONE REDS

1998	1999	2000	2001
★★★★	★★★	★★★★	★★★

recommended white & rosé wines

2000 M. Chapoutier La Bernardine, Châteauneuf-du-Pape 🍷 ★★★★ $$$
dry, medium-bodied, light oak, medium acidity   drink now–10 years
Chapoutier coaxes a cornucopia of citrus, pear, spice, and mineral flavors from the often dull Grenache Blanc.

2000 Domaine de l'Oratoire St-Martin, Côtes-du-Rhône 🍷 ★★★ $
dry, medium-bodied, no oak, medium acidity   drink now–4 years
A whimsical wine that sets floral notes amidst citrus and apple flavors.

2000 Domaine Petrus de Roy, Vin de Pays Vaucluse ♥ ★ ★ $ $
dry, medium-bodied, no oak, medium acidity   drink now–2 years
Looking for a fruity summer sipper? Look elsewhere. This is a smoky, mineral-laden white unlike any other in France.

2001 Château Val Joanis Rosé, Côtes du Lubéron ♥   ★ ★ $
dry, light-bodied, high acidity   drink now–2 years
The orange, light berry, and spice flavors of this rosé make nice summer sipping, especially with a firm chill.

2001 Perrin Réserve, Côtes-du-Rhône ♥   ★ ★ $
dry, medium-bodied, no oak, high acidity   drink now–3 years
Five grape varieties unite to provide peachy-keen flavor with a mineral edge.

2001 La Vieille Ferme Grenache Blanc-Roussanne-Ugni Blanc, Côtes du Lubéron ♥   ★ $
dry, medium-bodied, no oak, high acidity   drink now
This offers more fruit flavor than anyone has a right to expect for less than $10. Stock up.

recommended red wines

1999 Domaine Brusset Cuvée Homage à André Brusset, Côtes-du-Rhône Villages   ★ ★ ★ ★ $ $ $ $
dry, full-bodied, heavy tannin, medium acidity   drink in 2–15 years
As good as wines from nearby Châteauneuf-du-Pape, with intense dark fruit, nut, and mineral flavors.

2000 Domaine de Vieux Télégraphe, Châteauneuf-du-Pape   ★ ★ ★ ★ $ $ $
dry, full-bodied, heavy tannin, medium acidity   drink in 3–15 years
V.T.'s profound, stony, moonscape vineyards produce profound, stony flavors, yet deep fruit and smoke flavors assert themselves throughout. Great wine.

1999 Château La Nerthe, Châteauneuf-du-Pape   ★ ★ ★ $ $ $
dry, full-bodied, heavy tannin, high acidity   drink in 2–12 years
Classic Châteauneuf, with concentrated fruit shackled in tannin. Give it time to show its best.

1999 E. Guigal, Châteauneuf-du-Pape   ★ ★ ★ $ $ $
dry, full-bodied, heavy tannin, medium acidity   drink now–10 years
Not as lush as previous vintages of Guigal Châteauneuf, yet offering a macedoine of fruit flavors spiced with oak.

2000 Coudoulet de Beaucastel, Côtes-du-Rhône ★★★ $$
dry, full-bodied, heavy tannin, medium acidity   drink in 1–6 years
The "second" wine from Châteauneuf producer Château de Beaucastel bursts
with berry flavors balanced by lots of mineral and a pleasingly bitter edge.

2000 Domaine da la Charbonnière, Vacqueyras ★★★ $$
dry, full-bodied, medium tannin, medium acidity   drink now–6 years
A one-time sleeper of Châteauneuf-du-Pape has been waking locals up lately
with delicious wines like this charred berry-laden red.

2000 Domaine de la Janasse Les Garrigues,
Côtes-du-Rhône ★★★ $$
dry, full-bodied, medium tannin, medium acidity   drink in 1–8 years
Grenache goes *garrigue* (the name for the local scrubland) as old vines pick
up flavors of wild herbs and earth, adding complexity to the spicy fruit.

2000 Domaine de l'Oratoire St-Martin Cuvée Prestige,
Côtes-du-Rhône Villages Cairanne ★★★ $$
dry, full-bodied, medium tannin, medium acidity   drink now–8 years
Beauty more than skin deep, with an enchanting deep purple robe providing
seductive cover for intense blackberry, pepper, and herb flavors.

1999 Domaine des Grands Devers Syrah,
Côtes-du-Rhône ★★★ $$
dry, full-bodied, heavy tannin, medium acidity   drink now–5 years
Smoky oak and mineral flavors add a sultry edge to this berry-filled Syrah.

1999 Domaine Petrus de Roy, Côtes du Ventoux ★★★ $$
dry, full-bodied, heavy tannin, medium acidity   drink now–5 years
So heavily mineral, the bottle should be hard to lift. Make the effort for its
blackberry and coconut delights.

2000 Eric Texier, Côtes-du-Rhône Villages St-Gervais ★★★ $$
dry, full-bodied, medium tannin, medium acidity   drink now–8 years
The little-known village of St-Gervais offers a wine thick with creamy dark fruit
and hazelnut essence.

1999 Domaine Nôtre Dame de Cousignac, Côtes-du-Rhône ★★★ $
dry, full-bodied, medium tannin, medium acidity   drink now–5 years
Salt of the earth and a whole lot more, this rich, black wine blows most other
Côtes-du-Rhône wines away.

1999 Perrin, Gigondas ★★ $$
dry, medium-bodied, heavy tannin, high acidity   drink now–8 years
Fresh as a breeze sweeping through the lavender-scented hills of the southern Rhône, this high-acid, fruity red is a good choice for lamb stews.

2000 Domaine Duseigneur, Lirac ★★ $
dry, full-bodied, heavy tannin, medium acidity   drink now–6 years
Lyrical Lirac, with baritone notes of black currant, black berry, and violet.

2000 Domaine La Millière, Côtes-du-Rhône Villages ★★ $
dry, medium-bodied, medium tannin, medium acidity   drink now–3 years
Cedar and lavender fragrances waft through a river of cassis flavors in this wonderfully aromatic wine.

1999 Domaine Rabasse Charavin, Côtes-du-Rhône Villages ★★ $
dry, medium-bodied, medium tannin, medium acidity   drink now–5 years
A tobacco-scented, juicy blackberry-flavored wine made by one of the few women winemakers in the Rhône.

1999 Jean-Luc Colombo Les Abeilles, Côtes-du-Rhône ★★ $
dry, full-bodied, heavy tannin, medium acidity   drink now–5 years
An innovative winemaker offers an affordable pour that modernists and traditionalists alike can appreciate, full of spicy, earthy, berry flavors.

2000 Paul Jaboulet-Aîné Parallèle 45, Côtes-du-Rhône ★★ $
dry, medium-bodied, medium tannin, medium acidity   drink now–3 years
Easy to find, easy to enjoy, Parallèle offers simple berry flavors accented by tingly minerals.

2000 Delas St-Esprit, Côtes-du-Rhône ★ $
dry, full-bodied, heavy tannin, medium acidity   drink now–3 years
A bit of a trickster, with floral scents turning to tannic berry and balsam flavors.

2000 Domaine de l'Ameillaud Vin de Pays, Vaucluse ★ $
dry, medium-bodied, medium tannin, medium acidity   drink now–1 year
Enjoyable drinking with solid fruit flavors and chewy tannin at a bargain price.

WINES WE WISH WE HAD MORE ROOM FOR

1999 M. Chapoutier La Bernardine, Châteauneuf-du-Pape ★★★ $$$ dry, medium-bodied, medium tannin, medium acidity, drink in 2–12 years; **1999 Domaine de l'Oiselet, Vacqueyras** ★★ $ dry, medium-bodied, heavy tannin, high acidity, drink in 1–6 years; **1999 Domaine Pélaquié, Côtes-du-Rhône** ★★ $ dry, medium-bodied, medium tannin, high acidity, drink now–5 years; **1999 Domaine Rabasse Charavin, Côtes-du-Rhône** ★★ $ dry, light-bodied, medium tannin, medium acidity, drink now–2 years ; **2000 M. Chapoutier Belleruche, Côtes-du-Rhône** ★★ $ dry, medium-bodied, medium tannin, medium acidity, drink now–3 years; **2000 Jonquières St-Vincent, Côtes-du-Rhône** ★ $ dry, medium-bodied, medium tannin, high acidity, drink now–3 years; **2000 La Vieille Ferme, Côtes du Ventoux** ★ $ dry, medium-bodied, medium tannin, medium acidity, drink now–2 years

southwest

Le Sud-Ouest, land of the Three Musketeers, is about as swashbuckling as wine gets in France. From the southernmost edge of Bordeaux to the Pyrenees Basque country, Southwest wines are brash and bold, with a bit of nobility thrown in for good measure. It is here that some of France's heartiest reds are found, as well as wines elegant enough to be mistaken for Bordeaux. Learn to pronounce some of the Basque names and you'll be well ahead of the game.

grapes & styles

Different parts of the Southwest bring different grapes. Bergerac, immediately to Bordeaux's south, makes reds and whites that closely resemble common Bordeaux wines in style and grape varieties. Cahors and Madiran stand out for red wines. Cahors wines are based on Malbec (called Auxerrois in Cahors), and are stereotypically so intense that they're called "black wines." Madiran is even blacker and more tannic—no surprise given the name of its main grape, Tannat. Basque country wines, made from indigenous grapes whose names puzzle all but a few red-nosed linguists, are hard and hearty. Jurançon is known for its full-bodied, spicy whites, and Gascogne produces light- to medium-bodied wines from international varieties as well as a few from local grapes, though those are more usually distilled into brandy.

at the table

Drink white and red Bergerac wines as you would those from Bordeaux. Jurançon's nutty, acidic white wines are good with chunky country pâtés and dry, sharp sheep's milk cheeses. Cahors is best sampled with hearty foods such as a lamb stew, ideally with black olives. The powerful flavors of Madiran's red wines require dishes like grilled hanger steak *(onglet)* or, even better, the region's famous stick-to-your ribs cassoulet.

the bottom line Wines from Gascogne, Jurançon, and Bergerac can be found for under $15. Cahors and Madiran can be picked up for under $15, too, though it might be worth spending more to buy an older vintage that is ready to drink.

recommended white wines

2000 Château de la Colline Sec, Bergerac ★ ★ ★ $
dry, medium-bodied, light oak, medium acidity   drink now–4 years
With spicy pear and mineral flavors, this resembles good white Bordeaux, but costs far less.

2000 Clos Lapeyre Sec, Jurançon ★ ★ $
dry, medium-bodied, light oak, high acidity   drink now–4 years
A dry Jurançon, yet rich with creamy, nutty citrus flavors.

2001 Domaine de Pellehaut Cuvée Harmonie,
Vin de Pays des Côtes de Gascogne ★ ★ $
dry, light-bodied, no oak, high acidity   drink now
There's a compelling currylike note to this herbaceous, mineral-studded wine, a unique and easily enjoyed aperitif.

2001 Domaine des Cassagnoles, Gascogne ★ $
dry, light-bodied, no oak, high acidity   drink now
Sancerre-like flavors for a song.

2000 Domaine du Mage, Vin de Pays des Côtes de Gascogne ★ $
dry, light-bodied, no oak, high acidity   drink now
Don't give it a second thought: just enjoy its green apple crispness and lemon-fresh lightness.

recommended red wines

1999 Château Lagrezette, Cahors ★ ★ ★ $ $
dry, full-bodied, heavy tannin, medium acidity   drink now–12 years
Ripe fruit and floral flavors give a dandyish first impression, but the smoky, meaty, mineral qualities say salt of the earth.

1998 Château La Coustarelle Grande Cuvée Prestige,
Cahors ★ ★ ★ $
dry, full-bodied, heavy tannin, medium acidity   drink now–10 years
Swashbucklingly spicy and full of fortifying cherry flavor, this wine could inspire any musketeer to heroic deeds.

1998 Caves Plaimont Chevalier d'Antras, Madiran ★ ★ $
dry, full-bodied, heavy tannin, medium acidity   drink now–6 years
With profound minerals, tannin, and black fruit, this Madiran needs hearty food like braised lamb or cassoulet: all else will be overwhelmed.

1999 Château Lamartine, Cahors ★ ★ $
dry, full-bodied, heavy tannin, high acidity   drink in 2–10 years
Black magic: black cherry, licorice, and smoky mineral flavors at a bargain price.

1998 Château Le Cléret, Côtes de Bergerac ★ ★ $
dry, medium-bodied, heavy tannin, medium acidity   drink now–4 years
With zingy berry, spice, and vanilla, this fills in for a respectable Bordeaux for a
fraction of the price.

1998 Domaine Capmartin Vieilles Vignes, Madiran ★ ★ $
dry, full-bodied, heavy tannin, medium acidity   drink in 1–10 years
A big, brooding beast of a wine, with spicy, black-as-night fruit guaranteed to
turn your teeth dark purple.

2000 Domaine Chiroulet, Vins de Pays des Côtes de Gascogne ★ ★ $
dry, full-bodied, medium tannin, medium acidity   drink now–6 years
A burlesque of bawdy fruit and spice flavors is whipped into shape by mineral
and tannin.

1998 Domaine Lapeyre, Béarn ★ ★ $
dry, full-bodied, medium tannin, medium acidity   drink now–4 years
A little-known appellation stands out with this wine's bold fruit and spice flavors.

2000 Jean-Luc Matha Cuvée Lairis, Marcillac ★ ★ $
dry, medium-bodied, medium tannin, high acidity   drink now–1 year
The antidote to the heavy, tannic reds of France's Southwest, this is tart, peppery, and elegant.

FAVORITE WINE COCKTAILS

Kir White wine with a splash of crème de cassis.
Substitute Champagne for a Kir Royale.

Bellini White peach juice and Prosecco, a favorite at
Hemingway's old digs, Harry's Bar in Venice.

Sangria Red wine with Cointreau or Triple Sec, orange
and pineapple slices, orange juice, sugar, and club soda.

Mimosa Orange juice and Champagne. Without it,
brunch wouldn't be as fun.

Glühwein/Mulled wine Heated and infused with
spices, orange peel, and often a splash of brandy.

Wassail Bowl Wine warmed with with sweet spices,
roasted apples and brown sugar, and sometimes ale.

italy

Italy may be one of the most challenging wine-producing countries to get to know, but it's also one of the most rewarding. With twenty wine-growing regions and some 2,000 grape varieties, Italy offers a wine for every taste and occasion.

on the label

Label practices are as diverse as wine styles in Italy. Some wines take the name of their region of origin, such as Barolo and Chianti. Others are identified by a region-specific style, such as Amarone. And yet others emphasize the grape alone, especially those from German-influenced northern regions, or the grape in conjunction with a place, such as Barbera d'Alba.

There is also a classification scheme designed after the French model. Wines made in accordance to specific rules are entitled to official status, known as the *Denominazione di Origine Controllata* (DOC). Wine from regions traditionally considered "noble" are given the slightly higher status of *Denominazione di Origine Controllata e Garantita* (DOCG). A decade ago, a wine that failed to meet the requirements for DOC status was simply classified as *vino da tavola,* or "table wine," regardless of its quality. In 1992, however, the excellence of many of those wines led the government to add *Indicazione Geografica Tipica* (IGT), roughly equivalent to France's *Vin de Pays.* These wines must come from certain regions, as stated on the label, and are allowed to include grape varieties that are not officially considered traditional to that area.

northern italy

With France, Switzerland, Austria, and Slovenia as neighbors, the northern regions of Italy provide a nearly encyclopedic variety of wine styles.

Featured Wine-Growing Regions

trentino-alto adige & friuli-venezia giulia

In Alpine Trentino-Alto Adige, German-speaking locals live in houses worthy of Hansel and Gretel and drink wines made from Germanic grapes like Müller-Thurgau, Riesling, and Gewürztraminer. Friuli is just next door, but here varieties like Tocai Friulano and Ribolla Gialla hint at Slavic influences from neighboring Slovenia, while the centuries-old existence of so-called "international" varieties reflects the influence of former Roman, Hapsburg, Byzantine, and Venetian rulers. Both regions produce Italy's most exciting white wines, as well as some of its most interesting reds.

145

white wines

Trentino-Alto Adige's alpine climate and sun-drenched valleys make for exceptional, lean-bodied Chardonnay and Pinot Grigio, as well as racy Riesling, Gewürztraminer, and Müller-Thurgau. Friuli produces excellent Pinot Grigio, too, but the aromatic Tocai Friulano, herbaceous Sauvignon Blanc and full-bodied Ribolla Gialla particularly stand out here.

at the table
Rich Tocai Friulano is often paired with pork, though it complements lobster or grilled tuna as well. Ribolla Gialla, with a nearly creamy texture, is wonderful with seafood risotto. Crisp, fresh Pinot Grigios and Sauvignon Blancs provide a counterpoint to fried calamari or a seafood stew. The slightly sweet, exotic flavors of Gewürztraminer and Müller-Thurgau are natural matches for Asian-fusion dishes.

the bottom line The lighter the white wine, the lighter the damage to your pocketbook: Appealing Pinot Grigios and Sauvignon Blancs can be found for $10, but $20-plus buys more substantial versions. $25 buys some of the better Tocai Friulano and Ribolla Gialla.

recommended wines

1997 Gravner Ribolla Gialla, Collio ★★★★ $$$$
dry, full-bodied, medium oak, high acidity   drink now–10 years
A Ribolla crafted with a Michelangelo-like touch: brawny in flavor, rippling in structure, yet extraordinarily modest and fine.

2000 Jermann Capo Martin, Venezia Giulia ★★★ $$$
dry, medium-bodied, medium oak, high acidity   drink now–8 years
A wonderful ménage of oak, fruit, and fine mineral flavors from one of the finest producers in Italy's Northeast.

2001 Ronco del Gelso Latimis, Isonzo del Friuli ★★★ $$$
dry, light-bodied, no oak, high acidity   drink now–12 years
Utterly charming, with light fruit blossom and citrus flavors, this develops nutty, spicy, and lemon curd flavors with age.

2001 Schiopetto Tocai Friulano, Friuli　　　　　★★★ $$$
dry, medium-bodied, no oak, high acidity　　　　drink now–4 years
This Tocai Friulano starts off on a typical meaty and nutty note before exploding
into pure fruit and minerals. Delicious.

2000 Vie di Romans Flors di Uis, Friuli　　　　★★★ $$$
dry, medium-bodied, no oak, high acidity　　　　drink now–4 years
Four grape varieties make for a multiflavored, multilayered blend with floral,
lime, spice, smoke, and a sharp mineral edge.

2000 Bastianich Vespa Bianca, Friuli　　　　　★★★ $$
dry, medium-bodied, light oak, high acidity　　　drink now–4 years
NYC restaurateurs Lidia and Joseph Bastianich put out this nutty, lime- and
mineral-laden wine.

2001 Peter Zemmer Gewürztraminer, Alto Adige　　★★★ $$
dry, medium-bodied, no oak, high acidity　　　　drink now–6 years
Tense Gewürz, with lush fruit, floral, and stone flavors tightly restrained.

2000 Walter Filiputti Poiesis, Colli Orientali del Friuli　★★★ $$
dry, medium-bodied, light oak, high acidity　　　drink now–4 years
An unusual blend of Chardonnay, Tocai, Pinot Bianco, and Picolit makes an
unusual, smoke-infused, orange honey- and mineral-flavored wonder.

**2001 Pojer e Sandri Palai Dolomiti Müller-Thurgau,
Alto Adige**　　　　　　　　　　　　　　★★★ $
dry, full-bodied, no oak, high acidity　　　　　drink now–3 years
Bursting with explosive lime and herb flavors and peppered with chilelike
spice, this may be the best Müller-Thurgau in the world.

2001 Tenuta Beltrame Chardonnay, Friuli　　　　★★★ $
dry, medium-bodied, no oak, high acidity　　　　drink now–6 years
Mineral-streaked autumn fruit flavors make a good case for Italian Chardonnay.

2000 Abbazia di Novacella Sylvaner, Alto Adige　　★★ $$
dry, medium-bodied, no oak, high acidity　　　　drink now–3 years
Sly Sylvaner, showing subtle fruit and haunting smoke and mineral flavors.

2001 Livio Felluga Esperto Pinot Grigio, Friuli-Venezia Giulia　★★ $
dry, medium-bodied, no oak, medium acidity　　　　　drink now
Felluga's regular Pinot Grigio is better, but give this sophisticated (and cheaper)
version a try.

2000 Rocca Bernarda Tocai Friulano, Colli Orientali del Friuli　★★ $
dry, medium-bodied, no oak, high acidity　　　　drink now–8 years
Smoky notes blow off to reveal mouthwatering almond and citrus flavors.

2001 Pighin Pinot Grigio, Collio ★ $
dry, light-bodied, no oak, high acidity drink now
Tasty fruit motivated by brisk acidity make this Pinot Grigio a natural for summer sipping.

WINES WE WISH WE HAD MORE ROOM FOR
2000 Jermann Riesling Afix, Venezie ★★★★ $$$ dry, light-bodied,
no oak, high acidity, drink now–5 years; **2000 Keber Sauvignon Blanc,
Collio** ★★★ $$ dry, medium-bodied, no oak, high acidity, drink now–3
years; **2000 La Cadalora Traminer Aromatico, Trentino** ★★★ $ dry,
medium-bodied, no oak, high acidity, drink now–6 years; **2001 Brigl Pinot
Grigio, Alto Adige** ★ $ dry, light-bodied, no oak, high acidity, drink now

red wines

Merlot and Pinot Noir (often spelled "Nero") do well in both Friuli
and Trentino-Alto Adige, but the most interesting wines may
come from Friuli's meaty, smoky Refosco and herbaceous
Schioppettino. Teroldego Rotaliano, another local grape, makes
relatively light-bodied, smoky wines with red berry flavors.

at the table

Drink Refosco, Schioppettino, and Teroldego with roasted
meats; venison or wild boar would be especially good. Try
Merlot with roast lamb or braised brisket.

the bottom line Since the region's red wines are relatively unknown, they can be bargains, with Merlots that rival
many from California starting at $11, and Refosco and
Teroldego starting at $10 and ranging to $30. Schioppettino
hovers between $20 and $30.

recommended wines

1999 Bastianich Calabrone Rosso, Friuli ★★★★ $$$
dry, full-bodied, medium tannin, medium acidity drink now–10 years
A spectacular blend of native Refosco and Pignolo with Cabernet and Merlot,
giving dark berry and deep mineral flavors as tightly and intricately woven as
any Missoni design.

1994 Ronchi di Cialla Schioppettino di Cialla,
Colli Orientali del Friuli　　　　　　　★★★★ $$$
dry, medium-bodied, medium tannin, high acidity　　drink now–5 years
Pomegranate, rose water, and oriental nut flavors remind you that Italy's outlet
to the East is but a short distance away.

1994 Ronchi di Cialla Refosco di Cialla,
Colli Orientali del Friuli　　　　　　　　★★★ $$$
dry, medium-bodied, medium tannin, high acidity　　drink now–8 years
A beautiful example of the advantages age brings: Refosco's rough edges are
softened to smoky fruit, mineral, and smooth spice.

1999 Conti Formentini Tajut Merlot, Collio　　　★★ $$$
dry, full-bodied, heavy tannin, medium acidity　　drink now–8 years
If you want plummy, velvety Merlot, look elsewhere. This is all about Collio's
soils, with peppery mineral flavors that add piquancy and texture.

2000 Walter Filiputti Pignolo Riserva,
Colli Orientali del Friuli　　　　　　　　　★★ $$$
dry, full-bodied, heavy tannin, medium acidity　　drink now–12 years
A beautiful tapestry of a wine, with plush cherry flavors woven against a waft
of smoky tobacco flavors and a weft of deep minerals.

2000 Foradori Teroldego Rotaliano, Trentino　　　★★ $$
dry, medium-bodied, medium tannin, medium acidity　drink now–4 years
If you like ease of berry flavors but want the challenge of smoke, minerals, and
spice, this local grape is for you.

1999 Tenuta Beltrame Tazzelenghe, Venezie　　　★★ $$
dry, medium-bodied, heavy tannin, high acidity　　drink now–6 years
"Tazzelenghe" means "tongue-cutter" in Friulano, a description of this grape's
high acidity and rough tannin. Though no soft sipper, it is tamer than that, with
spicy red berry flavors.

2000 Cavit Collection Pinot Noir, Venezie　　　　★★ $
dry, medium-bodied, medium tannin, high acidity　　drink now–3 years
It ain't Burgundy, but it's full of tasty fruit flavors and costs a whole lot less.

WINES WE WISH WE HAD MORE ROOM FOR
1998 Villa Russiz Graf de La Tour Merlot, Collio ★★★ $$$ dry, full-
bodied, heavy tannin, medium acidity, drink in 1–8 years; **1999 Conti
Formentini Cabernet Franc, Collio** ★★ $ dry, full-bodied, medium tan-
nin, medium acidity, drink now–5 years; **2000 Scarbolo Merlot, Collio**
★★ $ dry, medium-bodied, medium tannin, medium acidity, drink now–4
years; **2001 Anime Merlot, Friuli Isonzo** ★ $ dry, medium-bodied, heavy
tannin, medium acidity, drink now–4 years

piedmont

Relatively isolated from the rest of Italy with France to the west, Switzerland to the north, and the Alps on three sides, Piemontese winemakers have developed wines suitable for every occasion, from sparkling wines for toasting to powerful, elegant reds meant for long aging, and dessert wines to finish the meal.

white wines

Cortese-based wines like Gavi di Gavi have gained wide popularity in recent years, with Milanese *fashionistas* and diners along the Ligurian coast comparing them to white Burgundy. That might be a stretch, but they are worth trying. More interesting is Arneis, especially from Roero. California Chardonnay lovers should look to Langhe for Chardonnay with similarly ripe tropical fruit and vanilla flavors but more acidity. To end a meal, look for the light, flowery, off-dry bubbly called Moscato d'Asti.

at the table

Gavi is a perfect companion for grilled bass or scampi, or pasta dressed with an earthy pesto. Arneis works, too, but it can also stand up to mushroom-stuffed chicken breasts. Try Chardonnay from Langhe with veal *saltimbocca.*

the bottom line
If Piedmont whites suffer from one problem, it's price. Gavi and Arneis run $12 to $40, while Chardonnay starts at $25 and rises up to $50.

recommended wines

2000 Les Crêtes Chardonnay, Vallée d'Aosta   ★ ★ ★ ★ $ $ $
dry, medium-bodied, light oak, high acidity   drink now–10 years
Northwest of Piedmont, Valle d'Aosta makes wines more French than Italian, which may explain why this nutty, restrained Chardonnay is so fine.

1999 Bastia Chardonnay, Langhe ★★★ $$$
dry, medium-bodied, medium oak, high acidity   drink now–6 years
Barolo master Conterno Fantino fashioned this Chardonnay, a vibrant blend of lime and coconut flavors.

2000 La Scolca Gavi dei Gavi (black label) ★★★ $$$
dry, medium-bodied, no oak, high acidity   drink now–3 years
One of the best Gavi available, full of stony flavors with a spritz of lime that would complement fish grilled with herbs.

1999 Piero Busso Bianco, Langhe ★★★ $$
dry, full-bodied, heavy oak, medium acidity   drink now–6 years
With lots of oak and fruit flavors as concentrated as citrus marmalade, this smoky Chardonnay-Sauvignon Blanc blend is rich enough for veal scallopini.

2000 Vietti Arneis, Roero ★★ $$
dry, medium-bodied, no oak, high acidity   drink now–2 years
A bright, fresh, appley white with engaging pepper and floral notes.

2000 Tenuta Santa Seraffa Le Colombare Gavi di Gavi ★★ $
dry, medium-bodied, no oak, high acidity   drink now–2 years
Smoke and stone notes add complexity to tart apple and lime flavors.

2001 Castelvero Cortese ★ $
dry, light-bodied, no oak, high acidity   drink now
This light-hearted summer wine could add life to any party.

red wines

Nebbiolo (also called Spanna), the noble grape of Piedmont, is responsible for the legendarily powerful Barolo and the softer—though by no means effeminate—Barbaresco. Both are heavy, tannic wines that need age. Barbera and Dolcetto grapes traditionally provide easy-drinking, fruity reds, but some Superiore versions and examples from modern producers provide more serious, ageworthy wines. Of course, the region also hosts international stars like Pinot Noir, Cabernet Sauvignon, and Merlot.

at the table
There's no better match for well-aged Barolo or Barbaresco than risotto showered with white truffle shavings. For a less extravagant meal, try oxtail braised in red wine. If you have to

open these wines before they've aged at least five years, decant them several hours before serving. Then pour with a charred rib steak. Basic Barbera and Dolcetto wines are perfect for grilled chicken, burgers, or pasta, while Superiore versions can step up to braised short ribs or wild mushroom pasta.

the bottom line Barbaresco starts at around $25, Barolo a bit higher, and both can soar over $100 for some single-vineyard wines. But Nebbiolo-based wines from less prestigious parts can be a bargain at only $15 or so. Basic Barbera and Dolcetto start at $9 and run from $15 to $35 for more substantial bottles, with a few touted Barberas topping out at $80.

BAROLO & BARBARESCO

It used to be that Barolos were unapproachable for a decade or more, but innovative winemakers have lowered the required aging in barrels from three years to two for basic Barolo (with an extra year for Riservas), and implemented techniques such as shorter maceration times and the use of small, new oak barrels to make wines that are still plenty tannic yet approachable much earlier. Barbaresco has undergone similar changes, which is to be expected since many winemakers make both wines, even from the same vineyard. For both wines, winemakers commonly list the vineyard on the label.

what to buy BAROLO & BARBARESCO

1993	1994	1995	1996	1997
★★★	★★	★★★★	★★★★	★★★★

1998	1999	2000	2001
★★★	★★★	★★★★	★★★★

recommended wines

1998 Ceretto Bricco Rocche, Barolo ★★★★ $$$$
dry, full-bodied, heavy tannin, high acidity   drink in 3–30 years
A wine for the ages, with Herculean fruit, bitter chocolate, and licorice flavors that should last decades. Superb.

1999 Moccagatta Cole, Barbaresco ★★★★ $$$$
dry, full-bodied, heavy tannin, high acidity   drink in 2–12 years
Plush as crushed velvet, with dark fruit and mineral flavors smoothed with the
vanilla flavors given by small French oak barrels, this is sensuous Barbaresco.

1997 Anselma Vigna Rionda, Barolo ★★★★ $$$
dry, medium-bodied, medium tannin, medium acidity drink now–15 years
A superbly balanced berry, tobacco, leather, and anise-filled wine with charm
that brings a smile to the face.

1997 Vietti Castiglione, Barolo ★★★★ $$$
dry, full-bodied, heavy tannin, high acidity   drink in 3–15 years
Major wine, thick with smoky, spicy berry, and mineral flavors filling out its
mass, this has the stuffing to last years.

1997 Ascheri Sorano, Barolo ★★★ $$$$
dry, medium-bodied, medium tannin, medium acidity drink in 2–12 years
A powerful Barolo in the old style: lean, somewhat astringent, with lots of
smoke, leather, spice, and mineral notes making the fruit flavors complex. Give
it some time, and then pour it with game birds or wild mushroom pasta.

1999 Cascina Luisin Sorì Paolin, Barbaresco ★★★ $$$$
dry, full-bodied, heavy tannin, medium acidity   drink in 1–10 years
From a vineyard named for an uncle who left home for America, this wine
offers honest-to-goodness stick-to-your-ribs roasted berry, eucalyptus, and
home-is-where-the-heart-is flavors.

1998 La Spinona Bricco Faset, Barbaresco ★★★ $$$$
dry, medium-bodied, medium tannin, high acidity   drink in 2–10 years
This wine barks licorice and lavender at first approach, but has wags of berry
when you actually taste it. A mineral bite makes you stand back again.

1997 Michele Chiarlo Cerequio, Barolo ★★★ $$$$
dry, full-bodied, heavy tannin, medium acidity   drink in 1–15 years
This Barolo may be readily approachable in its youth, but it will only get better
with time, as the mineral flavors give more space for the fruit to expand and
for the underlying complexity to come to the fore.

1999 Poderi Colla Tenuta Roncaglia, Barbaresco ★★★ $$$
dry, medium-bodied, medium tannin, medium acidity drink in 3–15 years
Strong tannins leave the mouth cotton-dry, but wait awhile and the fruit, min-
eral, and spice should come into fine balance.

1998 Viberti Buon Padre, Barolo ★★★ $$$
dry, medium-bodied, heavy tannin, high acidity   drink in 2–12 years
The "good father" provides, here giving peppery, earthy, sweet cherry flavors.

BARBERA & DOLCETTO

The best Barberas can fill in for a Barolo or Barbaresco, only they are ready to drink much sooner. Dolcettos are usually slightly lighter. The best examples of each tend to come from delimited areas (DOCs or DOCGs) such as Alba or Dogliani, which will be indicated on the label. Versions labeled Superiore have spent at least one year in barrels.

what to buy BARBERA & DOLCETTO

1993	1994	1995	1996	1997
★★★	★★	★★★★	★★★★	★★★★

1998	1999	2000	2001
★★★	★★★	★★★★	★★★

recommended wines

1999 Hasae Quorum, Barbera d'Asti ★★★★ $$$$
dry, full-bodied, heavy tannin, medium acidity   drink now–10 years
Five top Barbera producers come together to make a superb fruit-filled, herb, and mineral-rich wine.

**2000 Pecchenino Siri d'Jermu,
Dolcetto di Dogliani** ★★★ $$$
dry, full-bodied, heavy tannin, high acidity   drink in 1–8 years
Dark Dolcetto: dark cherry, dark chocolate, dark mineral, and dark pepper. Excellent.

2000 Giacomo Conterno, Dolcetto d'Alba ★★★ $$
dry, full-bodied, medium tannin, medium acidity   drink now–5 years
Last chance to sample a Barolo master's art at a low price: Conterno ripped out his Dolcetto after the 2000 vintage.

2000 Mossio, Dolcetto d'Alba ★★★ $$
dry, medium-bodied, medium tannin, medium acidity   drink now–4 years
Dolcetto's soft side, with plenty of luscious fruit.

2000 Poderi Luigi Einaudi Vigna Tecc, Dolcetto di Dogliani ★★★ $$
dry, medium-bodied, medium tannin, medium acidity   drink now–6 years
When euros are short, try this smoky, full-flavored, affordable Dolcetto from an excellent Barolo producer.

1999 Prunotto Pian Romualdo, Barbera d'Alba   ★★★ $$
dry, full-bodied, heavy tannin, high acidity   drink in 2–12 years
Serious, single-vineyard Barbera, this cherry, mint, and mineral-flavored wine
needs time to realize its potential.

1998 Attilio Ghisolfi Vigna Lisi, Barbera d'Alba   ★★ $$$
dry, full-bodied, medium tannin, high acidity   drink now–5 years
Barbera's big, juicy, berry flavors are made more complex here by notes of
burnt sugar, vanilla, and minerals.

1999 Ceretto Piana, Barbera d'Alba   ★★ $$
dry, full-bodied, medium acidity, high acidity   drink now–6 years
The big easy, with fleshy fruit and melt-in-your-mouth smoked meat qualities,
all supported by minerals.

1999 Vicara, Barbera del Monferrato Superiore   ★★ $$
dry, medium-bodled, medium tannin, medium acidity   drink now–4 years
Monferrato's hallmark tobacco and mineral notes are in force in this fruity
wine. Try Vicara's single-vineyard Barberas for even greater effect.

2000 Villa Sparina Bric Maioli, Dolcetto d'Acqui   ★★ $$
dry, medium-bodied, medium tannin, high acidity   drink now–5 years
The wispy herb and red berry aromas give an impression of frivolity, yet the
charry fruit and bitter herb and mineral characteristics prove otherwise.

2000 Santero Bio Nature, Barbera del Monferrato   ★★ $
dry, medium-bodied, medium tannin, medium acidity   drink now–4 years
Like the ladybug on the label, this is a charming, organically grown wine with
pretty red berry flavors.

2001 La Sera Il Falò, Piedmont   ★ $
dry, medium-bodied, light tannin, medium acidity   drink now
Barbera as it used to always be: simple, juicy, and fun.

OTHER PIEDMONT REDS

Light, fruity, and sometimes slightly sweet and effervescent,
Freisa makes one of Italy's most charming wines. It's best lightly
chilled before serving. More attention, however, is paid to wines
made from Nebbiolo, the best of which can approach Barolo
wines in size and compexity. In addition, following the lead of
Tuscan vintners and their Super Tuscan wines, many innovative
Piemontese vintners are combining classic local grapes with
international varieties, making some impressive—and expen-
sive—red wines.

recommended wines

1998 Gaja Sperss, Langhe ★★★★ $$$$
dry, full-bodied, heavy tannin, medium acidity   **drink in 3–20 years**
This exceptional, multilayered wine made by Piedmont's wine master Angelo Gaja defies designation. Suffice it to say that it is made from Nebbiolo grown in a top Barolo vineyard.

1999 Cascina Bongiovanni Faletto, Rosso delle Langhe ★★★ $$$
dry, full-bodied, heavy tannin, medium acidity   **drink now–10 years**
Fueled by Barbera, Nebbiolo, and Cabernet, this "Super Piedmont" will take off into something great once the oak tones down a bit.

1998 Poderi Colla Bricco del Drago, Langhe ★★★ $$$
dry, medium-bodied, medium tannin, medium acidity **drink now–12 years**
Easy Dolcetto and tougher Nebbiolo create a Barolo-like blend with earth and berry flavors.

1998 Travaglini, Gattinara ★★★ $$$
dry, medium-bodied, heavy tannin, high acidity   **drink now–8 years**
The warped bottle is not a sign of a warped wine. Fully Nebbiolo, there's plenty of smoke and cedar, yet the cherry flavor is the star. Look for the Riserva as well, for even more truffley, earthy flavor.

2000 Cascina Chicco Mompissano, Nebbiolo d'Alba ★★★ $$
dry, full-bodied, heavy tannin, high acidity   **drink now–8 years**
Open this now if you like chewy wines, or cellar it to get to those spicy berry, coffee, and vanilla flavors.

1998 Ceretto Monsordo, Rosso delle Langhe ★★★ $$
dry, medium-bodied, heavy tannin, high acidity   **drink now–6 years**
Cabernet's pepper, Syrah's smoke, Nebbiolo's breadth, Pinot Noir's finesse and a dash of soft Merlot add up to very good wine.

1997 Coppo Mondaccione Freisa, Piedmont ★★ $$$
dry, medium-bodied, medium tannin, medium acidity **drink now–3 years**
Here's a charmer made from Freisa, a Piedmont grape that doesn't aspire to be anything more than fun.

1999 Monchiero Carbone Srü, Roero ★★ $$$
dry, full-bodied, medium tannin, high acidity   **drink in 2–8 years**
It seems impossible, but here's a good Nebbiolo—berry-laden, mineral, and smoky—without a Barolo price.

veneto

One of Italy's most productive regions for both wine and food, Veneto has been blessed and cursed by its success. Many wines such as Prosecco, Soave, and Valpolicella have reached such fame that quantity now far outweighs quality. Luckily, with so much wine, there is room for plenty of excellent wines, from sparkling through to dessert wines.

white wines

Veneto's predominant white wine is Soave, made from the local Garganega grape with up to 15 percent of Chardonnay, Pinot Bianco, or Trebbiano allowed. Though the majority are lackluster, the best Soave is full of citrus and mineral flavors. A few producers outside of Soave, in areas such as Lugana, are making some terrific wines from local grapes like Pinot Grigio, Pinot Bianco, and Tocai. And don't forget the region's wildly popular sparkling wine, Prosecco, which begins nearly every Veneto meal. See page 269 for recommendations.

at the table

The simplest Soave needs the simplest environment: a glass in the afternoon, or before dinner with light appetizers. Soave Classico and single-vineyard versions are made for chicken piccata or any baked white fish. If you are lucky enough to have an older Soave, pull it out for a fresh pasta tossed with butter and shaved truffles. The bright acidity of a good Pinot Grigio pairs well with fried clams or breaded veal cutlets. Lighter blends can stand in for simple Soaves, while richer blends need richer dishes like a seafood risotto.

the bottom line A simple Soave should not cost more than $8, but to find out how good it can be, fork over a few dollars more for a Classico, or as much as $35 for a single-vineyard version. Pinot Grigios tend to run an affordable $8 to $15, while blends can range from $10 to $50 for the most sophisticated examples.

recommended wines

2000 Tamellini Le Bine, Soave Classico Superiore   ★ ★ ★ $ $
dry, full-bodied, no oak, high acidity   drink now–4 years
Master of the Soave universe, Tamellini captures the sun in this wine's spicy, concentrated pineapple flavors and plumbs the depths of the earth with its profound minerality.

1999 Vignalta Sirio Oro Dry Muscat   ★ ★ ★ $ $
dry, light-bodied, no oak, high acidity   drink now–2 years
As seductive as a siren, with citrus blossom and mineral flavors that call out for another sip.

2001 Gini, Soave Classico Superiore   ★ ★ ★ $
dry, medium-bodied, no oak, high acidity   drink now–2 years
With vibrant orange and apple flavors, Gini's "basic" Soave leaves most Soave in the dust (or the drain).

2000 Gini Maciete Fumé   ★ ★ $ $
dry, medium-bodied, medium oak, high acidity   drink now–5 years
Oak barrel fermentation adds a tropical twist to Gini's Sauvignon, full of creamy mango flavors rather than typical grassiness.

2001 Bertani Due Uve, Venezie   ★ ★ $
dry, light-bodied, no oak, high acidity   drink now
Two grapes double the enjoyment, as Pinot Grigio's light tropical fruit sambas with Sauvignon's breezy grass flavors.

2001 Cavalchina, Bianco di Custoza   ★ ★ $
dry, medium-bodied, no oak, high acidity   drink now–3 years
Green apple aromas predict a light, snappy wine, but there's more weight in its apple and citrus flavors than expected.

1999 Serego Alighieri Bianco delle Possessioni   ★ ★ $
dry, medium-bodied, no oak, high acidity   drink now–3 years
A blend of the indigenous Garganega with Sauvignon Blanc spawns this lightly nutty, flower-scented, passion-fruited wine.

2000 Bolla Tufaie, Soave Classico   ★ $
dry, medium-bodied, no oak, medium acidity   drink now–2 years
Easy to find and easy to enjoy, with nutty fruit and mineral flavors.

2001 Villa Teresa Pinot Grigio   ★ $
dry, light-bodied, no oak, high acidity   drink now–1 year
Candied lemon flavors contrast with austere minerals for an intriguing balance.

red wines

Veneto's best-known red wine is Valpolicella. It's made mainly from the aromatic Corvina grape (with bits of Rondinella and Molinara) and it can be quite attractive when not thin and lackluster from overproduction. Wines from the geographically defined zone of Valpolicella Classico are usually better than regular Valpolicella, while those labeled Superiore are even better, as they are required to have higher alcohol levels (i.e., more concentration) and to age for a year in barrels. Amarone is a more intensely flavored subspecies of Valpolicella, made from the same varieties, partially dried before pressing. Ripasso wines fall somewhere in between, having been made by steeping Valpolicella in the must (the leftover pulp from grapes pressed for wine) of Amarone. There is also a sweet version of Amarone labeled Recioto. The Veneto is also known for the light-bodied wines of Bardolino, as well as wines from international grape varieties, particularly Merlot.

at the table

Choose a light Valpolicella for Italian cold cuts like bresaola; a richer Classico for baked pastas like manicotti. Superiore versions and Amarone are excellent with robust, sweet-spicy dishes like a lamb tagine with prunes or lamb shanks braised with cloves and cinnamon.

the bottom line
Look past basic Valpolicellas that cost more than $10; Classicos and Superiores are only a couple of dollars more and are much better. Amarones fall mostly between $30 and $80, although older wines and Amarones from top producers like Quintarelli and Dal Forno can run into the $100-plus price range .

recommended wines

1998 Allegrini La Poja ★★★★ $$$$
dry, full-bodied, heavy tannin, high acidity drink in 2–12 years
One for the cellar, with full, spicy, wild berry flavors, maple, and an appealing burnt sugar bitterness.

1997 Acinum, Amarone della Valpolicella Classico ★★★ $$$
dry, full-bodied, heavy tannin, high acidity   drink in 1–15 years
This might be delicious now for its thick, velvety ripe fruit and smoky earth, leather, and spice flavors, but to open it today means to miss out on a spectacular experience in the future.

1997 Bolla, Amarone della Valpolicella Classico ★★★ $$$
dry, full-bodied, heavy tannin, high acidity   drink in 2–12 years
Valpolicella is what Bolla does best, as evidenced in this wine's full, roasted fruit flavors gracefully mulled with smoke, mineral, and spice notes.

1997 Cesari, Amarone della Valpolicella ★★★ $$$
dry, full-bodied, heavy tannin, high acidity   drink in 2–12 years
Espresso-thick and fuelled by oak-induced smoke and vanilla notes, this bittersweet wine will never let you forget the meaning of Amarone.

1998 Corte Sant'Alda Ripasso, Valpolicella Superiore ★★★ $$$
dry, medium-bodied, medium tannin, high acidity   drink now–6 years
Here's a Valpolicella with Amarone aspirations, offering concentrated, sophisticated, and spicy flavors.

1998 Masi Costasera,
Amarone della Valpolicella Classico ★★★ $$$
dry, full-bodied, heavy tannin, high acidity   drink in 3–10 years
Concentrated fruit tangles with leather, mineral, and spice components; it's delicious now, but will be even better after time has worked the kinks out.

1995 Sartori Corte Brà, Amarone ★★★ $$$
dry, full-bodied, heavy tannin, high acidity   drink now–10 years
This may have a few extra years of age, but that doesn't mean it's settled. Enjoy the rivalry of fruit, minerals, and spice, now and in the coming years.

2000 Acinum, Valpolicella Classico Superiore ★★ $$$
dry, medium-bodied, medium tannin, high acidity   drink now–3 years
As fresh as Acinum's Amarone is intense, this fruity wine is just the thing for picnics or simple pastas.

2000 Maculan Brentino, Veneto ★★ $$
dry, full-bodied, medium tannin, medium acidity   drink now–6 years
Here's a juicy, spicy Merlot-Cabernet with a Veneto touch.

1999 Cesari Mara Vino di Ripasso,
Valpolicella Classico Superiore ★★ $
dry, full-bodied, heavy tannin, high acidity   drink now–4 years
The benefits of recycling: spent must (pulp) from Amarone is used to fortify regular Valpolicella, adding impressive body and spice.

WINES WE WISH WE HAD MORE ROOM FOR
1996 Santi Proemio, Amarone della Valpolicella ★ ★ ★ $ $ $ dry, full-bodied, heavy tannin, high acidity, drink now–12 years; **1999 Allegrini Palazzo della Torre** ★ ★ ★ $ $ dry, medium-bodied, medium tannin, high acidity, drink now–8 years; **1998 Domini Veneti, Amarone della Valpolicella** ★ ★ ★ $ $ dry, full-bodied, heavy tannin, medium acidity, drink now–8 years; **2000 Masi Modello delle Venezie** ★ ★ $ dry, medium-bodied, medium tannin, high acidity, drink now–3 years

central italy

North to South, Italy is filled with great history and culture, but for many, the heart of the country lies in its six central regions. Just as it is impossible to picture the Renaissance without Rome, Siena or Florence, Italian cuisine is unimaginable without Parmigiano-Reggiano or *ragù* Bolognese, not to mention wines such as Chianti, Frascati, Lambrusco, and Orvieto—all of which we owe to central Italy.

tuscany

As Tuscan "trattorias" have become ubiquitous across the U.S., Chianti has evolved from light, astringent plonk poured from straw-covered *fiaschi* to a gracious and noble wine. Tuscany's plain old *vini da tavola*—now elevated to "Super Tuscan" status—incite as much excitement among wine press followers as Superman did among *Daily Planet* readers.

white wines

Compared to red wine, white wine in Tuscany seems nearly an afterthought. Trebbiano, the dominant grape, generally offers only productivity to growers, acidity and wetness to consumers. Vernaccia di San Gimignano is far more interesting, with refreshing citrus flavors with a bitter almond finish and good acidity; older styles tend to take on a pleasingly nutty, oxidized flavor and have more power than the fresh, fruity, new-style wines. Chardonnay has found its way into the region with few obvious successes, except perhaps in producers' pocketbooks.

at the table

Nutty, old-style Vernaccia matches wonderfully with roasted free-range chicken or a traditional Tuscan bean soup. Modern styles have the freshness for fried artichokes or stuffed zucchini blossoms. Match Trebbiano and Chardonnay blends with herbed chicken breasts.

the bottom line
Local varieties such as Vernaccia, Grechetto, Vermentino, and Trebbiano are usually priced under $12, though Riserva versions may climb to $20. Good Tuscan Chardonnay runs about $25.

recommended wines

2000 Antinori Vermentino, Bolgheri ★★★ $$
dry, full-bodied, no oak, high acidity   drink now–3 years
In a red wine region, this white wine holds its ground with a concentrated mélange of fruit and mineral flavors.

1999 Ruffino La Solatia Chardonnay, Toscana ★★★ $$
dry, full-bodied, medium oak, medium acidity   drink now–8 years
A good argument for Tuscan Chardonnay: creamy, with lush honey, orange, and passion fruit flavors.

2000 Castello del Terriccio Rondinaia, Toscana ★★ $$$
dry, medium-bodied, no oak, high acidity   drink now–2 years
A Chardonnay that's more than the sum of its parts: vibrant citrus and pear flavors take on a caramel edge, without any help from oak.

2001 Castello Banfi San Angelo Pinot Grigio, Montalcino ★★ $$
dry, light-bodied, no oak, high acidity   drink now–1 year
One of the first Tuscan Pinot Grigios is also one of the most charming, with crisp and clean fruit flavors.

**2000 Tenuta Le Calcinaie Vigna ai Sassi,
Vernaccia di San Gimignano** ★★ $$
dry, medium-bodied, light oak, high acidity   drink now–3 years
Exceptional Vernaccia, with lovely, nutty flavors that have brightness and snap.

2001 Geografico, Vernaccia di San Gimignano ★ $
dry, light-bodied, no oak, high acidity drink now
With vibrant citrus flavors and lively acidity, this Vernaccia will add spark to a simple fish dinner.

2000 I Campetti L'Accesa Malvasia, Toscana ★ $
dry, medium-bodied, no oak, high acidity drink now–2 years
Aromatic as a breeze blowing through wildflowers, surprisingly stony, too.

2000 Teruzzi & Puthod, Vernaccia di San Gimignano ★ $
dry, light-bodied, no oak, high acidity drink now
Light lemon and lime flavors might interject, but it's the minerals that do the talking here. Chill well.

red wines

Tuscany is red wine territory. Sangiovese is the grape of choice, typically producing medium- to full-bodied wines with cherry, leather, and herb flavors and thirst-quenching acidity. Vintners have traditionally blended it with other red or white grapes, but 100 percent Sangiovese wines are becoming more common, as are wines made with foreign varieties like Cabernet Sauvignon and Syrah. When these wines do not meet DOC standards, they are often labeled "Toscana," although the popular moniker "Super Tuscan" more appropriately captures their quality and full-bodied, full-flavored profile (not to mention price tag).

CHIANTI

The heart of Tuscan wine country, Chianti is a large region. The most famed of its seven zones is Chianti Classico, between Florence and Siena, though Chianti Rùfina and Chianti Colli Fiorentini are also well regarded. Traditionally, Chianti was a Sangiovese-based wine blended with other indigenous red and white varieties and aged in big, old oak barrels. Modern styles tend to be richer, as they can contain 100 percent Sangiovese, or up to 15 percent Cabernet Sauvignon, Merlot, and Syrah. Modernists often age their wines in small, new oak barrels which contribute mellow vanilla flavors. Riserva wines, with higher alcohol levels and at least twenty-seven months of barrel aging, are some of the finest wines in Italy.

at the table

The pleasingly fruity and astringent flavors of simple Chianti are great for pizza and spaghetti with meatballs. Classicos and Chiantis from designated subregions have enough body and flavor to serve with chicken cacciatore. Reserve Riservas for venison or a *bistecca alla fiorentina.*

the bottom line Basic Chiantis run $9 to $12; Classicos, $11 to $27; and Riservas, $14 to $83. Wines from lesser-known subregions such as Rùfina are often good value.

what to buy CHIANTI

1993	1994	1995	1996	1997
★★★	★★★	★★★★	★★★	★★★★

1998	1999	2000	2001
★★★	★★★	★★	★★

recommended wines

1998 Badia a Coltibuono Classico Riserva　★★★★ $$$
dry, full-bodied, medium tannin, high acidity　drink now–15 years
Whereas Castel 'in Villa (below) speaks of the ages, this wine speaks of today and the future, with silky fruit, lavender, leather, and chocolate flavors that seem to go on forever.

1995 Castel 'in Villa Classico Riserva　★★★★ $$$
dry, medium-bodied, heavy tannin, medium acidity　drink now–20 years
Aged longer before release than most, this Chianti's dry cherry, wild herb, and profound mineral flavors express themselves with confidence.

1999 Castello di Monsanto Classico Riserva　★★★ $$$
dry, medium-bodied, medium tannin, high acidity　drink now–10 years
Classical Chianti, with bright cherry flavors and aromatic earthy notes presented with tremendous finesse.

1999 Fontodi Classico　★★★ $$
dry, medium-bodied, heavy tannin, medium acidity　drink now–5 years
The first whiff brings earthy, smoky aromas of fall; the first sip, the juicy ripe fruit flavors of summer.

1998 Ruffino Ducale Traditional Classico Riserva   ★★★ $$
dry, medium-bodied, medium tannin, high acidity   drink now–6 years
From a well-known Chianti producer, this (and its more esteemed gold-labeled
sibling) stands out with flavors and acidity that beg for a great meal.

1998 Melini Vigneti La Selvanella Classico Riserva   ★★ $$
dry, medium-bodied, medium tannin, high acidity   drink now–12 years
Dark, smoky fruit flavors are given extra charm with graceful floral notes.

1998 Tenuta di Nozzole Classico Riserva   ★★ $$
dry, full-bodied, heavy tannin, high acidity   drink now–10 years
Mineral notes punctuate velvety smooth fruit flavors for this long-lived Chianti.

1999 Casina di Cornia Classico   ★★ $
dry, medium-bodied, medium tannin, high acidity   drink now–4 years
Foresty flavors of nuts and berries play alongside earthy, peppery flavors in
this *vino biologico* (organic wine).

1999 Lanciola, Colli Fiorentini   ★★ $
dry, medium-bodied, heavy tannin, high acidity   drink now–4 years
As smoky and appetite-arousing as the scent of truffled, roasted meat.

2000 Straccali Classico   ★ $
dry, medium-bodied, medium tannin, medium acidity   drink now–2 years
Bright, acidic cherry flavors rounded out with a little vanilla are perfect drink-
ing for a casual mid-week meal.

2000 Villa Giulia Alaura   ★ $
dry, medium-bodied, medium tannin, medium acidity   drink now
The perfect pizza wine, with dry, herbal cherry flavors for less than $10.

WINES WE WISH WE HAD MORE ROOM FOR
1998 Cecchi Messer Pietro di Teuzzo Classico Riserva ★★★ $$$
dry, full-bodied, medium tannin, medium acidity, drink now–12 years; **1999
Borgo Salcetino Classico** ★★ $$ dry, medium-bodied, heavy tannin,
medium acidity, drink now–6 years; **1998 Nipozzano Riserva, Rùfina**
★★ $$ dry, medium-bodied, medium tannin, medium acidity, drink now–2
years; **2000 Piazzano Rio Camerata** ★ $ dry, medium-bodied, medium
tannin, high acidity, drink now–8 years

MONTALCINO

Brunello di Montalcino is one of the most sought-after Italian
wines, revered for its balance of power and finesse. Made solely
from Brunello, the local name for Sangiovese, Brunellos di

Montalcino are famously dry and tannic, with strong yet delicate flavors of dried cherries, cedar, and leather. Long-lived wines, Brunellos require at least four years of age before release, five for Riserva wines, and they can often handle more. Rosso di Montalcino, sometimes called "Baby Brunello," is often made from younger vines and aged for only a year in barrel, and so is ready to drink sooner.

at the table
Brunello's ideal match is game birds wrapped in prosciutto and roasted, though leg of lamb would also be perfectly appropriate. Full-bodied but less powerful, Rossos can be enjoyed with lamb chops or steaks.

the bottom line Brunello is expensive: noteworthy bottles start at $45 and climb over $100 for top Riservas. If you want one to drink tonight, look for older vintages, or settle for a Rosso di Montalcino at $18 to $30 while the Brunello mellows.

recommended wines

1997 Castello Banfi Poggio Alle Mura, Brunello di Montalcino ★★★★ $$$$
dry, full-bodied, heavy tannin, high acidity   drink in 3–20 years
Though it seems every Tuscan vintner is releasing a Brunello these days, this stands out with herbs, spice, black berry, and sweet oak flavors.

1995 Fanti Riserva, Brunello di Montalcino ★★★★ $$$$
dry, full-bodied, heavy tannin, high acidity   drink now–15 years
"Riserva" here means more fruit, more spice, more balance, more deliciousness all around.

1997 Gaja Rennina, Brunello di Montalcino ★★★★ $$$$
dry, full-bodied, heavy tannin, medium acidity   drink in 2–15 years
Brunellos from 1997 tend to be so fleshy that they lose some of Brunello's characteristics, but not Rennina.

1997 Livio Sassetti Pertimali, Brunello di Montalcino ★★★★ $$$$
dry, full-bodied, heavy tannin, high acidity   drink in 2–20 years
Exquisite wine, with berry, smoke, and earthy mineral flavors that seem to have infinite depth.

1997 Camigliano, Brunello di Montalcino ★★★ $$$
dry, full-bodied, heavy tannin, high acidity   drink in 2–15 years
A brute of a Brunello, with intense dark fruit, herbs, minerals, and spice that will become more appealing as they soften with time.

1995 Geografico, Brunello di Montalcino ★★★ $$$
dry, full-bodied, heavy tannin, high acidity   drink in 2–10 years
Dry cherry, leather, coal, oil, mineral: this has all the firm, lasting flavors that Brunello brings to mind.

1997 Marchesato degli Aleramici, Brunello di Montalcino ★★★ $$$
dry, full-bodied, heavy tannin, high acidity   drink now–10 years
Brunello, ready to go, with Rubenesque chocolate and cherrylike flavors and fragrant herbs.

1999 Ciacci Piccolomini d'Aragona Fonte,
Rosso di Montalcino ★★★ $$
dry, medium-bodied, medium tannin, medium acidity   drink now–6 years
This doesn't tower like Ciacci's Brunello, but the mixed fruit and sassy licorice flavors stand tall.

1997 Casanova di Neri Tenuta Nuova,
Brunello di Montalcino ★★ $$$
dry, full-bodied, heavy tannin, medium acidity   drink in 2–10 years
Rustic but refined, here's a country gentleman sort of Brunello, with earthy cherry and dry violet flavors.

2000 Il Poggione, Rosso di Montalcino ★★ $$$
dry, medium-bodied, heavy tannin, high acidity   drink now–5 years
A Rosso aiming for Brunello status, with more dense fruit and spicy flavors than expected.

1999 Castello Banfi, Rosso di Montalcino ★★ $$
dry, medium-bodied, heavy tannin, medium acidity   drink now–5 years
So tasty with sticky berry, roasted meat, and herb flavors, you'll be tempted to eat this with your fingers.

OTHER TUSCAN REDS

Vino Nobile di Montepulciano is generally fuller bodied but less elegant than Chianti, a reflection of the warmer climate of Montepulciano and the difference in the local Sangiovese clone, Prugnolo Gentile. Nobile wines require two years of barrel aging, while the lighter Rosso di Montepulciano wines are not required to spend any time in barrels.

Carmignano, northwest of Florence, is unique in Tuscany for requiring the addition of Cabernet Sauvignon to its Sangiovese base. The resulting wines are usually more full and tannic than Chianti, but less acidic.

Morellino di Scansano is a 100 percent Sangiovese wine whose name—"little cherry of Scansano"—hints at its flavor.

Super Tuscan is a term you'll never see on a label, but whisper the words to any Italian wine enthusiast and you're likely to get a smiling nod of recognition. The term refers to a wine made outside the bounds of DOC bureaucracy, employing practices and grape varieties that, until recently, have not been regarded as traditional to the region. This includes French varieties like Cabernet Sauvignon, Merlot, and Syrah, often blended with local Sangiovese, as well as 100 percent Sangiovese. Since these wines did not fit into any official category until recently, bureaucrats filed them in the lowly *vino da tavola* classification. As it became clear that these wines were among Italy's best, the classification IGT (*Indicazione Geografica Tipica*) was added in 1992.

at the table

Drink Morellino, Carmignano and Montepulciano as you would Chiantis of similar levels. Super Tuscans are a good alternative to Bordeaux in class and quality, and match well with steaks (especially a T-bone, Florentine-style) or rich dishes like osso buco.

the bottom line Simple Morellinos, Carmignanos, and Montepulcianos fetch no more than $10, but $35 a bottle is not unheard of, especially for Carmignano. For years, Super Tuscan meant "super expensive." Prices haven't come down for the category's elites, which run over $100, but there are a handful at $10, several around $20, and a bunch between $30 and $50.

what to buy SANGIOVESE-BASED WINES

1995	1996	1997	1998	1999	2000
★★★★	★★★	★★★★	★★★	★★★	★★

what to buy SUPER TUSCANS

1996	1997	1998	1999	2000
★★★	★★★★	★★★	★★★	★★★

recommended sangiovese-based wines

**1999 Fattoria Le Pupille Poggio Valente,
Morellino di Scansano**   ★ ★ ★ ★ $$$
dry, full-bodied, heavy tannin, medium acidity   **drink now–8 years**
Simply exceptional, and exceptionally smoky, with concentrated fruit, mineral, and herb flavors in perfect harmony.

**1997 Mauro Vannucci Piaggia Riserva,
Carmignano**   ★ ★ ★ $$$
dry, full-bodied, medium tannin, medium acidity   **drink now–10 years**
This is as concentrated as Sangiovese can be, its balance maintained by the impressive framework of minerals.

**2000 Villa Patrizia Le Valentane,
Morellino di Scansano**   ★ ★ ★ $$$
dry, full-bodied, heavy tannin, medium acidity   **drink now–8 years**
Morellino means "little cherry" but there's nothing little about this, with its lush black cherry and bitter chocolate flavors.

1999 Villa di Capezzana, Carmignano   ★ ★ ★ $$
dry, full-bodied, medium tannin, medium acidity   **drink now–15 years**
The small region of Carmignano puts out some big wines, like this beautiful red with nut and mineral notes streaming through the cherry flavors.

1999 Boscarelli, Vino Nobile di Montepulciano   ★ ★ $$
dry, full-bodied, medium tannin, medium acidity   **drink now–8 years**
This may be easy to drink but it's more than a quaffer, with deep, dark cherry and licorice flavors.

2000 Selecaia Fassati, Rosso di Montepulciano   ★ ★ $$
dry, medium-bodied, medium tannin, medium acidity   **drink now–4 years**
Light licorice and cherry flavors are ready for a picnic or casual meal, especially if there's caponata on the menu.

1999 Val delle Rose, Morellino di Scansano   ★ ★ $$
dry, medium-bodied, medium tannin, medium acidity   **drink now–3 years**
Pure, smooth cherry flavors with a touch of tartness are perfect for roast duck with a sour cherry sauce.

2001 Fanti Rosso, Sant'Antimo   ★ ★ $
dry, medium-bodied, medium tannin, high acidity   **drink now–2 years**
Unexpected freshness from a wine made just outside of Montalcino, loaded with juicy, ripe berry and sweet spice flavors.

2000 Dei, Rosso di Montepulciano ★ $$
dry, medium-bodied, medium tannin, medium acidity   drink now–2 years
Dei makes some of Montepulciano's most noble wines. This is nobility done simple, full of fruit.

2000 Ambra Barco Reale, Carmignano ★ $
dry, medium-bodied, medium tannin, medium acidity   drink now–2 years
Give this simple, cheery, tart cherry-flavored red a slight chill and chill out: no thought needed.

2000 Avignonesi, Rosso di Montepulciano ★ $
dry, medium-bodied, medium tannin, medium acidity   drink now–3 years
An inviting, fruit- and flower-scented wine from a solid Montepulciano producer at an affordable price.

2000 Marchesi Antinori Santa Cristina, Toscana ★ $
dry, medium-bodied, medium tannin, high acidity   drink now–2 years
This affordable Sangiovese hits all the right notes: tart cherry, nuts, and spice, with bright, appetite-arousing acidity.

recommended super tuscans

1998 Castello Banfi Excelsus, Sant'Antimo ★★★★ $$$$
dry, full-bodied, heavy tannin, high acidity   drink in 2–10 years
Alongside chewy cassis and black berry flavors, Cabernet and Merlot develop an Italian accent of sweet spice and smoke in this benchmark Super Tuscan.

1998 Tenuta San Guido Sassicaia, Bolgheri ★★★★ $$$$
dry, full-bodied, medium tannin, medium acidity   drink now–10 years
Luxury defined, with super-suave blackberry flavor studded with notes of herb and minerals (diamonds, no doubt).

1999 Livernano Puro Sangue ★★★ $$$$
dry, full-bodied, heavy tannin, medium acidity   drink now–10 years
Smokier than your average Sangiovese (and bloodier, too, as Livernano notes in the name) with excellent fruit and spice flavors.

1999 Marchesi Antinori Tignanello ★★★ $$$$
dry, medium-bodied, heavy tannin, medium acidity drink in 2–10 years
A Tuscan titan, flexing its taut muscles with earthy, dry cherry flavors jacketed in fragrant leather.

1999 Ciacci Piccolomini Ateo ★★★ $$$
dry, full-bodied, medium tannin, medium acidity   drink now–10 years
Like Black Forest cake, with rich, creamy cherry and chocolate flavors.

2000 Gaja Ca' Marcanda Promis ★★★ $$$
dry, full-bodied, medium tannin, medium acidity   drink now–10 years
Angelo Gaja's magic for a relatively affordable price. Its dark berry and underlying herb and mineral notes are lovely.

1997 Terrabianca Campaccio ★★★ $$$
dry, medium-bodied, medium tannin, medium acidity   drink now–8 years
A mineral-rich wine sweetened by fruit and oak.

1997 Villa Monte Rico Vino da Tavola ★★★ $$$
dry, full-bodied, medium tannin, medium acidity   drink now–12 years
Many Super Tuscans focus on the "super," but this actually tastes Tuscan, with
red cherry, cedar, and leather notes.

1999 Cantina di Montalcino Poggio del Sasso ★★★ $$
dry, medium-bodied, medium tannin, medium acidity   drink now–5 years
Grown just outside of Montalcino, this may not bear that town's revered appel-
lation, but it sure tastes like it. Enjoy it like a Brunello.

2000 Biondi-Santi Sassoalloro ★★ $$$
dry, medium-bodied, medium tannin, medium acidity   drink now–8 years
Do winemakers dream of being pastry chefs? This wine's black cherry and bitter chocolate flavors say the answer is "yes."

1999 Marchesi de' Frescobaldi-Robert Mondavi Lucente ★★ $$$
dry, medium-bodied, heavy tannin, high acidity   drink in 1–6 years
The second-tier wine of a two-continent partnership combines Mondavi's
finesse with Frescobaldi's nobility in an affordable package.

1998 Marchesi Pancrazi Villa di Bagnolo Pinot Noir ★★ $$$
dry, medium-bodied, medium tannin, high acidity   drink now–4 years
This herbal Pinot shows off the grape's typical finesse with a distinctive
Tuscan flair.

1998 Tenuta Caparzo Borgo Scopeto Borgonero ★★ $$$
dry, medium-bodied, medium tannin, medium acidity   drink now–8 years
Toscana internazionale, with smooth red fruit and dark chocolate flavors that
don't taste particularly Tuscan, but do taste very good.

1999 Rovai Ca' del Vispo ★★ $$
dry, full-bodied, heavy tannin, medium acidity   drink now–5 years
An herb-laden, tart berry wine, heavy with minerals, too.

2000 Banfi Centine   ★ ★ $
dry, medium-bodied, medium tannin, medium acidity   **drink now**
Super Tuscans don't have to be super expensive, as this fruity, herbal blend of
Sangiovese, Cabernet, and Merlot shows.

other central italy

Surrounding Tuscany to the north, south, and east are five wine
regions with their own traditions of winemaking.

Abruzzi The Montepulciano grape finds its greatest expression
in the hands of a few winemakers in this province south of Le
Marche. Dark in color, rich in aroma and tannin, Montepulciano
d'Abruzzo is one of Italy's greatest red wine values. White wines
from the Trebbiano d'Abruzzo grape (different from Tuscany's
Trebbiano) can be outstanding.

Emilia-Romagna While this region's most exported wine is
the frothy, purple Lambrusco, there are some good white wines
made from Albana and Chardonnay grapes, and tasty reds from
Sangiovese, Barbera, and Cabernet.

Lazio Rome's province is best known for Frascati, a fresh, *friz-
zante* white wine based on Trebbiano and Malvasia grapes.
Light-bodied with snappy acidity, Frascati can be quite refreshing—just the thing to enjoy *la dolce vita*.

Le Marche In addition to its distinctive lemon- and almond-
tinged Verdicchio, Le Marche is undergoing a transformation
that is resulting in Sangiovese wines that rival those grown in
Chianti. Look also for wines from Rosso Piceno and Rosso
Cònero, which blend Sangiovese with Montepulciano grapes for
full-bodied, rich reds.

Umbria This small, land-locked province next to Tuscany is
best known for the dry white wine of Orvieto based on the local
Grechetto grape. In the last few years, however, Tuscan winemakers seeking new frontiers (and cheaper land) have set up
shop in Umbria to produce some impressively good Sangiovese.
Meanwhile, the Sagrantino grape has caught the attention of
avant-garde wine lovers, especially in the dark, smoky reds of
the Sagrantino di Montefalco DOCG.

at the table

Lazio's Frascati was made for *fritto misto* or simple, garlic-and-oil-dressed pastas. Richer, nuttier Albana from Emilia-Romagna matches the sweet-salty flavors of prosciutto di Parma. Sangiovese-based wines from any of these regions can be treated in the same way as Chianti: simple examples for pasta with Bolognese sauce and heavier versions for slowly braised beef or chunks of Parmigiano-Reggiano.

the bottom line Wines from all of these regions are often overlooked in favor of Tuscan reds and therefore can offer great value. Whites generally sell between $10 and $20; most reds range from $10 to $15, though some can hit $70.

recommended white wines

1998 Palazzone Campo del Guardiano Orvieto Classico, Umbria ★★★ $$
dry, medium-bodied, no oak, high acidity   drink now–5 years
Those who think Orvieto is only a simple, citrusy wine will have their heads turned with this zesty, full-bodied example.

2000 Bucci Verdicchio dei Castelli di Jesi Classico, Le Marche ★★★ $
dry, medium-bodied, light oak, high acidity   drink now–4 years
Give this some time in the glass and out will come confident and delicious smoky fruit flavors.

1998 Valentini, Trebbiano d'Abruzzo ★★ $$$$
dry, medium-bodied, no oak, high acidity   drink now–3 years
Ripe orange flavors are contrasted with nutty and mineral notes for a sweet and savory sip.

2000 Salviano di Salviano, Umbria ★★ $$
dry, medium-bodied, no oak, high acidity   drink now–3 years
Umbria has white wines beyond Orvieto, like this full, lightly floral, fruity blend of local Grechetto with Sauvignon Blanc and Chardonnay.

2000 Vallona Pignoletto Colli Bolognesi, Emilia-Romagna ★★ $$
dry, medium-bodied, no oak, high acidity   drink now–2 years
Bolognese wines are rare in the U.S., but this one is well worth searching out for its tasty tropical fruit flavors.

**2000 Tavignano Verdicchio dei Castelli di Jesi Classico,
Le Marche**   ★★ $
dry, medium-bodied, no oak, medium acidity   drink now–5 years
Verdicchio dressed by Valentino, with an elegant economy of smoky, mineral, and fruit flavors.

2000 Villa Simone Frascati Superiore, Lazio   ★ $
dry, light-bodied, no oak, high acidity   drink now
Charming, crisp, and flowery, no wonder Frascati is so popular in Rome.

recommended red wines

1997 Illuminati Lumen Controguerra Riserva, Abruzzo ★★★ $$$$
dry, full-bodied, medium tannin, medium acidity   drink now–10 years
A rich departure from Montepulciano, with spicy black cherry and vanilla flavors laced with smooth, bitter chocolate notes.

1998 Colpetrone Sagrantino di Montefalco, Umbria   ★★★ $$$
dry, full-bodied, heavy tannin, high acidity   drink now–10 years
Italian wine lovers in-the-know are flocking to Montefalco for wines like this powerful nectar of black cherry and sweet spice.

1999 Terre del Cedro Montepirolo, Emilia-Romagna   ★★★ $$
dry, full-bodied, heavy tannin, medium acidity   drink now–10 years
It might have taken Bordeaux grape varieties to do it, but Italy's gastronomic heart finally has a world-class wine to call its own.

1999 Le Terrazze Rosso Cònero, Le Marche   ★★★ $
dry, medium-bodied, medium tannin, medium acidity   drink now–6 years
Roasted fruit, mushroom, and nut flavors are perfect for a hearty stew.

**1998 Tre Monti Sangiovese di Romagna Superiore,
Emilia-Romagna**   ★★ $$
dry, medium-bodied, medium tannin, medium acidity   drink now–5 years
If there was ever a wine made for spaghetti Bolognese, this is it.

1999 Boccadigabbia Rosso Piceno, Le Marche   ★★ $
dry, medium-bodied, medium tannin, medium acidity   drink now–4 years
"Cage mouth" in Italian, Boccadigabbia locks down on the palate with vibrant cherry and smoke flavors.

2000 Cantina Zaccagnini, Montepulciano d'Abruzzo   ★★ $
dry, medium-bodied, medium tannin, high acidity   drink now–2 years
Juicy, tart Montepulciano, great for simple spaghetti and garlic bread.

2000 Illuminati Riparosso, Montepulciano d'Abruzzo ★ ★ $
dry, full-bodied, heavy tannin, medium acidity   **drink now–3 years**
While saving your dollars for Illuminati's Controguerra (above), try its sibling Riparosso. It offers much of the same for a lot less.

1999 Tenuta Cocci Grifoni Le Torri Rosso Piceno Superiore, Le Marche ★ ★ $
dry, medium-bodied, medium tannin, medium acidity   **drink now–5 years**
Lean but not mean, this offers a wonderful range of fruit and floral flavors.

NV Terrazzo C Ossor Orenoc Rosso Cònero, Le Marche ★ ★ $
dry, medium-bodied, medium tannin, medium acidity   **drink now–3 years**
Other than the region listed on the label, there's nothing backward about this soft, lightly spicy wine.

southern italy

For Italy's southern wine regions, the sun is both friend and foe. It fosters sweet, ripe fruit flavors, but its strong rays tend to burn off any balancing acidity, especially when the grapes are left to stew in traditional outdoor fermentation tanks. With better viticulture and new technology, such as temperature-controlled tanks, contemporary vintners in southern Italy are making some of the most interesting wines in the world.

Apulia More wine comes from Apulia ("Puglia" in Italian) than from any other region of Italy, and thankfully most of it will never grace these shores. But what does come here tends to be good, even excellent. Look for wines from Salice Salentino and Copertino, where Negroamaro makes wines that have grace and power in their black flavors. The dark, juicy wines that come from Primitivo grapes grown in Manduria are delicious alternatives to Zinfandel, to which the variety is related.

Basilicata Aglianico del Vulture has a forbidding name, but it's a delightful, Arab-spiced, rose-scented wine from Aglianico grapes grown around the Monte Vulture volcano. It is tannic when young, but lovely after a few years of aging.

Calabria Cirò is Calabria's best red. Based on Gaglioppo, the best Ciròs are full-bodied wines high in alcohol, red fruit flavors, and tannin.

Campania might be the best wine region in southern Italy, with its bold, sweet-spiced red wines from Aglianico, and white wines from the honey- and hazelnut-scented Fiano di Avellino and almondy Greco di Tufo. There's also renewed interest in Falanghina, the white wine grape on which the ancients' famed Falernum was based.

Sicily & Sardinia Long known for sweet Marsala and Moscato, Sicily is showing its potential with hearty red wines made with local grapes like Nero d'Avola and Frappato, and sometimes Merlot and Cabernet Sauvignon. It also boasts brisk, citrusy whites from Catarratto and Grillo, both of which are often blended with Chardonnay. Sardinia's Vermentino is completely different in style, with tropical flavors and thirst-quenching acidity. Some of Sardinia's finest reds are made from smooth, spicy Cannonau (Grenache) and Carignano (Carignan), long-ago migrants from Spain.

white wines

at the table

Fiano di Avellino needs delicate dishes like fish or poached chicken, while Greco di Tufo can take grilled mackerel or veal scallopini. A popular Sardinian Vermentino with a bright red prawn on its label suggests its perfect accompaniment: fresh shellfish, though it's great with grilled anchovies or sardines, too. Simple Sicilian blends are made for sipping by the seaside.

the bottom line Campania's white wines are bargain-priced at $12 to $15; Sicilian whites are often even cheaper. Enjoy Vermentino's simple charms for around $10.

recommended wines

2000 Planeta Cometa Fiano, Sicily   ★ ★ ★ $$$
dry, full-bodied, medium oak, high acidity   drink now–6 years
Fully Fiano, this has the lushness of Sicilian pastry made with nuts, spices, and dried fruit, without any of the stickiness.

1999 Antica Masseria Venditti Bacalat Solopaca,
Campania ★ ★ ★ $$
dry, full-bodied, light oak, medium acidity   drink now–3 years
A coliseum of stony, fascinating flavors like baked quince, nuts, and spice.

2000 B. Ferrara Vigna Cicogna Greco di Tufo, Campania ★ ★ ★ $$
dry, medium-bodied, no oak, high acidity   drink now–5 years
With weighty (not heavy) flavors of fruits, nuts, and stones, this classically
structured wine could have graced the cup of Bacchus himself.

2000 Mastroberardino Greco di Tufo, Campania ★ ★ ★ $$
dry, medium-bodied, no oak, medium acidity   drink now–3 years
A model Greco di Tufo, with smoky, dried orange peel, almond, and mineral
flavors.

2000 Cantine Antonio Caggiano Fiagre Bianco,
Campania ★ ★ $$
dry, medium-bodied, light oak, medium acidity   drink now–2 years
The honeyed floral scents and flavors buzz with bright, refreshing acidity.

2000 Rapitalà Casalj, Sicily ★ ★ $
dry, medium-bodied, medium oak, high acidity   drink now–2 years
A taste of Sicily, with lemon flavors and hints of dry apricot and spice.

2001 Argiolas Vermentino di Sardegna, Sardinia ★ $
dry, light-bodied, no oak, high acidity   drink now
Nothing like an ice-cold glass of lemonade on a hot summer day—unless
there's a bottle of this under-$10 charmer chilling in the fridge.

2001 Sella & Mosca Vermentino di Sardegna La Cala,
Sardinia ★ $
dry, medium-bodied, no oak, high acidity   drink now
A perfect summer sipper with palate-tingling lemon and orange and thirst-
quenching mineral flavors.

red wines

at the table

Southern red wines are universally full-flavored and robust, so
plan accordingly. Play the sweet spice of Campania's Aglianico
against lamb braised with apricots or prunes, and pair Apulia's
Primitivo as you would a Zinfandel, with spit-roasted pork, for
example. Sicilian reds seem designed for *braciola*, a dish of beef

rolled around a stuffing of bitter greens and cheese. Try duck braised with orange and almonds with a Cannonau from Sardinia. Non-meat-eaters will do well with sharp pecorino cheeses or roasted eggplant.

the bottom line Excellent southern Italian reds can be found in the $10 range, although a few extra dollars might buy a wine with some age on it, and therefore added complexity. Perhaps encouraged by Zinfandel prices in California, Primitivo wines are climbing in cost, but there are good values to be found for less than $18. A few exceptional southern Italian wines cost around $40.

recommended wines

1997 Struzziero Taurasi Riserva, Campania   ★★★★ $$$
dry, full-bodied, heavy tannin, high acidity   drink now–10 years
Aglianico as Aglianico should be: full-bodied and elegant, with floral and spice flavors and whisps of seductive smoke.

1997 Mastroberardino Naturalis Historia Irpinia, Campania   ★★★ $$$$
dry, medium-bodied, heavy tannin, high acidity   drink now–10 years
You can take the boy out of the country, but you can't take the country out of the boy. This deluxe Aglianico has seductive, polished fruit, floral and spice flavors, but maintains a rustic edge.

1998 Cantina Santadi Terre Brune Carignano del Sulcis Superiore, Sardinia   ★★★ $$$
dry, full-bodied, heavy tannin, high acidity   drink now–10 years
Deep black berry, sweet spice, and mineral flavors give a taste of Sardinia.

1999 Planeta Merlot, Sicily   ★★★ $$$
dry, full-bodied, heavy tannin, high acidity   drink in 1–12 years
Sicily may not be the fist place you'd look for Merlot, but this elegant, mineral-rich, and peppery red puts up a good argument for it.

1999 Tenuta Le Querce Rosso di Costanza Aglianico del Vulture, Basilicata   ★★★ $$$
dry, full-bodied, medium tannin, high acidity   drink in 1–8 years
With an orgy of sweet and savory flavors, this would have been as appropriate for ancient banquets as it is for a modern barbecue.

1998 Villa Matilde Falerno del Massico Vigna Camerato, Campania ★★★ $$$
dry, full-bodied, heavy tannin, medium acidity   drink in 2–10 years
A spectacular revival of ancient Rome's favorite Falernum, chewy with black cherry, mineral, and bitter chocolate flavors accented with floral and sweet spice notes.

2000 Castel di Salve Priante Salento Rosso, Apulia ★★★ $
dry, full-bodied, medium tannin, high acidity   drink now–6 years
A suave southern Italian with a coconut oil tan and Armani-slick berry flavors.

2000 Il Circo La Violetta Uva di Troia Castel del Monte, Apulia ★★ $$
dry, medium-bodied, medium tannin, medium acidity   drink now–2 years
California's restless Randall Grahm went to Apulia for the newest addition to his big top, a trollop of a wine with big and spicy cherry flavors tailor-made for *puttanesca*.

2000 Abbazia Santa Anastasia Nero d'Avola, Sicily ★★ $
dry, medium-bodied, medium tannin, medium acidity   drink now–6 years
Sicily's great grape (among countless others) is treated with a refined hand, but there are still copious amounts of smoky berry and mineral flavors.

2000 A-Mano Primitivo, Apulia ★★ $
dry, full-bodied, medium tannin, high acidity   drink now–3 years
An Irish-American in Apulia makes this smoky, berry-laden wine with an appealing bitter edge.

1998 Apollonio Copertino, Apulia ★★ $
dry, full-bodied, heavy tannin, high acidity   drink now–4 years
Juicy as a baked berry crisp, hearty as a salt-and-pepper-crusted roast beef. Where's dinner?

2000 Argiolas Perdera Isola del Nuraghi, Sardinia ★★ $
dry, full-bodied, medium tannin, high acidity   drink now–3 years
Tart tomato, dark black olive, and spicy, voluptuous, fruit flavors make this a perfect pizza wine.

1997 Candido Salice Salentino Riserva, Apulia ★★ $
dry, medium-bodied, medium tannin, high acidity   drink now–5 years
Lots for the money, with fragrant floral, sweet spice, and roasted cherry flavors, velvety smooth.

2000 Feudo Monaci Primitivo, Apulia ★★ $
dry, full-bodied, medium tannin, medium acidity   drink now–6 years
Spicy, juicy, tasty wine.

THE WORLD'S TEN MOST OVERLOOKED WINES

1 **Any white wine from Alsace** Rieslings and Gewürztraminer are the standouts, but all varieties from the region are great—and more than reasonably priced.

2 **Beaujolais** Cru Beaujolais (not Beaujolais Nouveau, but those with village names on the label) can have the depth of fine Burgundy at a fraction of the price.

3 **Barbera and Dolcetto** Examples from the best Piedmont producers can offer a taste of the region for a lot less than Barolo or Barbaresco.

4 **Finger Lakes wines** The best values in American wines come from this region of New York State, where world-class Riesling, excellent Gewürztraminer, plus some darn good Pinot Noir and Cabernet Franc are grown—and sold for a steal.

5 **Fino Sherry** All categories of Sherry, from bone-dry to sticky sweet, offer great value, but savory Finos are great lightly chilled as an aperitif as well as paired with tapas, soups or garlicky roast chicken.

6 **German Riesling** Arguably the most flexible wine in terms of food pairings, as well as one of the most fascinating in the range of flavors it can give, Riesling enjoys a bit more attention than it has in recent years, yet it is still possible to pick up a beautifully balanced example for a lot less than California wines of similar quality.

7 **Madeira** One of the most complex wines on earth, great with rich soups as well as desserts.

8 **Rosé from the south of France** Forget about sweet and insipid; these pink wines are dry and enticingly aromatic.

9 **Savennières** This Loire Chenin Blanc is delicious when young but becomes sublime with age.

10 **Sparkling wine** Popping a cork is simply too much fun to save for celebrations, and most sparklers are inexpensive, not to mention incredbily flexible with everything from fried chicken to a veal blanquette

2000 Feudo Monaci Salice Salentino, Apulia   ★★ $
dry, medium-bodied, medium tannin, medium acidity   drink now–3 years
A Neopolitan pizzeria, a scratchy recording of Caruso, a friendly but absent-minded waiter, and a bottle of this bright, light, spiced pleasure.

2001 Ocone Vin Giocondo Rosso, Campania   ★★ $
dry, medium-bodied, medium tannin, medium acidity   drink now–2 years
This is surprisingly good at the price, with fresh, easygoing strawberry and cream flavors.

1999 Rapitalà Nuhar, Sicily   ★★ $
dry, medium-bodied, medium tannin, medium acidity   drink now–3 years
Local Nero d'Avola combines with Cabernet for a velvety, slightly piquant, and low-priced Super Sicilian.

2000 San Francesco Cirò Rosso Classico, Calabria   ★★ $
dry, medium-bodied, heavy tannin, high acidity   drink now–3 years
Bitter herb and dry mineral notes give this tart, berried, Calabrian wine an *amaro* quality.

2001 Promessa Negroamaro, Apulia   ★ $
dry, medium-bodied, medium tannin, medium acidity   drink now–1 year
A simple, fruity, affordable red with generous, spicy flavors for barbecue.

2000 Terrale Primitivo, Apulia   ★ $
dry, medium-bodied, medium tannin, high acidity   drink now–3 years
As smoky as Mount Vesuvius, with rich, juicy flavors.

spain

Spain's wine history has been peppered with foreign involvement: first the British, who have dominated the Sherry trade for centuries; then the French, who fled their phylloxera-stricken vineyards for Rioja in the late 1860s; and finally the Americans, who supply the oak barrels that give Spain's wines their hallmark flavor. Nevertheless, Spanish vintners continue to put out refreshingly individual wines of high quality— at low prices.

on the label

Each region has specific wine regulations, but a few classifications are common throughout Spain. Wines labeled *Joven* (young) have seen little, if any, time in oak barrels. *Crianza, Reserva,* and *Gran Reserva* wines have been aged in oak barrels for a specified time, with Crianza requiring the least amount of time and Gran Reserva, the longest. Ironically, Crianza wines sometimes taste "oakier" than wines in the other categories.

rioja

white wines

Rioja's white wines are often overshadowed by its reds. But basic, light white Riojas can be refreshing any time, and aged Reservas or Gran Reservas can be some of the most complex, sophisticated whites around. While they might seem oxidized or

premarurely aged at first, a bit of air rubs the tarnish off, and lev-els of nutty, fruity, spice-laden flavors shine through. Snap them up when you find them: these unfashionable but delicious gems might soon be part of wine lore.

at the table

With high acidity and citrus flavors, young white Riojas are a refreshing match for a clam bake. Sip older wines with salty tapas like Serrano ham or strong cheeses such as Manchego

the bottom line White Riojas are a steal, with young ones under $10; aged wines, a few dollars more.

recommended wines

1991 R. López de Heredia Viña Gravonia   ★★★★ $$
dry, full-bodied, light oak, high acidity   drink now–8 years
Years of oak aging bring a spicy harmony of dry fruit and nut flavors. Memorable and delicious.

183

2001 Cune Monopole   ★ ★ ★ $
dry, medium-bodied, light oak, high acidity   drink now–10 years
Enjoy this now for its fresh and delightful grapefruit and mineral flavors, or let it age into a sumptuously rich, nutty, special-occasion pour.

1999 Martínez Bujanda Conde de Valdemar Finca Alto de Cantabria   ★ ★ ★ $
dry, medium-bodied, heavy oak, high acidity   drink in 2–12 years
Absolutely unique. Three years of oak aging show right now, but the mineral and apple flavors peek through. Give it time.

2001 Bodegas Montecillo   ★ ★ $
dry, medium-bodied, no oak, high acidity   drink now
The height of fresh and fruity, with crisp apple and whimsical fruit flavors.

2001 Marqués de Cáceres   ★ ★ $
dry, light-bodied, no oak, high acidity   drink now–2 years
Dreaming of a holiday on Mallorca? This light, tropical fruit- and mineral-flavored wine can carry you there.

rosé wines

Young Rioja *rosados* have a charming freshness and forward flavor. But the harder-to-find aged versions take on a compelling complexity rare in rosés.

at the table
Simple Spanish rosés have both the freshness for salads and the body to stand up to smoky cold cuts. Aged rosés are enjoyable on their own, or with roast ham.

the bottom line Fine, young Rioja rosé costs $8 to $10; good older vintages run about $15.

recommended wines

2000 Bodegas Faustino Faustino V Rosado   ★ $
dry, medium-bodied, high acidity   drink now
Faustino is usually the fruit lover's friend, but he's gone underground this year, with loads of mineral and herb flavors.

2000 El Coto de Rioja El Coto Rosé   ★ $
dry, medium-bodied, high acidity   drink now
Light cherry flavors with a bitter herb edge wash tapas down well.

2000 Marqués de Cáceres Rosé   ★ $
dry, light-bodied, high acidity   drink now
Orange and cranberry flavors plus crisp acidity equals one delicious *rosado*.

red wines

While a few wines from Ribera del Duero and Priorat might surpass Rioja in price and sometimes quality, no region's table wines have enjoyed as high a reputation for as long a time. The wines of Rioja offer power and finesse, with velvety smooth, vanilla-tinged plum and cherry flavors and excellent acidity. Tempranillo is the region's most common grape, although it is frequently blended with Garnacha and other indigenous varieties, or Cabernet Sauvignon. The American oak barrels in which Rioja is traditionally aged contribute the coconut, mint, and vanilla flavors that are hallmarks of Rioja. Today, however, some winemakers have reverted to French oak casks to make less oaky wines.

at the table
Spicy, vanilla-scented Riojas are ideal with roasted lamb, pork, or aromatic vegetable couscous dishes, especially with sweet spices like cinnamon, cloves, and nutmeg.

the bottom line Few places beyond Rioja offer fully-aged, ten-year-old wines for as little as $25. Young Crianzas can be found for less than $15; Reservas, for $15 to $50, and Gran Reservas for $23 to $100.

what to buy RIOJA REDS

1994	1995	1996	1997
★★★★	★★★★	★★★	★★★

1998	1999	2000	2001
★★★	★★	★★★	★★★★

recommended wines

1995 Cune Imperial Gran Reserva ★★★★ $$$
dry, full-bodied, heavy tannin, high acidity drink now–20 years
Full of mineral, leather, and spice aromas set against a background of sour cherry and pomegranate, this is what Rioja is all about.

1994 R. López de Heredia Viña Tondonia Reserva ★★★★ $$$
dry, full-bodied, heavy tannin, high acidity drink now–15 years
Traditional Rioja defined. Long years of oak aging bring an amazing display of smoky, tart fruit, herb and spice, and leather flavors.

1996 Bodegas Bretón Dominio de Conte Reserva ★★★ $$$
dry, medium-bodied, medium tannin, high acidity drink now–20 years
This suave Rioja shows off the vineyard from which it came with layers of dark berry, smoky tobacco, and mineral flavors.

1994 El Coto de Rioja Coto de Imaz Gran Reserva ★★★ $$$
dry, medium-bodied, heavy tannin, high acidity drink now–12 years
At first impression this seems slightly worn, but air (or time) seduces it from middle age to youthful fruit and floral notes.

1999 Bodegas Artadi Viñas de Gain ★★★ $$
dry, medium-bodied, heavy tannin, high acidity drink in 2–10 years
The fruit and spice flavors may be dense and concentrated, but they're light on their feet.

1998 Bodegas Otañon Crianza ★★★ $$
dry, full-bodied, heavy tannin, high acidity drink now–10 years
Good, solid Rioja, with dark fruit, cocoa, and spicy floral flavors.

1996 Bodegas Primicia Juan Ramón Reserva de Familia ★★★ $$
dry, full-bodied, heavy tannin, high acidity drink in 1–8 years
This is six years old, but it still needs time for the dark berry and coffee flavors to overcome the oak. Luckily, there's plenty of flavor to last.

1995 Martínez Bujanda Conde de Valdemar Gran Reserva ★★★ $$
dry, full-bodied, heavy tannin, high acidity drink now–15 years
Unlike many Gran Reservas that "suffer" from a lack of fresh fruit, this has loads of it, but it takes air to find it through the shell of earthy flavors.

1999 Bodegas Bretón Loriñon Crianza ★★★ $
dry, medium-bodied, medium tannin, high acidity drink now–6 years
The typically strong oaky edge of a Crianza jumps out of the glass first, but the cherry and mineral flavors catch up quickly. Good wine.

1996 Finca Valpiedra Reserva   ★★ $$$
dry, full-bodied, heavy tannin, high acidity   drink now–10 years
Peppery tannin give a rustic edge to this Rioja, but Middle Eastern flavors like pomegranate and sweet spice keep it from being rough.

1997 Bodegas Montecillo Reserva   ★★ $$
dry, medium-bodied, medium tannin, high acidity   drink now–8 years
Montecillo made no Gran Reserva wine in 1997, so its best grapes went into this classic Rioja, mouthwatering in its tart cherry, herb, vanilla-spice flavors.

1998 Marqués de Cáceres Crianza   ★★ $
dry, medium-bodied, medium tannin, high acidity   drink now–4 years
Even if you don't find the tiny "Crianza" on the back label, a taste will tell you this elegant, smoky red is more than ordinary.

2000 Bodegas Solar de Carrión Antaño Tempranillo   ★ $
dry, medium-bodied, medium tannin, high acidity   drink now–2 years
Rioja *fresca,* with bright cherry flavors and a little bit of spice, this is a terrific pour for casual occasions.

1998 Marqués de Arienzo Crianza   ★ $
dry, medium-bodied, medium tannin, high acidity   drink now–3 years
Arienzo consistently puts out a nice Rioja at a bargain price. Keep some on hand for tapas parties.

OAK BARRELS

Just as the grape variety, the region, and the method of making wine affects its taste, so does the type of barrels it is aged in, from the type of oak used to the size of the barrels, to how many times they've been used. French oak—currently the most coveted—imparts subtle spice and vanilla flavors. American oak contributes stronger spice and vanilla flavors along with a telltale taste of coconut. Slovenian oak, popular in Italy, falls somewhere between American and French oak. The smaller the barrel, the more wood flavors in the wine, since the wine has more contact with the wood than it would in large barrels. Also, wines in small barrels age more quickly because they are more exposed to air that seeps through the pores of the wood. And the older the barrel, the fewer wood flavors it imparts. After three to five years of use, a barrel has given up all its flavor to wine.

ribera del duero

Ribera del Duero has been home to Spain's most celebrated winery, Vega Sicilia, for more than a century, yet its wines were little known until the mid-1980s, when wine critic Robert Parker heaped praise on another local winery, Pesquera. Since then, the region has seen a flurry of new wineries. Like Rioja, Ribera del Duero wines are based on Tempranillo, but an allowance of up to 25 percent Cabernet Sauvignon, Merlot, and/or Malbec can give them more body and tannin than Riojas.

at the table
The bold flavors of Ribera del Duero reds are great with well-marbled steaks or thick-sliced prime rib.

the bottom line
Top Ribera del Duero wines run $50 to $230, but excellent drinking can be found for $15 to $30.

what to buy RIBERA DEL DUERO

1996	1997	1998	1999	2000	2001
★★★★	★★★	★★★	★★★	★★	★★★★

recommended wines

1999 Condado de Haza ★★★ $$
dry, full-bodied, heavy tannin, high acidity drink in 2–10 years
A multiplicity of flavors envelopes the tongue with each sip of this wine: first berry, then mineral, smoked meat, coffee, berry… you get the idea.

1999 Pesquera ★★★ $$
dry, full-bodied, medium tannin, high acidity drink now–6 years
The basic wine of famed winemaker Alejandro Fernández's line-up is no also-ran, with deep dark fruit punctuated with herb and mineral notes.

1998 Bodegas Parxet Tionio Crianza ★★ $$
dry, full-bodied, heavy tannin, high acidity drink in 2–8 years
This takes time to show its musky black fruit and mineral flavors. Have patience.

1998 Carmelo Rodero Crianza ★★ $$
dry, full-bodied, heavy tannin, high acidity drink in 2–10 years
Espresso-thick with similar flavors, this wine needs a thick, charred steak.

1998 Valdubón Crianza ★★ $$
dry, medium-bodied, medium tannin, medium acidity drink now–6 years
Sweet spice and blackberry flavors put up an easy façade; a core of iron keeps it serious.

1999 Bodegas Montegaredo Tinto Roble ★ $
dry, medium-bodied, medium tannin, medium acidity drink now–3 years
As Ribera prices escalate, it's a relief to find a pleasurable wine like this, with lightly spiced cherry flavors for a low price.

navarra, penedès, priorat

Navarra borders Rioja, but it has shared little of its neighbor's glory. As in Rioja, the focus is on red wines, though here Garnacha dominates and Tempranillo plays the supporting role. Cabernet, Merlot, and Syrah have also established a presence in the region, with notable success.

Penedès and Priorat are the most prominent wine regions in Catalonia. Penedès makes quality red and white wines from local grape varieties, but it's most famous for sparkling Cavas (see page 270). Priorat's steep, mineral-rich slopes produce some of Spain's suavest, most full-bodied red wines from Garnacha.

at the table
Penedès whites have the body for seafood paella. Rosés from Navarra have a dry, herb-tinged spiciness that stands up to tapas. Powerful, peppery Priorat reds require peppery, powerful foods, like lamb shanks braised with red peppers.

the bottom line
Good Navarra or Penedès wines cost about $10, though special selections fetch $20 or more. In contrast, high demand and little supply pushes Priorat reds to $30 to $60, with a few that reach $180.

recommended
white & rosé wines

2001 Les Brugueres, Priorat ♀ ★★★ $$
dry, medium-bodied, no oak, high acidity   drink now–4 years
There's more to this than simple summer sipping—a profound minerality
underlies the delicious citrus and peach flavors.

2001 Can Feixes Blanc Selecció, Penedès ♀ ★★★ $
dry, medium-bodied, no oak, high acidity   drink now–2 years
From one of Spain's best sparkling wine producers, a still wine loaded with
floral, citrus, and mineral flavors from gravel-rich soils.

2000 Segura Viudas Xarel-lo Creu de Lavit, Penedès ♀ ★★ $$
dry, medium-bodied, medium oak, high acidity   drink now–3 years
Oak scents pour from the bottle when this is first opened, but they marry so
well with the fruit it all tastes like peaches.

2001 Torres Viña Esmeralda, Penedès ♀ ★★ $
off-dry, light-bodied, no oak, high acidity   drink now
A touch of sweetness adds extra charm to this floral, fruity, aromatic wine.

2000 Bodegas Ochoa Rosado de Lagrima, Navarra ♀ ★ $
dry, medium-bodied, high acidity   drink now
Not just another pretty-in-pink rosé. Strawberry and vanilla flavors are backed
up by spice and an appealing earthiness. Lively acidity keeps it fresh.

recommended red wines

1999 Celler Vall Llach Vall Llach, Priorat ★★★★ $$$$
dry, full-bodied, heavy tannin, high acidity   drink in 2–10 years
This is mountain wine, with roasted meat, wild huckleberry, and mineral flavors with a campfire smokiness.

1999 Cervoles, Costers del Segre ★★★ $$
dry, medium-bodied, medium tannin, high acidity   drink in 1–6 years
Next to Penedès, Costers del Segre is an emerging region making very good
wine. This is one of the best, with nutty fruit, mineral, and leather flavors.

1997 Palacio de Otazu Crianza, Navarra ★★ $$
dry, medium-bodied, medium tannin, high acidity   drink now–6 years
Cabernet and Merlot bring richness and spice to Tempranillo's cherry and
pomegranate flavors.

1998 Segura Viudas Mas d'Aranyó Reserva, Penedès   ★ ★ $ $
dry, full-bodied, medium tannin, high acidity   drink now–6 years
This offers a fascinating array of flavors, from dark berry to green pepper, sweet spice to bitter chocolate.

1998 Torres Gran Coronas Cabernet Sauvignon, Penedès   ★ ★ $ $
dry, full-bodied, heavy tannin, high acidity   drink in 2–8 years
There's a bloody note to the meaty cherry fruit of this wine, making it a primally appealing match to a black-and-blue steak.

2000 Guelbenzu Azul, Ribera del Queiles   ★ ★ $
dry, full-bodied, heavy tannin, high acidity   drink now–8 years
Guelbenzu adds Cabernet and Merlot to Tempranillo for a modern wine with ripe fruit, spice, and herb flavors.

2000 Mas Igneus Barranc dels Clossos, Priorat   ★ ★ $
dry, medium-bodied, heavy tannin, high acidity   drink in 1–5 years
With Priorat prices skyrocketing, it's exciting to find a bargain like this earthy, spicy, cherry-filled wine.

1998 Beltran Crianza, Navarra   ★ $
dry, full-bodied, heavy tannin, high acidity   drink now–5 years
An enthusiastic chorus of sweet spice, stewed berry, and oak-derived vanilla flavors will sing with char-grilled lamb chops.

other regions

On Spain's Atlantic coast, Galicia makes some of the country's finest whites; the full-bodied Albariños from Rías Baixas are arguably the best. The appealing, berry-flavored red wines of Somontano and Toro's heavy-duty reds have yet to gain fame, but are worth notice, especially at the low prices they ask. And vintners in Valencia, Utiel-Requena, Jumilla, and Alicante, known historically for anonymous bulk wines, now produce reds many are happy to put their names on.

at the table
Galicia's simple white wines seem made for steamed clams or raw oysters, while richer Albariño wines are marvelous with lobster or grilled scallops. Most central and southern reds happily accompany rustic stews or a paella made with chicken or rabbit.

the bottom line Simple Galician white wines start at around $10; exemplary Albariño runs $15 to $20. The lesser-known red wines from these regions are hard to find here, and range from $9 to $20.

recommended white wines

2001 Lusco do Miño Albariño, Rías Baixas ★★★ $$
dry, medium-bodied, no oak, high acidity drink now–6 years
So stony, it's as if someone built a fortress to protect the vibrant lime flavors of this wine. Drink it now or cellar it.

2001 Morgadío Albariño, Rías Baixas ★★★ $$
dry, medium-bodied, no oak, high acidity drink now–6 years
Galicia, home to Rías Baixas, has been likened to Ireland for its Atlantic climate, but the tropical fruit flavors give an impression of the South Pacific.

2001 Pazo de Señorans Albariño, Rías Baixas ★★ $$
dry, medium-bodied, no oak, medium acidity drink now–3 years
Floral, light honey, and lime zest flavors will put a spring in anyone's step.

2001 Cuevas de Castilla Con Class, Rueda ★★ $
dry, light-bodied, no oak, medium acidity drink now–2 years
Classy and sassy, with bright fruit and fresh herb flavors.

2001 Martínsancho Verdejo, Rueda ★★ $
dry, medium-bodied, no oak, high acidity drink now–4 years
Lush and lazy as a tropical holiday, yet vibrant with acidity. Chill and enjoy.

recommended red wines

1999 El Vínculo, La Mancha ★★★ $$
dry, full-bodied, heavy tannin, high acidity drink now–5 years
Alejandro Fernández, the maestro of Ribera del Duero, becomes the man in La Mancha with this elegant wine with dry fruit and spice flavors.

2000 Bodegas Castaño Solanera Monastrell, Yecla ★★★ $
dry, full-bodied, medium tannin, medium acidity drink now–5 years
Spanish Monastrell wines are usually leaner than their French counterparts (where the grape is called Mourvèdre), but this version is full-bodied, with fruit, spice, and nut flavors.

1999 Bodega Pirineos Moristel, Somontano   ★★ $
dry, medium-bodied, medium tannin, high acidity   drink now–3 years
Floral and spice scents are only the beginning for this tart berry wine made
from a unique grape variety.

1996 Bodegas Félix Solís Viña Albali Reserva, Valdepeñas ★★ $
dry, full-bodied, medium tannin, medium acidity   drink now–5 years
A candy shop of flavors, with praline and chocolate notes and a whip of
licorice, yet dry enough for dinner.

1999 Bodegas Inviosa Lar de Barros Crianza,
Ribera del Guadiana   ★★ $
dry, full-bodied, medium tannin, medium acidity   drink now–3 years
Delicious wine, dripping with strawberry and spice.

1996 Torre Oria Reserva, Utiel-Requena   ★★ $
dry, full-bodied, medium tannin, medium acidity   drink now–5 years
From the arid hinterlands east of Valencia comes a meaty, herb, and berry
wine, perfect for your next barbecue.

2001 Bodegas Agapito Rico Carchelo, Jumilla   ★ $
dry, medium-bodied, medium tannin, medium acidity   drink now
Juicy fruit and a little spice make a solid, inexpensive wine.

1998 Marqués de Alicante Crianza, Alicante   ★ $
dry, medium-bodied, medium tannin, high acidity   drink now–2 years
Berry and mineral flavors make this a nice, simple quaff.

BY ANY OTHER NAME

Spain's three most important red grapes and its most
important white variety turn up all over, though you may
not know it as their names change from place to place:

Garnacha Grenache (France), Cannonau (Sardinia)

Tempranillo Tinto Fino (Ribera del Duero), Tinto del
Madrid or Tinto del Pais (Ribera del Duero), Tinto de Rioja
(Rioja), Tinto de Toro (Toro), Cencibel (La Mancha and
Valdepeñas), Tinta Roriz (Portugal)

Montastrell Mourvèdre (France), Mataro (Australia,
California, parts of France's Roussillon), Esparte (Australia)

Macabeo Viura (Rioja), Maccabéo or Maccabeu
(France)

portugal

Portugal's dry table wines long played second fiddle to its sweet, fortified Port, but Portuguese winemaking underwent a renaissance in the 1990s. Facilities were upgraded and techniques fine-tuned. Vintners did not, however, replace their local grape varieties, among the most diverse and unique collections in Europe. Today, wines from some producers are among the finest anywhere.

on the label

Few wine regions use as diverse a variety of grapes as Portugal. (Most of the country's grapes aren't even seen anywhere else.) Port, its most famous wine, can be blended from eighty different varieties. With so much to choose from, it isn't surprising that blends are the norm. That said, wines labeled with a variety must contain at least 85 percent of the named grape. And wines labeled DOC (*Denominação de Origem Controlada* in Portuguese) must meet specific rules governing the blend of grapes. For example, Bairrada must contain at least 50 percent Baga grapes. Wines labeled *Reserva* must achieve a half percentage more alcohol than the minimum required by the DOC. *Garrafeira* wines are required to spend two years in wood casks plus a year in bottle. Port and Madeira are covered in Fortified & Dessert Wines, page 274.

white wines

grapes & styles

Portugal's best-known white wine is Vinho Verde, or "green wine," a light-bodied, low-alcohol, high-acid white with a slight sparkle usually meant to be consumed within the year it is

released. Most Vinho Verde is made from undistinguished (and unidentified) varieties, but Vinhos Verdes made from Alvarinho (Spain's Albariño) can sometimes have so much more body and flavor that they can age for years. Whites from other regions of Portugal, like the Dão, Douro, and Bucelas, are often excellent.

at the table

Light-bodied and low in alcohol, Vinho Verde is a refreshing summer pour, served chilled with luncheon salads or as an aperitif. Alvarinho can take on richer dishes like crab or lobster. Whites from other regions tend to have the body for grilled chicken or swordfish steaks.

portugal **whites**

the bottom line Most Vinho Verde is perfectly priced for summer parties at under $10. Alvarinho's quality warrants the extra $5 or $10 charge. Whites from other areas tend to fall in the $8 to $15 range.

recommended wines

2001 Portal do Fidalgo Alvarinho, Vinho Verde ★ ★ ★ $$
dry, full-bodied, no oak, high acidity drink now–3 years
Portugal's Brazilian connection is suggested by the juicy, tropical fruit- and rainforest nut-scented wine.

2001 Antonio Esteves Ferreira Soalheiro Alvarinho, Vinho Verde ★ ★ ★ $
dry, medium-bodied, no oak, high acidity drink now–3 years
Vinho Verde at its best, showing the depth of flavor possible from Alvarinho with spicy herb, mineral, and lemon oil flavors.

2001 Arca Nova, Vinho Verde ★ ★ $
dry, light-bodied, no oak, high acidity drink now
Archetypal Vinho Verde, with smoky lime and dry honey flavors.

2001 Borges Quinta de Simaens, Vinho Verde ★ ★ $
dry, light-bodied, no oak, high acidity drink now
The accent's on "verde" here: green herb, green apple, and green papaya.

2000 Casa de Saima, Bairrada ★ ★ $
dry, light-bodied, no oak, high acidity drink now
Here's a summery wine, full of zesty lime flavors, enchanting floral scents and mouthwatering minerals and acidity.

2001 Cooperativa de Ponte de Lima Adamado, Vinho Verde ★ ★ $
dry, medium-bodied, no oak, high acidity drink now
Just $7 gets you a floral, peachy summer quencher.

1999 Luis Pato Vinhas Velhas, Bairrada ★ ★ $
dry, medium-bodied, no oak, high acidity drink now–3 years
This offers tons of minerals, plus pear, lemon, and smoke flavors.

2000 Morgado de Sta. Catherina, Bucelas ★ ★ $
dry, full-bodied, medium oak, medium acidity drink now–5 years
A Portuguese version of Chardonnay, this offers lots of mineral, smoke, and lemon notes smoothed with buttery flavor.

2000 Quinta da Romeira Arinto, Bucelas   ★ ★ $
dry, medium-bodied, no oak, high acidity   drink now–2 years
Allow a few minutes in the glass for the ripe cheese aromas to dissipate, and a creamy apple and lemon flavor takes center stage.

red wines

grapes & styles

Not so long ago, Portuguese reds were charming for their love-able rusticity, but they were generally rather clumsy affairs. Today, better viticultural and vinification techniques are creating international-caliber wines that manage to maintain a distinct Portuguese identity. Some Cabernet Sauvignon and even a little Merlot has crept into Portugal, but indigenous varieties like Baga, Touriga Francesa, Touriga Nacional, and Tinta Roriz pre-vail, making full-bodied red wines that often offer many of the berry and sweet spice flavors of Port wines, but in a dry, tannic fashion. Many examples also age very well.

at the table

The hearty, aromatic reds of the Dão, Bairrada, or the Douro match well with spiced dishes like lamb shanks braised with Moroccan spices, chile-rubbed pork loin, or meaty bean stews like Brazil's *feijoada*. The sophisticated, mature flavors of Garrafeira wines go well with gamey meats, rack of lamb, and mushroom-laced dishes.

the bottom line Word has been getting out about Portugal's reds: though there are still good wines at $8 to $12, count on paying $15 to $18 for more substantial examples, and up to $65 for the best.

recommended wines

1997 Duas Quintas Reserva, Douro   ★ ★ ★ $$$
dry, full-bodied, heavy tannin, high acidity   drink in 2–10 years
As piquant, fruity, and chocolaty as a *mole* sauce—and just as complex and delicious. It will only get better with time.

197

portugal **reds**

1999 J. Portugal Ramos Marquês de Borba Reserva, Alentejo ★★★ $$$
dry, full-bodied, heavy tannin, high acidity   drink in 2–15 years
Don't drink this just because you're looking for a Portuguese wine. Drink it because it's a world-class wine, rich with fruit, oak, and spice flavors so dense and ripe they take on a tarry edge.

1999 Quinta do Vale Meão, Douro ★★★ $$$
dry, full-bodied, heavy tannin, high acidity   drink in 2–15 years
This aims for the bleachers with its deep flavors of dark fruit, dark spice, and vanilla. Lay this one down.

2000 Luis Pato Vinhas Velhas, Beiras ★★★ $$
dry, medium-bodied, heavy tannin, high acidity   drink in 3–15 years
The essence of Portugal in juicy red fruit, sweet and peppery spices, and floral notes, all exhibited with understated grace.

1999 Globus, Ribatejo ★★★ $
dry, medium-bodied, medium tannin, high acidity   drink now–12 years
The broad cherry and spice flavors of this modern Ribatejo red would please anyone the world over.

1999 Quinta do Crasto, Douro ★★★ $
dry, medium-bodied, medium tannin, high acidity   drink now–8 years
A fine, old-fashioned Port producer makes a fine, modern table wine, rich in berry, cedar, lavender, and spice notes.

1997 Cartuxa Evora, Alentejo ★★ $$
dry, medium-bodied, medium tannin, high acidity   drink now–6 years
As fragrant as a bed of roses, with dry berry and earthy spice flavors too. Have this with roast pig.

1999 Casa de Santar Reserva, Dão ★★ $$
dry, full-bodied, heavy tannin, high acidity   drink now–6 years
This captures the flavor of the Dão region in earthy, roasted fruit flavors with plenty of warm spice.

1999 Quinta da Mimosa, Palmela ★★ $$
dry, full-bodied, heavy tannin, medium acidity   drink now–8 years
Loaded with sweet, dark berry and peppermint flavors, this would match a lamb-and-prune tagine brilliantly, especially on a cold night.

1999 Altano, Douro ★★ $
dry, medium-bodied, medium tannin, high acidity   drink now–3 years
Earthy and easy-drinking, this has lots of berry flavors augmented with herb notes and plenty of verve.

2000 Casa Agricola Cortes de Cima Chaminé, Alentejo ★★ $
dry, full-bodied, medium tannin, medium acidity   drink now–5 years
Fresh cherry-berry flavors come alive with vibrant acidity and peppery tannin.

2000 Casa Santos Lima Alicante Bouschet, Estremadura ★★ $
dry, full-bodied, medium tannin, medium acidity   drink now–6 years
Said to come from Spain's Alicante region, Alicante Bouschet is right at home
in Portugal, making an intensely colored wine full of black berry, oak, and
tobacco flavors.

2000 Falua Aragonês, Ribatejo ★★ $
dry, full-bodied, heavy tannin, medium acidity   drink in 2–10 years
Rich berry flavors turn dry with the handfuls of spice and mineral notes.

2000 Quinta de la Rosa, Douro ★★ $
dry, medium-bodied, medium tannin, high acidity   drink now–3 years
Spiced cherry flavors enlivened with vibrant acidity can brighten up anything
from roast chicken to lamb chops.

**1999 José Maria da Fonseca Periquita,
Terras do Sado** ★ $
dry, medium-bodied, medium tannin, high acidity   drink now–2 years
Always reliable and always cheap. The tart red fruit bolstered by lots of acidity
matches grilled burgers or *linguiça* sausages just right.

FAME HAS ITS DRAWBACKS

It took a war between England and France to make
Portuguese wines known to the English-speaking public,
but, ironically, these same circumstances also kept
Portugal's best table wines from being known to the
world. In the late 17th century, British merchants, cut off
from ready supplies of inexpensive Bordeaux wines (imagine that!), discovered the lush reds of Portugal's mountain-
ous Douro region. However, as the wines tended to be
inconsistent from year to year and were difficult to preserve during the haul from the Douro to Britain, it became
the norm to fortify them with brandy. The English Port wine
industry was thus born, and the excellent dry red wines of
the Douro were forgotten. Over the past decade, however,
Port wine houses like Quinta do Crasto and Ramos-Pinto
have introduced wines that may earn the Douro's dry
wines a place next to their Ports.

germany

Long gone are the days when German wine was synonymous in America with insipid *Liebfraumilch* like Blue Nun. Today, German wines have regained much of their pre-World War II luster in the U.S. market. After years of hard work, German vintners are once again producing a wide range of high-quality wines, from crisp sparklers to luscious dessert wines.

grapes & styles

Of the many grape varieties grown in Germany, Riesling reigns above all others in quality and quantity. Müller-Thurgau runs a close second in terms of quantity, though most of it is made into wines of little consequence. Fine whites are also made from Silvaner, Gewürztraminer, Kerner, and Scheurebe. Red wine production in Germany is small but growing. The finest examples are made from Spätburgunder (Pinot Noir) and Dornfelder.

on the label

With long, unfamiliar names in Gothic script, German wine labels may be intimidating, but they are actually quite informative. Nearly every label will list not only the winery, but also the grape, region, village, and sometimes even the vineyard in which the grapes were grown.

German wines are also classified by quality. One of the more basic classification levels is QbA (*Qualitätswein bestimmter Anbaugebiete),* for quality wine from one of thirteen regions. A step up is QmP (*Qualitätswein mit Prädikat,* or quality wine with distinction, often called simply *Prädikatswein*), for wines categorized according to the ripeness of the grapes at harvest. The categories start at *Kabinett,* for the lightest wines, and move up in richness to *Spätlese, Auslese, Beerenauslese* (BA), and *Trockenbeerenauslese* (TBA), for the ripest and richest wines.

While ripeness often corresponds to the sweetness of the wine, there is much variation. Some vintners print *trocken* ("dry") or *halbtrocken* (literally "half-dry") on their labels to indicate that a wine is dry or off-dry, but even so, styles vary between producers and regions. That said, most Auslese is almost dessert-sweet, and BA and TBA wines are always sweet, with an especially luscious quality from the botrytis, or "noble rot," that affects the grapes before harvest. A separate category is *Eiswein,* an extremely sweet wine made from grapes that are left to freeze on the vine. Since it's the water in the grapes that freezes, when the frozen grapes are pressed, only the flavorful juice is extracted, making for an intensely sweet and concentrated elixir. Eiswein is not affected by botrytis. (For sweet wines, see Fortified and Dessert Wines, page 274.)

201

lay of the land

Differences among Germany's major wine regions are often overlooked, but variations in terrain, soil, and climate create profoundly different results, and allow other grape varieties to thrive.

Mosel-Saar-Ruwer Rieslings grown along the steep banks of the Mosel River, as well as along its southerly tributaries, the Saar and Ruwer, are revered for their crisp acidity and fruity yet mineral flavors. Wines from the Mosel are usually fuller in body than those from the Saar and Ruwer.

Rheingau This region is so closely identified with Riesling that the variety is often left off the label. Rheingau Riesling tends to be fuller in body with riper fruit flavors than those from the Mosel.

Rheinhessen Rheinhessen may be infamous for sweet, insipid Liebfraumilch like Blue Nun and Black Tower, but even the Blue Nun has seen the error of her ways and is now attaching her name to wines of better quality. Wines from the steep Rheinterrasse subregion are particularly good.

Pfalz Riesling still dominates in the Pfalz, but Germany's sunniest wine region nurtures grape varieties that don't do very well in other regions, such as Gewürztraminer, Weissburgunder (Pinot Blanc), Grauburgunder (Pinot Gris), and Scheurebe.

Other regions Look to Baden for aromatic Pinot Blanc and Pinot Gris, and to the Mittelrhein for steely, high-acid Rieslings. Franken is unique not only for its short, round bottles, but also for its wide array of grapes, such as Silvaner, Kerner, and Bacchus.

white wines

RIESLING

For many people, Riesling is the world's white grape *sans pareil*. Not only does it give bold, citrusy fruit flavors kept light and refreshing with naturally high acidity, but it is particularly adept at reflecting the mineral qualities of the soil in which it grows. The wines are also impressively long-lived, developing richer flavors and sometimes oddly compelling kerosene-like aromas.

at the table

German Riesling is one of the most versatile wines with food. Clear fruit flavors and mouthwatering acidity make it a natural for fish and seafood, while the slight sweetness of some Rieslings goes well with sweet and spicy dishes like pad thai or chile-spiced fried snapper. Older Rieslings have the richness and acidity to pair with Wienerschnitzel or even duck *à l'orange*.

the bottom line Simple Rieslings from outstanding producers can be found for as little as $7. A few outstanding, top-of-the-line wines will run $80 or more, but many excellent choices can be found for $35 or less.

what to buy RIESLING

1997	1998	1999	2000	2001
★★★	★★★	★★★★	★★	★★★★

recommended wines

2000 A. Christmann Idig Königsbach Spätlese Trocken, Pfalz　　　　★★★★ $$$
dry, medium-bodied, no oak, high acidity　　　drink now–20 years
Wow. Explosive with strawberry, mango, and mineral flavors.

2000 Georg Breuer Berg Schlossberg Rüdesheim, Rheingau　　　　★★★★ $$$
dry, full-bodied, no oak, high acidity　　　drink now–12 years
One of Rheingau's most dynamic producers combined with one of its best vineyards makes for a work of art of glazed fruit and fine mineral flavors.

2001 Müller-Catoir Haardter Burgergarten Spätlese, Pfalz　　　　★★★★ $$$
off-dry, medium-bodied, no oak, high acidity　　　drink now–25 years
Simply one of the world's best wines. Don't even think about opening it now; lose it in the cellar for a decade and it will reward.

2001 Weingut Dr. Crusius Niederhäuser Felsensteyer Spätlese, Nahe　　　　★★★★ $$$
off-dry, medium-bodied, no oak, high acidity　　　drink now–15 years
Ripe pear and apricot flavors show the power of our closest star and haunting musk notes point to the mysteries of the earth.

germany **whites**

2000 Weingut Wwe. Dr. H. Thanisch Bernkasteler Doctor Spätlese,
Mosel-Saar-Ruwer ★★★★ $$$
off-dry, full-bodied, no oak, high acidity drink now–15 years
Doctors on double duty offer an herb- and spice-laden wine with very ripe
peachlike flavors. It has the stuffing to last years.

2000 Robert Weil Estate Kabinett Halbtrocken, Rheingau ★★★★ $$
dry, medium-bodied, no oak, high acidity drink now–10 years
Robert Weil is the star of the Rheingau; this wine, with its mineral, toasted nut,
herb, and lime flavors, can explain why.

1996 von Othegraven Kanzem Altenberg,
Mosel-Saar-Ruwer ★★★★ $$
dry, full-bodied, no oak, high acidity drink now–20 years
Just released, this luscious, nutty, mineral-laden Riesling shows what a few
years does to a wine from a great vintage.

2001 Wittman Kirchspiel Trocken, Rheinhessen ★★★ $$$
dry, light-bodied, no oak, high acidity drink now–15 years
Limestone-rich soils give great smoky mineral flavors; fruit pushes through
like grass through cracks in the stones.

2001 Dönnhoff Estate, Nahe ★★★ $$
dry, medium-bodied, no oak, high acidity drink now–10 years
A great value from a superb producer, with sweet peachy flavor countered
with dry mineral and spice notes.

2001 Joh. Jos. Christoffel Ürziger Würzgarten Kabinett,
Mosel-Saar-Ruwer ★★★ $$
off-dry, medium-bodied, no oak, high acidity drink now–12 years
One taste of this wine explains that *"Würzgarten"* means "spice garden." Its
ripe fruit flavors provide a juicy platform.

2000 Johannishof Johannisberger Vogelsang Kabinett,
Rheingau ★★★ $$
off-dry, medium-bodied, no oak, high acidity drink now–8 years
A lusty, full-flavored Riesling, with musky, vibrant fruit and mineral flavors.

2001 Messmer Burrweiler Schlossgarten Kabinett, Pfalz ★★★ $$
dry, medium-bodied, no oak, high acidity drink now–10 years
Mesmerizing, with concentrated, spicy fruit flavors plus vibrant acidity.

2001 Selbach-Oster Bernkasteler Badstube Kabinett,
Mosel-Saar-Ruwer ★★★ $$
dry, medium-bodied, no oak, high acidity drink now–10 years
Here's a weighty one, with heavy-duty fruit and mineral flavors.

2001 Weingut Alfred Merkelbach Erdener Treppchen Auslese,
Mosel-Saar-Ruwer ★★★ $$
off-dry, medium-bodied, no oak, high acidity   drink now–20 years
Take grapes of Auslese ripeness, ferment them until almost dry, and the
resulting wine will be intense and spicy like this mineral-packed example.

2000 Weingut Bürklin-Wolf Estate, Pfalz ★★★ $$
dry, medium-bodied, no oak, high acidity   drink now–8 years
Absolutely terrific wine, with ripe tropical fruit and mineral flavors for a surprisingly low price.

2001 Weingut Eugen Müller Forster Ungeheuer Kabinett,
Pfalz ★★★ $$
dry, medium-bodied, no oak, high acidity   drink now–12 years
Like a reliable friend, Müller offers a lot, but asks for little. Minerally citrus and
peppery spice flavors offer much pleasure.

2000 Weingut Fritz Haag Estate Kabinett,
Mosel-Saar-Ruwer ★★★ $$
dry, medium-bodied, no oak, high acidity   drink now–8 years
Fresh herb and lemon flavors are great on their own, but together in this wine
they are electric.

2001 Weingut Weingart Bopparder Hamm Feuerlay Spätlese,
Mittelrhein ★★★ $$
off-dry, full-bodied, no oak, high acidity   drink now–12 years
Palate-gripping mineral flavors and searing acidity hold the honeyed apricot
flavors firm and long, an intense and impressive wine from an often over-
looked region.

2000 Weingut Willi Haag Brauneberger Juffer Spätlese,
Mosel-Saar-Ruwer ★★★ $$
off-dry, medium-bodied, no oak, high acidity   drink now–3 years
Intense lime and lime blossom flavors and a bit of mineral make for lip-
smacking drinking.

2001 Dr. Fischer Ockfener Bockstein Kabinett,
Mosel-Saar-Ruwer ★★★ $
dry, medium-bodied, no oak, high acidity   drink now–6 years
Nearly every wine from this producer offers good value. Here, lime, herb, and
mineral flavors are framed by searing acidity.

2000 Karthäuserhof Estate, Mosel-Saar-Ruwer ★★★ $
off-dry, full-bodied, no oak, high acidity   drink now–5 years
Stunning value from non-classified wine, with luscious fruit, mineral, and herb
flavors. Stock up.

germany **whites**

1999 Sibyl Qualitätswein, Nahe ★★★ $
dry, medium-bodied, no oak, high acidity   drink now–8 years
California winemaker Zelma Long produced this intense, grapefruit, nut, and
mineral-flavored wine.

2001 von Othegraven Maria v. O., Mosel-Saar-Ruwer ★★★ $
dry, full-bodied, no oak, high acidity   drink now–10 years
The fruit flavors of this mineral-rich wine are ambrosial; Othegraven's "prestige" wines arc cvcn more sublime.

**2000 Weingut Dr. von Bassermann-Jordan Estate Trocken,
Pfalz** ★★★ $
dry, medium-bodied, no oak, high acidity   drink now–5 years
Thrills come cheap in this bone-dry wine full of citrus and mineral flavors.

**2001 Weingut Eugen Wehrheim Niersteiner Orbel Spätlese,
Rheinhessen** ★★★ $
off-dry, medium-bodied, no oak, high acidity   drink now–8 years
A delicious, harmonious ensemble of fruit and mineral flavors.

2000 Weingut Pfeffingen Estate Dry, Pfalz ★★★ $
dry, medium-bodied, no oak, high acidity   drink now–8 years
A fusillade of tangerine and mineral flavors shoot from glass to mouth.

**2000 Dr. Loosen Erdener Treppchen Kabinett,
Mosel-Saar-Ruwer** ★★ $$
off-dry, medium-bodied, no oak, high acidity   drink now–5 years
Exuberant as a garden approaching full bloom, the citrus, tropical fruit, and
spice flavors come up everywhere.

**2001 Graf von Schoenborn Hattenheimer Pfaffenberg Kabinett,
Rheingau** ★★ $$
off-dry, medium-bodied, no oak, high acidity   drink now–4 years
The spicy, smoky, citrus flavors play well off sweet and savory Asian dishes.

2001 Toni Jost Bacharacher Hahn Kabinett, Mittelrhein ★★ $$
dry, medium-bodied, no oak, high acidity   drink now–8 years
Glazed fruit and spice flavors combine with sweet, lemony herbal notes.

2000 Weingut Reichsrat von Buhl Armand Kabinett, Pfalz ★★ $$
dry, light-bodied, no oak, high acidity   drink now–5 years
From a great Pfalz estate, a light wine full of vibrant citrus and mineral flavors.

2000 Dr. Loosen Dr. "L.", Mosel-Saar-Ruwer ★★ $
off-dry, medium-bodied, no oak, high acidity   drink now–2 years
Peach and pear lushness for a low price.

2001 J. & H.A. Strub Niersteiner Kabinett, Rheinhessen ★★ $
dry, light-bodied, no oak, high acidity drink now
Keep a one-liter bottle of this wonderfully light and lively—and cheap—
Riesling in the fridge all year long.

2001 Lingenfelder Bird Label, Pfalz ★★ $
dry, light-bodied, no oak, high acidity drink now
Fun and easy to enjoy. Musk and smoke notes add depth to the fruit.

**2001 Schumann Nägler Johannisberger Erntebringer Kabinett,
Rheingau** ★★ $
off-dry, medium-bodied, no oak, high acidity drink now–8 years
Light tropical punch and flinty mineral flavors make a tasty wine.

**2001 Paul Anheuser Schlossboeckelheimer Koenigsfels Kabinett,
Nahe** ★ $
dry, medium-bodied, no oak, high acidity drink now–2 years
Perhaps it's the power of suggestion, but this is as refreshing as a cold pilsner
with nutty and dry mineral flavors and a hoplike floral quality.

2001 W. Ailenz Ayler Kupp Qualitätswein, Mosel-Saar-Ruwer ★ $
dry, light-bodied, no oak, high acidity drink now
A one-liter bottle offers room for a lot of wine, and this citrusy Riesling fills it
up with personality.

OTHER WHITE WINES

Adventurous drinkers are well rewarded in Germany. Scheurebe,
a cross of Silvaner and Riesling, gives rich wines with aromatic
flavors like cassis, grapefruit, and honey. Kerner and Huxelrebe,
two other crosses, can produce distinctive wines.
Grauburgunder (more commonly known as Pinot Gris), makes
full-bodied wines in warmer areas such as Pfalz. Silvaner and
Müller-Thurgau (also a cross) are major grape varieties, but with
notable exceptions, they tend to produce tart, insipid wines.

at the table

Most German white wines share Riesling's high acidity, aromatic
flavors, and hint of sweetness and can be enjoyed as Riesling
would. More pungently flavored wines, like Scheurebe, are
especially good with sweet and spicy foods.

the bottom line Non-Riesling wines tend to top out
at $20, though some exceptional examples run a little more.

what to buy OTHER WHITE WINES

1997	1998	1999	2000	2001
★★★	★★★	★★★★	★★	★★★★

recommended wines

2001 Müller-Catoir Haardter Burgergarten Muskateller Kabinett Trocken, Pfalz   ★★★★ $$$
dry, medium-bodied, no oak, high acidity   drink now–6 years
Lovers of the steely, dry floral, and herb charms of dry Muscat wines will find no better example in the world than this, just one of the exceptional wines from this revered producer.

2000 Wisching Iphöfer Kronsberg Scheurebe Kabinett Trocken, Franken   ★★★★ $$
dry, full-bodied, no oak, high acidity   drink now–10 years
Franken wines have a small but fanatical following. You'll see why after a sip of this intensely herbal, bone-dry yet almost oily Scheurebe.

2001 Fitz-Ritter Dürkheimer Spielberg Chardonnay Spätlese, Pfalz   ★★★ $
dry, medium-bodied, no oak, high acidity   drink now–8 years
In a world awash in Chardonnay, Germany stands out for its lack. Here's a rare example, with ripe but very dry fruit flavors and loads of minerals. Pour it in place of a more expensive Burgundy.

2000 Heinrich Seebrich Niersteiner Oelberg Gewürztraminer Spätlese, Rheinhessen   ★★★ $
off-dry, medium-bodied, no oak, high acidity   drink now–8 years
This offers a succulent luau of grilled pineapple, honeysuckle, and herb flavors balanced by loads of minerals.

1999 Fürst Müller-Thurgau Kabinett, Franken   ★★ $$
dry, medium-bodied, no oak, high acidity   drink now–3 years
Fürst doesn't use Franken's traditional squat bottle for this untraditional Müller-Thurgau, rich with ripe tropical fruit and lots of minerals.

2001 Lingenfelder Grosskarlbacher Burgweg Scheurebe Kabinett Halbtrocken, Pfalz   ★★ $$
dry, light-bodied, no oak, high acidity   drink now–5 years
Need an evening wake-up call? Lingenfelder makes a Scheurebe that buzzes with catty, pungent, green herb aromas and shakes with minerals.

2000 Weinhaus Heger Pinot Gris Qualitätswein Trocken,
Baden ★★ $$
dry, medium-bodied, light oak, high acidity   drink now–6 years
Not many German wines employ oak, but it's used here to give the smoke, mineral, and lime flavors a warm, toasty edge.

2000 Graf von Schoenborn Schloss Hallburg Silvaner Kabinett
Trocken, Franken ★★ $
dry, medium-bodied, no oak, high acidity   drink now–3 years
This is so dry it's hard to imagine there's any room for flavor, but lime, almond, and tart plum flavors are all there.

2000 Weingut Ernst Bretz Bechtolscheimer Petersberg Kerner
Spätlese, Rheinhessen ★★ $
off-dry, medium-bodied, no oak, high acidity   drink now–3 years
Wild and super, with flavors of ground hazelnuts, pungent bitter herbs, smoky tobacco, and zesty lime.

2001 Weingut Köster-Wolf Albiger Schloss Hammerstein
Müller-Thurgau, Rheinhessen ★ $
dry, light-bodied, no oak, high acidity   drink now
Light citrus and nut flavors add a festive note to everyday drinking.

CLASSIC AND SELECTION WINES OF GERMANY

To lure customers who are intimidated by German wine labels with their Gothic lettering and Byzantine classifications like *"Spätlese halbtrocken,"* the German Wine Board introduced two new classifications that took effect with the 2000 vintage: Classic and Selection. This system doesn't supercede QbA and QmP classifications (see page 200), but rather allows vintners to choose a simplified label to describe their wines. "Classic" denotes a wine made from a grape traditional to its region and vinified dry; wines bearing this designation cannot list a village or vineyard on the label. "Selection" wines must be made from traditional grapes hand-picked from a specific vineyard at higher ripeness levels; these wines will list the vineyard, region, and grape, but cannot use extraneous descriptive terms like *"halbtrocken."* While in theory wines labeled Classic and Selection are dry, sweetness levels still vary. But the labels sure are easier to read.

austria

In addition to meeting the strictest production standards in the world, Austria's wines have been enriched by the influence of its many winegrowing neighbors. German traditions are most obvious, but Italian, Hungarian, Slovakian, and Slovenian sensibilities are also evident. Thanks to this cross-pollination as well as a diversity of climates and grapes, Austria offers an exciting array of wines.

grapes & styles

Bone-dry white wines dominate in Austria. Local variety Grüner Veltliner surpasses all in quantity, uniqueness, and many would argue, quality, though partisans of Austria's superb Rieslings might disagree. Other interesting whites include widely-grown Welschriesling and relatively rare Furmint.

Austria's red wines don't receive the same level of acclaim as the whites, though increasingly, they are worthy of attention. Look for juicy Zweigelt, delicate Blauer Portugieser, peppery, Blaufränkisch (or Lemberger), or Blauburgunder (Pinot Noir).

on the label

Austrian wines are labeled by variety and region. In addition, Austria uses a classification system similar to Germany's to indicate wines of good *(Qualitätswein)* and excellent *(Prädikatswein)* quality. The terms *Kabinett, Spätlese, Auslese, Beerenauslese,* and *Trockenbeerenauslese* (see Germany, page 200) are also used to indicate ripeness levels of grapes at harvest. However, an Austrian wine is likely to be drier than its German counterpart.

Vintners in the highly-regarded Wachau use a different sys-

NIEDEROSTERREICH

Kamptal
Kremstal
Wachau
Traisental
Carnuntum
Neusiedlersee
Thermenregion
Neusiedlersee-Hügelland

Weinviertel
Donauland

• VIENNA

SALZBURG •

BURGENLAND

STEIERMARK

Featured
Wine-Growing
Regions

tem. *Steinfeder* indicates the lightest wines, meant for drinking within the year they were made; *Federspiel* is slightly richer, and *Smaragd*, a reference to a sun-loving lizard found in between the vines, is applied to wines substantial enough to age.

lay of the land

Niederösterreich Austria's largest wine region, with eight subregions: Carnuntum, Donauland, Thermenregion, Traisental, Weinviertel, Kamptal, Kremstal, and Wachau. The last three put out some of Austria's most intense Veltliners and Rieslings.

Burgenland Austria's warmest region, on the eastern border with Hungary. The Neusiedlersee and Neusiedlersee-Hügelland subregions excel in white dessert wines. Mittelburgenland and Südburgenland specialize in dry red wines.

Steiermark Close to Slovenia and northern Italy, Steiermark (Styria) doesn't make a lot of wine, but its Sauvignon Blanc and Chardonnay stand out.

Vienna One of the few capital cities in the world with a productive wine industry, Vienna supplies both local wine taverns (*Heurigen*) and outsiders with fresh Grüner Veltliner.

white wines

GRÜNER VELTLINER

Most Grüner Veltliner wines are simple and fresh, designed to flow freely through the taps of local wine taverns. The bottles that find their way across the ocean, though, are among the most captivating wines made anywhere, with flavors often described as lemon, flowers, smoke, white pepper, and even lentils.

at the table

Grüner Veltliner's complex and pleasantly vegetal flavors stand up to foods that kill most wines, like asparagus and artichokes. But the pairing doesn't have to be extreme: simple examples are light and fresh enough for anytime, while Smaragds are rich enough for veal schnitzel or chicken Florentine.

the bottom line Some wonderful, simple Grüner Veltliners are less than $12, but most cost over $25.

what to buy WHITE WINES

1997	1998	1999	2000	2001
★★★★	★★★	★★★★	★★★★	★★★

recommended wines

2001 Weingut Bründlmayer Ried Lamm, Kamptal ★★★★ $$$$
dry, full-bodied, no oak, high acidity   drink now–20 years
The Hapsburgs couldn't have commissioned a more luxurious wine than this, with velvety fruit and spice, plus a treasure chest of mineral flavors.

2001 Nikolaihof Im Weingebirge Smaragd, Wachau ★★★★ $$$
dry, full-bodied, no oak, high acidity   drink now–20 years
A spectacular wine from a biodynamic winery that exudes life from within its smoky mineral and dry fruit flavors.

2001 Nigl Kremser Freiheit, Kremstal ★★★ $$
dry, medium-bodied, no oak, high acidity   drink now–4 years
Foreplay to Nigl's more expensive wines, Freiheit tantalizes with its smoky fruit and almond flavors while you save up for the others.

2000 Freie Weingärtner Terrassen Federspiel, Wachau ★★ $$
dry, medium-bodied, no oak, high acidity   drink now–5 years
Textbook Grüner Veltliner from one of the world's best cooperatives, with both refreshing citrus flavor and engaging earth and herb notes.

2001 E. & M. Berger, Kremstal ★★ $
dry, light-bodied, no oak, high acidity   drink now
With lime, herb, smoke, and mineral flavors, this is a terrific bargain at the price—and it's a one-liter bottle.

2001 Weingut Walter Glatzer Kabinett, Carnuntum ★★ $
dry, light-bodied, no oak, high acidity   drink now
Herb flavors sing, backed by a harmony of lime flavors.

RIESLING

While Grüner Veltliner has its fanatics, others consider Riesling the most noble grape in the country. It is unique, making aromatic wines drier than those from Germany and more full-bodied than their Alsatian counterparts.

at the table

The dryness of Austrian Riesling makes it a good match for rich dishes like roast duck, Wienerschnitzel, or mushroom stroganoff.

the bottom line Because of their excellent quality, Austrian Rieslings offer value, but not low prices. While a few odd bottles run less than $15, count on spending $25 and up.

recommended wines

2001 Nigl Privat, Kremstal ★★★★ $$$$
dry, full-bodied, no oak, high acidity   drink now–20 years
Arguably first among equals in the pantheon of great Austrian wines, Nigl once again puts forth an astounding wine of perfectly ripe fruit and peppery mineral flavors.

2001 Weingut Bründlmayer Steinmassel, Kamptal ★★★★ $$$
dry, medium-bodied, no oak, high acidity   drink now–15 years
The power of Austria's sunny, warm summers is reflected in the richness of the fruit, mineral, and spice flavors. It will only get better with time.

austria **whites**

**2000 Weingut Prager Weissenkirchen Steinriegl Smaragd,
Wachau** ★★★★ $$$
dry, full-bodied, no oak, high acidity   drink now–15 years
The brawny fruit and mineral flavors are enjoyable now, but let it age a bit to
really flex its muscles.

**2000 Franz Hirtzberger Steinterrassen Spitz Federspiel,
Wachau** ★★★ $$$
dry, medium-bodied, no oak, high acidity   drink now–12 years
The cooler climate in the western end of the Wachau allows for a graceful,
almost feminine expression of fruit, smoky mineral, and floral flavors.

2001 Nikolaihof vom Stein Federspiel, Wachau ★★★ $$$
dry, medium-bodied, no oak, high acidity   drink now–12 years
"Stein" ("stone" in German) says it all: flinty, smoky, and austere, this is all
about the soil in which it grew. Impressive.

2000 Freie Weingärtner Terrassen Federspiel, Wachau ★★★ $$
dry, medium-bodied, no oak, high acidity   drink now–4 years
An exemplary Austrian Riesling at an exemplary price, with as many of the
juicy citrus, spice, and mineral flavors as other wines costing far more.

2001 Hirsch Zöbing, Kamptal ★★★ $$
dry, medium-bodied, no oak, high acidity   drink in 1–12 years
The juicy pear and toasted almond flavors are delicious now, but give them
time and they will grow so big they may explode.

2001 Salomon Pfaffenberg, Kremstal ★★★ $$
dry, medium-bodied, no oak, high acidity   drink now–10 years
Almond and mineral notes add depth to bright grapefruit flavors.

2001 Schloss Gobelsburg vom Urgestein, Kamptal ★★★ $$
dry, medium-bodied, no oak, high acidity   drink now–10 years
Young Michael Moosbrugger ferments ripe grapes absolutely dry, producing a
wine infused with the essences of pear and pineapple without any of their
weight; only mineral flavors tether it to the earth.

2001 E. & M. Berger Spiegel Kabinett, Kremstal ★★ $$
dry, medium-bodied, no oak, high acidity   drink now–5 years
An austere, mineral- and smoke-filled Riesling for those who like wine dry.

OTHER WHITE WINES

Though part of the international grape repertory, Weissburgunder
(Pinot Blanc), Sauvignon Blanc (sometimes called Muskat-
Sylvaner), and Chardonnay (locally called Morillon) have been

Austrian staples for more than a century. Furmint, a grape shared by one-time co-national Hungary, makes fascinating wines in the eastern part of Austria.

at the table

Welschriesling and Weissburgunder match well with the usual suspects like grilled chicken cutlets or roast turkey. Sauvignon Blanc is a good choice with lake trout or perch, while richer Chardonnay does well with roasted salmon, or even roast pork.

the bottom line Welschriesling, Weissburgunder, and Furmint sell for between $9 and $35. Sauvignon Blanc and Chardonnay run $13 to $50.

recommended wines

2001 Jamek Ried Kollmitz Federspiel Muskateller, Wachau ★ ★ ★ ★ $$$
dry, light-bodied, no oak, high acidity   drink now–5 years
Magical: from a puff of smoke appears an exuberant bone-dry display of honeysuckle, pear, and mineral flavors.

2001 Polz Steirische Klassik Sauvignon Blanc, Steiermark ★ ★ ★ $$$
dry, medium-bodied, no oak, high acidity   drink now–4 years
With Sauvignon Blanc as full of ebullient passionfruit and herb flavors as this, New Zealand had better watch its back.

2001 Gross Grauburgunder, Steiermark ★ ★ ★ $$
dry, medium-bodied, light oak, high acidity   drink now–5 years
Pinot Gris done the Austrian way, with spicy herb, lime, and deep mineral flavors that come from gravel and slate soils.

2001 Heidi Schröck Furmint, Neusiedlersee-Hügelland ★ ★ ★ $$
dry, medium-bodied, no oak, high acidity   drink now–5 years
Reflecting a long-shared history, Schröck uses the grape behind Hungary's famed Tokaji wine to make a fine, dry wine with nut, spice, and flower flavors.

2000 Höpler Pinot Blanc, Burgenland ★ $
dry, medium-bodied, no oak, high acidity   drink now–3 years
Simply citrus at first, honeyed nut and light flower flavors develop with a little air. A terrific choice for picnics.

switzerland

Switzerland has a great wine tradition, but for decades its wines were rarely exported. In recent years, however, trade barriers have fallen, making it possible for customers abroad to enjoy some of Switzerland's impeccably made wines.

grapes & styles

Switzerland's most common grape is Chasselas, a variety also found, but widely ignored, in Alsace. Depending on where it is grown, Chasselas can be flowery, intensely mineral, or mouth-wateringly citric. In the Valais region, it is called "Fendant." Other quality white grapes include Pinot Gris and Petite Arvine. Red wines are principally made from Pinot Noir and Gamay, which, when blended together, take the name "Dôle" in the Valais, though Merlot reigns in the Italian-speaking region of Ticino, and Syrah grows in the francophone Valais.

on the label

If a white wine isn't labeled with a grape, assume it is made from Chasselas. Unlabeled reds are likely blends. Most wines will bear the name of the region in which they were grown, too.

at the table

With its strong acidity, Chasselas from Neuchâtel is great with raw shellfish, while the less acidic versions from the Vaud pair well with rich seafood dishes like sole Mornay. The minerality of Valais Fendant will cut through rich pâté or complement breaded chicken breasts. Pinot Gris stands up to cheese fondue; Petite Arvine is complex enough for pork loin or sage-crusted veal. Drink Merlot with roast beef; the richer Dôle, with lamb or duck.

the bottom line
The few Swiss wines available in the U.S. range from $18 to $60, with most under $35.

Thurgau
Schaffhausen
ZURICH •
Neuchâtel
• BERN
Lake Geneva
• LAUSANNE
Dézaley
Rhône River
Vaud
• GENEVA
Aigle
Valais
Ticino

Featured
Wine-Growing
Regions

recommended wines

**2000 Jean et Pierre Testuz Grand Cru L'Arbalète,
Dézaley** 🍷 ★★★★ $$$
dry, full-bodied, light oak, medium acidity   drink now–11 years
One hundred percent Grand Cru Chasselas, one hundred percent pleasure.

2000 Henri Badoux de Père en Fils Les Murailles, Aigle 🍷 ★★★ $$$
dry, light-bodied, no oak, high acidity   drink now–4 years
Subtle pear, mineral, and herb flavors play together in complex harmony.

**1999 F.lli Valsangiacomo Riserva di Bacco Merlot dei Colli del
Mendrisiotto, Ticino** 🍷 ★★★ $$
dry, full-bodied, medium tannin, medium acidity   drink now–8 years
Smooth berry flavors feel simple until sultry, smoky mineral notes emerge.

2000 François Gilliard Les Murettes Fendant de Sion, Valais 🍷 ★★★ $$
dry, medium-bodied, no oak, high acidity   drink now–4 years
A wallop of flower, honey, and citrus flavors rush through a bed of stones.

2000 Château d'Auvernier, Neuchâtel 🍷 ★★ $$
dry, medium-bodied, light oak, high acidity   drink now–4 years
Juicy grapefruit flavors are enveloped by clouds of minerals and smoke.

2000 Chanteauxvieux Dôle du Valais 🍷 ★ $$
dry, medium-bodied, medium tannin, medium acidity   drink now–1 year
A simple blend of Pinot Noir and Gamay brings cherry and light smoke flavors.

2000 Pierrafeu Fendant du Valais 🍷 ★ $$
dry, light-bodied, no oak, medium acidity   drink now–2 years
Charming fruit and stony flavors; a simple white wine for light dishes.

greece

Some of the most highly prized wines in the ancient world came from Greece, and if you think that Greek wine today is limited to harsh retsina, think again. Contemporary winemakers are taking advantage of the country's diverse terrain, micro-climates, and the many indigenous grape varieties to make Greece one of today's most exciting wine-producing regions.

grapes & styles

International favorites like Cabernet Sauvignon and Chardonnay are playing an increasing role in Greek viticulture, but indigenous grapes provide far more interesting wines. The white wine grape Savatiano is the most common. Although pine resin is often added to it to make Greece's distinctive retsina, vintners are now using Savatiano to make some fruit-juicy, simple (and some-times inspired) nonresinated whites. Santorini whites, made from Assyrtiko, are powerful, mineral-filled wines with electric acidity. Mantinia, in the Peloponnese, specializes in Moscofilero, a pink-skinned grape capable of giving both wonderfully floral whites and exotically spiced rosés.

In the realm of red wines, Agiorgitiko rules the Peloponnese, where it produces copious quantities of cheap, plummy, easy-to-drink wines and a handful of hillside wines with the same beguiling plumminess and plenty of tannin, too. The best are from Neméa. In the continental climate of the north, Náoussa has built its fame on Xinomavro. These reds are true to the grape's name—literally "acid-black"—when young, but with a decade or more of aging, its earthy, trufflelike flavors and struc-ture invite comparisons to Italy's Nebbiolo wines. Some recent, spicy, Rhône-like Syrahs suggest that there is serious potential for this grape here as well.

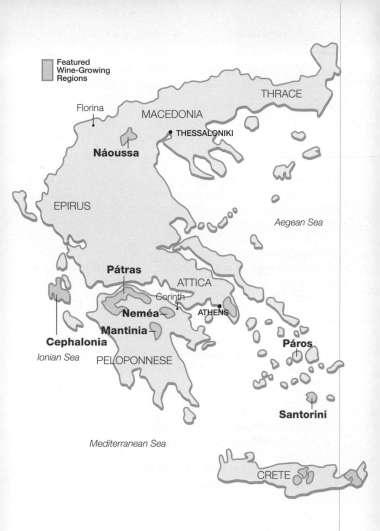

Featured Wine-Growing Regions

THRACE

MACEDONIA

Florina

Náoussa

● THESSALONIKI

EPIRUS

Aegean Sea

Pátras

ATTICA

Corinth

Neméa

ATHENS

Mantinia

Cephalonia

Páros

Ionian Sea

PELOPONNESE

Mediterranean Sea

Santorini

CRETE

white wines

at the table

Light Greek whites seem made for *mezes*, Greek appetizers
such as piquant olives, salty cheeses, and garlicky dips.
Assyrtiko, on the other hand, can grace a grilled sea bass as
easily as a leg of lamb. And spicy, floral Moscofilero finds reso-
nance in exotically-spiced dishes, say a Moroccan *bisteeya*.

bottom line Greek whites are veritable bargains, rarely
surpassing $15, though a few creep over $20.

recommended wines

2000 Boutari Kallisti, Santorini   ★ ★ ★ ★ $$
dry, medium-bodied, light oak, high acidity   drink now–10 years
A hint of oak gives the tight, limey, mineral flavors of Assyrtiko a lovely breadth and fullness, as well as the richness to age.

NV Gai'a Ritinitis Nobilis, Retsina   ★ ★ ★ ★ $
dry, medium-bodied, light oak, high acidity   drink now
Whereas most retsina is at best indifferent, this is art. Its vibrantly fresh, lightly resinous flavors are perfect with mezes.

2000 Kourtaki Assyrtiko, Santorini   ★ ★ ★ $
dry, medium-bodied, no oak, high acidity   drink now–1 year
With its beautiful balance of citrus, berry, hazelnut, and mineral flavors, this would be a good value at double the price. But at $12 a double bottle, it's stupendous.

2000 Ktima Kyr-Yianni Samaropetra, Florina   ★ ★ ★ $
dry, light-bodied, no oak, medium acidity   drink now
Gewürztraminer and Sauvignon Blanc are combined with Greece's Roditis for an exotically fragrant and spicy white.

2000 Creta Olympias, Crete   ★ ★ $
dry, medium-bodied, no oak, medium acidity   drink now
With fleshy fruit and dry minerals, this is a terrific choice to chill for a picnic.

2001 Domaine Tselepos Moscofilero, Mantinia   ★ ★ $
dry, full-bodied, no oak, medium acidity   drink now–1 year
Light floral notes set off rich, spicy peach fruit, making for a heady, mouthfilling white wine.

2001 Gai'a Nótios, Peleponnese   ★ ★ $
dry, medium-bodied, no oak, high acidity   drink now
Tangerine dreams, as the flowery Moscofilero grape is blended with citrusy Roditis. Great with prosciutto and figs.

2000 Gentilini Classico, Cephalonia   ★ ★ $
dry, full-bodied, light oak, medium acidity   drink now–3 years
As layered as baklava, with flavors of fruit, butter, and flowery honey.

2000 Oenoforos Asprolithi, Pátras   ★ ★ $
dry, medium-bodied, no oak, high acidity   drink now–2 years
A taste of the Peloponnese in a bottle, with lemon and melon flavors mixed with almond and mineral notes.

red wines

at the table

The simple berry goodness of bargain-priced southern reds is just the thing for grilled sausages or lamb kebabs. The Barolo-like earthy pleasures of Xinomavro are as fitting with rosemary-roasted leg of lamb as they are with a Piemontese-inspired wild mushroom pasta.

the bottom line Good, simple, juicy southern red wines can be found for $8; a few dollars more will buy a bit more complexity. Most Greek reds top out at $15, though a few exceptional examples have crept up over $40.

recommended wines

2000 Boutari Merlot-Xinomavro, Imathia   ★ ★ ★ $ $
dry, full-bodied, medium tannin, high acidity   drink now–8 years
Opposites attract, as hard-nosed Xinomavro offers smoky meat and wild herb flavors that marry beautifully with Merlot's soft-hearted berry notes.

1997 Ktima Kyr-Yianni Ramnista, Náoussa   ★ ★ ★ $ $
dry, medium-bodied, heavy tannin, high acidity   drink in 2–10 years
How many flavors can there be in one wine? In this Xinomavro, innumerable. To sample: cherry, vanilla, wild mushroom, fennel, Middle Eastern spice, leather...

1999 Skouras Grande Cuvée, Neméa   ★ ★ ★ $ $
dry, full-bodied, heavy tannin, medium acidity   drink in 2–10 years
Agiorgitiko shows its dark, complex side with smoky berry, mineral, coffee, and rum flavors. This deserves time.

2000 Domaine Constantin Lazaridi Amethysos, Macedonia ★ ★ $ $
dry, full-bodied, heavy tannin, high acidity   drink in 1–6 years
A place that claims Alexander the Great as a local son needs a big wine, and with ripe cherry and cassis flavors, smoke, and peppery tannin, this is it.

2000 Gai'a Nótios, Neméa   ★ ★ $
dry, full-bodied, heavy tannin, medium acidity   drink now–3 years
An exceptional everyday wine, full of rustic but plush plum flavors suffused with smoke and accented with pepper.

eastern europe

During the Cold War, state-run wine companies across Eastern Europe produced great quantities of decent, but hardly exciting wines. Since the fall of the Berlin Wall in 1989, however, the region's quality wines, such as Hungary's revered Tokaji, are once again the focus of international interest.

grapes & styles

Slovenia Only borders separate Slovenia's main wine regions from their neighbors in Italy and Austria; even many of their grapes are the same. Primorska makes aromatic dry whites and brash reds similar to those of nearby Friuli in Italy; Ljutomersko-Ormoske, bordering Austria's Steiermark, puts out crisp, dry whites from grapes like Pinot Blanc and spicy Gewürztraminer.

Hungary Known for its sweet Tokaji Aszú wines based on Furmint grapes (see Fortified and Dessert Wines, page 274), Hungary also makes terrific dry whites from the same variety, as well as Traminer, Sauvignon Blanc, and Chardonnay. Some reds from Bordeaux varieties show promise.

Bulgaria Bulgaria excels at high-quality, low-priced Cabernet Sauvignon; it also makes good Merlot and some Chardonnay. More interesting are the full-bodied reds from local Melnik and Mavrud varieties that should appear in U.S. markets soon.

Croatia Apart from Slovenia, Croatia makes the finest wines in the former Yugoslavian countries. Inland regions specialize in dry white wines such as Laski Rizling (not the same as Riesling), Traminer, and Pinot Blanc, while coastal regions grow reds, the best of which is Plavac Mali, a relative of California's Zinfandel.

white wines

at the table

Treat dry white varietals as you would their kin from other countries. Serve Pinot Blanc or Gewürztraminer from Slovenia or Croatia with fresh trout or fried calamari; dry Hungarian Furmint with more substantial dishes like roast chicken.

the bottom line Eastern Europe offers a bargain bonanza of white wines. While long-lived, sweet Tokaji can command $30 to $80, dry whites rarely top $10, save for a few Slovenian whites that hit $30.

recommended wines

1999 Movia Turno, Brda, Slovenia ★★★★ $$
dry, medium-bodied, light oak, high acidity drink now–10 years
Pinot tricolor: Pinots Noir, Gris, and Blanc go into this unique wine, layered with flavors ranging from citrus to tropical, to apple, minerals, nuts, and herbs.

223

eastern europe **whites**

1999 Grgich Posip, Cara, Croatia ★★ $
dry, medium-bodied, medium oak, high acidity   drink now–2 years
Intense lime and mineral flavors rounded by some oak make fascinating and unique drinking.

2000 Avia Pinot Grigio, Primorski Region, Slovenia ★ $
dry, light-bodied, no oak, high acidity   drink now
With Italy just across the border, it isn't surprising that Slovenia makes Pinot Grigio, the candied lemon flavors taste fine.

2000 Avia Riesling, Primorski Region, Slovenia ★ $
off-dry, light-bodied, no oak, high acidity   drink now
Chill well and enjoy the easy lime and vanilla flavors on a hot day.

2000 Bagueri Chardonnay, Goriska Brda, Slovenia ★ $
dry, medium-bodied, light oak, high acidity   drink now–2 years
If you like your Chardonnay lemony with just a whisper of oak, this light, crisp wine is for you.

2000 Bagueri Sauvignon, Goriska Brda, Slovenia ★ $
dry, medium-bodied, no oak, high acidity   drink now–1 year
Unusually florid Sauvignon Blanc, with tart citrus flavors and a green edge.

red wines

at the table

Cabernet and Merlot are made in an international style, so think lamb or beef, or vegetable kebabs. Dry Plavac Mali is perfect with the richness of baked ham or goulash.

the bottom line With a couple of exceptions, most Eastern European reds sell for under $10. Quality can be inconsistent, but with low prices, one can afford an off bottle or two.

recommended wines

1993 Movia Veliko Rosso, Goriska Brda, Slovenia ★★★ $$$
dry, medium-bodied, medium tannin, medium acidity   drink now–6 years
This dry, smoky, berry-flavored blend shows why Slovenia is thought by many to have the greatest fine wine potential in Eastern Europe.

1999 Grgich Plavac Mali, Dingac, Croatia ★★★ $$
dry, medium-bodied, medium tannin, high acidity   drink now–5 years
Mike Grgich has won accolades for his Napa wines; in his native Croatia, he earns smiles for this juicy, dry cherry-flavored wine.

1999 Quercus Cabernet Sauvignon, Goriska Brda,
Slovenia ★★ $
dry, medium-bodied, medium tannin, high acidity   drink now–4 years
Smooth berry flavors peppered with herb notes make for good wine.

2000 Vini Cabernet Sauvignon, Sliven, Bulgaria ★★ $
dry, medium-bodied, medium tannin, medium acidity   drink now–4 years
Bulgaria grows more Cabernet than almost any other country, and they know what to do with it, as this fruity, spicy wine shows.

2000 Avia Merlot, Primorski Region, Slovenia ★ $
dry, medium-bodied, medium tannin, high acidity   drink now
Merlot's plummy flavors with lots of acidity for just $4.

1999 Bagueri Merlot, Brda, Slovenia ★ $
dry, full-bodied, medium tannin, high acidity   drink now–3 years
With an impressive Darth Vader-like bottle you might not expect much inside, but the dry berry flavors and high acidity are tasty.

2000 Egervin Bulls Blood, Eger, Hungary ★ $
dry, full-bodied, medium tannin, high acidity   drink now–3 years
Thick and rich, with meaty, ripe berry flavors.

2000 Four Seasons Reserve Cabernet Sauvignon, Taraclia,
Moldova ★ $
dry, medium-bodied, medium tannin, high acidity   drink now–5 years
Most Moldovan wines (even reds) are sweet, but this cassis and appealingly camphor-scented wine shows they can do dry, too.

2000 Garling Collection Black Monk, Trifesti, Moldova ★ $
off-dry, medium-bodied, medium tannin, high acidity   drink now
This off-dry red, with sour cherry and spice flavors, would be good with a spicy meat stew (and an open mind).

1998 Laura Cabernet Sauvignon, Murfatlar, Romania ★ $
dry, medium-bodied, medium tannin, high acidity   drink now–2 years
Appealing, ripe strawberry flavors have a hint of sweet spice.

1999 Laura Pinot Noir, Murfatlar, Romania ★ $
dry, medium-bodied, medium tannin, high acidity   drink now–3 years
Pinot's cherry and smoke flavors at a very affordable price.

middle east & north africa

Middle Eastern peoples have been making wine for millennia. Even after the rise of teetotaling Islam in the 7th century C.E., non-Muslims in the region continued to make and enjoy wine. Some Muslims did, too, taking their cue from more lenient wine references in the Qur'an. Today, wine is still made across North Africa and the Middle East, with some of the best examples coming from Lebanese vintners who survived their country's civil war and Israeli wineries established in the Golan Heights after the region was captured from Syria in 1967.

grapes & styles

Morocco, Tunisia, Algeria Most North African wines are based on southern French varieties introduced during the French occupation from 1830 to 1962. The wines resemble the simple, sturdy wines of France's Languedoc, whose climate is similar.

Lebanon Lebanon grows French varieties like Cabernet Sauvignon, Carignan, Chardonnay, and Cinsault, but several indigenous varieties appear in blends. For years, three producers, Château Musar, Château Kefraya, and Ksara, dominated the wine scene, but recent foreign investment has triggered explosive growth. At their best, Lebanese wines are superb.

Israel Most of Israel's vineyards are on the warm, humid coast, but the best wines come from vineyards in the Golan Heights planted with Cabernet Sauvignon, Merlot, and Sauvignon Blanc.

Featured
Wine-Growing
Countries

Turkey Although Turkey is overwhelmingly Muslim, its secular governments have encouraged winemaking since the republic's founding in the 1920s. Along with Georgia and Armenia (which strictly speaking are not part of the Middle East), Turkey is one of the area's important wine producers. Turkish dry and off-dry white wines and dry reds are made from a combination of French and indigenous grapes.

Georgia Georgian wine has long been celebrated throughout the Russo-influenced world. Most of it, both red and white, is semisweet, but vintners eager to please foreign buyers are fine-tuning their dry wines. Rkatsiteli is the most successful grape, making white wines that can resemble Loire Valley Chenin Blanc.

Armenia Grapes have been grown on Mount Ararat since Noah landed his arc there. Little is available in the U.S., and the wines that do make it here, red or white, are likely to be sweet.

white wines

at the table

Follow the "when in Rome" (or "when in Beirut") approach when pairing Middle Eastern wines. Lebanese blends are especially good with fish in *tarator,* a tahini, lemon, and parsley sauce. Georgian Rkatsiteli is terrific with chicken with *satsivi,* a walnut sauce. Drink international varieties such as Chardonnay and Sauvignon Blanc as you would versions from California.

the bottom line Lebanese and Israeli whites are the most consistent in quality and rarely cost more than $18. North African wines cost between $7 and $10, and Georgian Rkatsiteli rarely breaks $8, cheap enough to try without worry.

recommended white wines

1997 Château Musar, Beka'a Valley, Lebanon ★★★★ $$$
dry, full-bodied, light oak, high acidity drink now–8 years
Made from indigenous Lebanese grapes, this superb wine just oozes honey-nut, stone, and zesty citrus flavors.

2000 Golan Heights Winery Yarden Katzrin Chardonnay, Galilee, Israel ★★★ $$$
dry, full-bodied, heavy oak, medium acidity drink now–6 years
Following the California model, this is oaky, waxy Chardonnay, full of buttery, tropical fruit flavors.

2000 Kavaklidere Selection Beyaz Narince de Tokat, Turkey ★★★ $
dry, full-bodied, medium oak, medium acidity drink now–5 years
"Narince" is Turkish for a type of orange, which, with nuts and mineral flavors, pretty much sums this one up.

2000 Château Kefraya La Dame Blanche, Beka'a Valley, Lebanon ★★ $
dry, medium-bodied, no oak, high acidity drink now–2 years
Three southern French grape varieties feel right at home in Lebanon, offering light, candied citrus flavors.

2001 Château Ksara Blanc de Blancs, Beka'a Valley, Lebanon ★★ $
dry, light-bodied, no oak, high acidity drink now
Light-bodied, but smoldering with smoke and citrus flavors, this is great with grilled trout.

2001 Château Ksara Cuvée du Pape Chardonnay, Beka'a Valley, Lebanon ★★ $
dry, medium-bodied, light oak, high acidity drink now–5 years
This Chardonnay seems to have sucked up the herbs and sunshine of its warm environment.

1995 JSC Corporation Tsinandali, Kakheti, Georgia ★★ $
dry, light-bodied, light oak, high acidity drink now–3 years
Lightly resinous, this would be delicious served cold with mezes.

2000 Kavaklidere Çankaya Emir de Nevsehir, Turkey ★ ★ $
dry, medium-bodied, no oak, high acidity drink now–2 years
With a coastline that covers three seas, Turkey needs a good fish wine. The
zingy apple and citrus flavors of this do the trick.

1996 Tbilvino Tsinandali, Kakheti, Georgia ★ ★ $
dry, full-bodied, light oak, high acidity drink now–3 years
Smoky, with slightly nutty apple and citrus flavors, this is rich and acidic
enough to match roast pig.

1997 Tbilvino Vazisubani, Kakheti, Georgia ★ ★ $
dry, medium-bodied, light oak, high acidity drink now–3 years
A blend of Rkatsiteli and Mtsvane permeated with pomegranate, walnut, and
mineral flavors, this is unique and compelling.

red wines

at the table

The finest Lebanese red wines can substitute for good-quality
Bordeaux with roast leg of lamb, or serve them with shish
kebabs for an authentic touch. Ripe, rich, North African reds are
good with grilled *merguez* sausages. Turkish reds are made for
Turkish meat dishes like spicy *adana kebab*, made from ground
lamb and hot pepper. Match dry Georgian reds to roast pork,
and try off-dry versions with smoked meats.

the bottom line Bargains abound: North African
wines cost $7 to $10; Turkish wines, a couple of dollars more.
Dry Georgian reds sell for $8 to $20; semisweet versions are
slightly higher. Lebanese wines are the most expensive at $12 to
$22, with a few exceptional examples nearing $50. Israeli reds
rarely top $30.

recommended red wines

1995 Château Musar, Beka'a Valley, Lebanon ★ ★ ★ ★ $ $ $
dry, full-bodied, medium tannin, high acidity drink now–12 years
The Middle East's most celebrated winery shows its art with supremely balanced, ripe berry, herb, and spice flavors.

229

1998 Golan Heights Winery Yarden Cabernet Sauvignon, Galilee, Israel ★★★ $$$
dry, full-bodied, heavy tannin, medium acidity   drink now–10 years
A kosher wine that is more evocative of Napa Cabernet Sauvignon than Manischewitz.

1999 Château Ksara Cuvée Speciale Cabernet Sauvignon, Beka'a Valley, Lebanon ★★★ $$
dry, full-bodied, heavy tannin, medium acidity   drink in 1–9 years
Scents of the wild herbs that make Lebanon's famed *za'atar* spice mixture permeate this wine, together with dark cherry flavors that pleased Arab poets for centuries.

1998 Kavaklidere Selection Kirmizi Oküzözü d'Elazig, Turkey ★★★ $
dry, medium-bodied, heavy tannin, medium acidity   drink now–5 years
A wine for pashas, full of dark fruit and mineral flavors, but with noble grace. Excellent.

1999 Hochar Père et Fils, Beka'a Valley, Lebanon ★★ $$
dry, full-bodied, medium tannin, medium acidity   drink now–4 years
Château Musar's second-tier wine is nearly as interesting as its first, with full, very ripe blue and black berry flavors.

1998 Amazir Beni M'tir, Morocco ★★ $
dry, medium-bodied, medium tannin, medium acidity   drink now
A souk's worth of flavors, spice, pomegranate, and dry herbs in a bottle.

BACCHIC BARD OF ARABIC POETRY

If there was a Shakespeare-equivalent in the vast opus of Arabic poetry, it would be the 8th-century poet Abu Nawwas. During the early days of the Abbasid empire (750–1258 C.E.), Abu Nawwas was at the forefront of a literary movement known as *al-khamarriyah*, or wine poetry, that is still considered a classic of Arabic literature. In his intricate poems, Abu Nawwas created a dialectic between the glories of wine and the Islamic milieu in which he lived, managing, in the end, to reconcile hedonism with spirituality. Although Abu Nawwas was condemned by the puritans of his and other ages for his poetry and his reportedly licentious lifestyle, he enjoyed the support of the Abbasid court during his life, and the admiration of the broader Arab nation in the 1,200 years since his death.

1999 Château Kefraya Les Bretèches,
Beka'a Valley, Lebanon ★★ $
dry, full-bodied, heavy tannin, medium acidity   drink now
This Rhône-style blend pays homage to Lebanon's French connection in grapes as well as *garrigue,* those dry herb flavors of southern France.

1999 Château Ksara Réserve du Couvent,
Beka'a Valley, Lebanon ★★ $
dry, full-bodied, heavy tannin, high acidity   drink in 2–8 years
A massive wine, full of smoke, mineral, tannin, and dark fruit. Give it time and have it with charred meat.

1998 Château Romain, Coteaux du Zaccar, Algeria ★★ $
dry, medium-bodied, medium tannin, medium acidity   drink now–2 years
Ancient Romans used to import Algerian wine, but it's unlikely what they drank had the finesse of this light cherry- and spice-scented wine.

2000 Tbilvino Mukuzani, Kakheti, Georgia ★★ $
dry, full-bodied, heavy tannin, high acidity   drink now–4 years
Full of charred mineral, mulberry, and herb flavors, this is a different and interesting wine.

2000 Tbilvino Khvanchkara, Racha, Georgia ★ $$
medium-sweet, medium-bodied, medium tannin, medium acidity drink now
Semisweet berry and spice flavors are unusual but tasty, especially with a spice-rubbed roast leg of lamb.

2000 Kavaklidere Yakut Oküzözü d'Elazig, Turkey ★ $
dry, medium-bodied, heavy tannin, high acidity   drink now
Juicy, red-fruited, Beaujolais-like fruit flavors have enough tannin to take on grilled beef kebabs.

NV Sidi Mustapha Marrakech Private Reserve, Morocco ★ $
dry, medium-bodied, medium tannin, medium acidity   drink now
Marrakesh's Djama'a F'naa is a cacophony of sounds, sights, smells, and flavors. This wine captures its ambience perfectly.

australia

Around the time Mel Gibson lost his accent, Australian wines began to flood the U.S. market. Their rich flavors, full body, and affordable prices were very appealing, but their sameness didn't spark much excitement among wine cognoscenti. That's changed now, as many small-production wines that show off Australia's varied micro-climates and styles have joined the lower-priced offerings on U.S. wine store shelves.

on the label

It's customary for the labels on Australian wines exported to the U.S. to list the grapes in the wine, even if it is a blend, as well as its region, as long as 85 percent of the wine was grown there.

white wines

CHARDONNAY

There was a time when it seemed that every Australian Chardonnay came in a buttery, tutti-frutti style that stressed size over finesse. However, it's now possible to find Australian Chardonnays tangy with citrus, herbal, and mineral flavors, and little to no oak. Some of the leanest styles come from Western Australia, where Indian Ocean breezes keep vineyards cool.

at the table

Rich, buttery Chardonnay matches best with rich, buttery foods, like lobster dipped in drawn butter or grilled salmon. Pull out subtler styles for light fish or sage-stuffed chicken breasts.

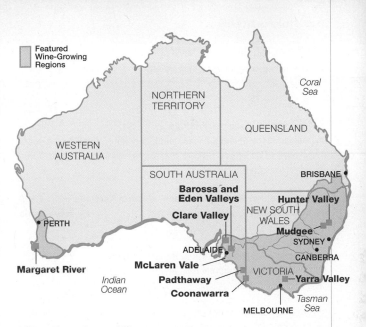

Featured Wine-Growing Regions

Coral Sea

NORTHERN TERRITORY

QUEENSLAND

WESTERN AUSTRALIA

SOUTH AUSTRALIA

BRISBANE

Barossa and Eden Valleys

Hunter Valley

Clare Valley

NEW SOUTH WALES

Mudgee

SYDNEY

PERTH

ADELAIDE

CANBERRA

Margaret River

McLaren Vale

VICTORIA

Yarra Valley

Indian Ocean

Padthaway

Coonawarra

Tasman Sea

MELBOURNE

the bottom line It's still hard to beat Australia when it comes to quality Chardonnay under $10. Quality rises with each dollar spent, and some excellent wines can be purchased for $22 to $25, though prices can reach $70 or more.

recommended wines

1998 Coldstream Hills Reserve, Yarra Valley ★★★★ $$
dry, medium-bodied, medium oak, medium acidity drink now–10 years
A unique Chardonnay, with every note of fruit and mineral flavors polished with age.

2001 Cape Mentelle, Margaret River ★★★ $$
dry, medium-bodied, light oak, high acidity drink now–6 years
The coolness of Western Australia gives this Chardonnay restrained and sophisticated fruit and mineral flavors.

2001 Shaw & Smith Woodside Unoaked, Adelaide Hills ★★★ $$
dry, medium-bodied, no oak, high acidity drink now–5 years
With no wood in the way, Chardonnay's citrus and mineral flavors sing.

2001 Penfolds Thomas Hyland, Adelaide Hills ★★★ $
dry, medium-bodied, medium oak, high acidity drink now–8 years
An elegant wine with floral notes and citrus flavors deepened by smoky wood.

233

australia **whites**

2001 Rosemount Hill of Gold, Mudgee ★★ $$
dry, full-bodied, medium oak, high acidity drink now–6 years
The gold is in the luscious, sweet pineapple flavors, which give way to a multitude of savory mineral and smoky oak notes.

2001 Lindemans Reserve, Padthaway ★★ $
dry, medium-bodied, medium oak, medium acidity drink now–3 years
Always reliable, Lindemans Reserve is brassy in color and brassy in flavor, with peach pie flavors burnished with oak.

2000 Plantagenet Omrah Unwooded, Western Australia ★★ $
dry, medium-bodied, no oak, high acidity drink now–5 years
Bright, juicy fruit and vibrant acidity, unfettered by oak.

1999 Simon Gilbert Card Series, Hunter Valley ★★ $
dry, medium-bodied, medium oak, medium acidity drink now–4 years
Easy-drinking, with creamy caramel flavors joined by some citrus.

2001 Wynns Coonawarra Estate, Coonawarra ★★ $
dry, medium-bodied, light oak, high acidity drink now–4 years
Luscious tropical fruit flavors with a macadamia nut richness that would go well with fish served with mango salsa.

2001 Abbey Rock, South Eastern Australia ★ $
dry, medium-bodied, light oak, high acidity drink now
Lovely fruit flavors with a dash of vanilla make a good choice for picnics.

WINES WE WISH WE HAD MORE ROOM FOR
2000 Ninth Island, Tasmania ★★ $$ dry, medium-bodied, no oak, high acidity, drink now–3 years; **2001 Wolf Blass, South Australia** ★★ $ dry, medium-bodied, light oak, high acidity, drink now; **2001 Angove's Bear Crossing, South Australia** ★ $ dry, medium-bodied, light oak, high acidity, drink now; **2001 Rosemount Estate, South Eastern Australia** ★ $ dry, full-bodied, heavy oak, medium acidity, drink now

OTHER WHITE WINES

Beyond the displays of inexpensive Aussie Chardonnay lie some of Australia's finest whites. Semillon, the classic white grape from Bordeaux, offers full-bodied orange and nut flavors that take on marmalade qualities with a few years of age. Some of the best, ageworthy versions come from the Hunter Valley in New South Wales. Semillon is also blended with Sauvignon Blanc to create a wine with similar flavors but higher acidity. Riesling, arguably Australia's most exciting white wine, is storming U.S.

markets with its dry lime, peach, and mangolike flavors. Look especially for examples from South Australia's Clare Valley. Keep an eye out for Rhône varieties Marsanne and Roussanne, too, which give wines with dry, honeyed almond and orange flavors.

at the table

Young Semillon has a balanced richness that makes a luxurious match for sautéed scallops or buttery crabs, though make sure to stash a few bottles in the cellar, too: it will only get more luxurious with age. With its bright acidity, Sauvignon Blanc goes well with simpler seafood dishes or even raw shellfish. And Australian Riesling, with its combination of luscious fruit flavors and high acidity, pairs wonderfully with everything from mild fish like sautéed trout to a richer seared tuna, or even duck or goose.

the bottom line Often overshadowed by Chardonnay, Australia's other whites generally sell for $15 or less, though some of the best examples cost a few dollars more. Australian Rieslings cost $15 to $60.

recommended wines

2001 Grosset Polish Hill Riesling, Clare Valley ★★★★ $$$
dry, medium-bodied, no oak, high acidity   drink now–15 years
One of the finest wines in the world, with deep mineral, citrus, and slight herb flavors in perfect proportion.

2001 Clonakilla Viognier, Canberra ★★★ $$$
dry, medium-bodied, no oak, high acidity   drink now–4 years
Light and luscious at once, this offers a base of fruit and mineral flavors draped in a diaphanous sheet of floral scents.

1998 Tim Adams Semillon, Clare Valley ★★★ $$
dry, full-bodied, medium oak, high acidity   drink now–8 years
Four years of age has brought on baked apple and nut flavors, but this still has citrusy verve and mineral profundity. Fantastic wine.

2001 Pikes Riesling, Clare Valley ★★★ $
dry, medium-bodied, no oak, high acidity   drink now–6 years
There may be plenty of stony flavor here, but the juicy tropical fruit flavors are the real draw.

235

1999 Tahbilk Marsanne Nagambie Lakes, Central Victoria ★ ★ ★ $
dry, full-bodied, no oak, high acidity   drink now–10 years
Honeyed nut and intense fruit flavors make this as fine, or even finer, than
some Rhône examples. A favorite.

2001 Brokenwood Semillon, Lower Hunter Valley   ★ ★ $$
dry, light-bodied, no oak, high acidity   drink now–8 years
Right now, this offers pleasant, light citrus and herb flavors, but it has the
potential to evolve into a rich nectar of nutty, orange fruit.

2000 Cockfighter's Ghost Semillon, Hunter Valley   ★ ★ $$
dry, medium-bodied, no oak, high acidity   drink now–4 years
Unlike the "marmalade" flavors typical of Aussie Semillon, this is pure citrus
zest and fresh herbs.

2000 Nepenthe Sauvignon Blanc, Adelaide Hills   ★ ★ $$
dry, medium-bodied, no oak, high acidity   drink now–2 years
Homer wrote that if one drinks the nectar from Nepenthe, all one's sorrows
will go away. Good advice.

2000 Trevor Jones Boots White, Barossa Valley   ★ ★ $$
dry, medium-bodied, no oak, high acidity   drink now–2 years
Aromatherapy you can drink, with intense lime zest, floral, and mineral notes.
Delicious.

2001 Hope Estate Verdelho, Hunter Valley   ★ ★ $
dry, full-bodied, no oak, high acidity   drink now–4 years
Guava and pineapple flavors take the lead in this surprisingly ripe and floral
Verdelho from New South Wales.

2001 Rosemount Estate Sauvignon Blanc,
South Eastern Australia   ★ ★ $
dry, medium-bodied, no oak, high acidity   drink now–2 years
Rosemount's Sauvignon Blanc offers New Zealand-like exotic fruit and grass
flavors with admirable restraint.

2000 Wirra Wirra Vineyards Scrubby Rise White,
McLaren Vale   ★ ★ $
dry, medium-bodied, no oak, high acidity   drink now–2 years
Fun in the sun, with tropical fruit, pear, and refreshing herbal flavors with a
pinch of spice.

2001 Lindemans Cawarra Semillon-Chardonnay,
South Eastern Australia   ★ $
dry, medium-bodied, light oak, high acidity   drink now–2 years
An inexpensive white with ripe fruit flavors and a tobacco smoke edge.

red wines

SHIRAZ

If there is one grape that sets Australia's wine industry apart from all others, it is Shiraz. Named for the city in Iran where the grape is thought to have originated, Australia's Shiraz tastes much different from France's Syrah, the same grape, with mellower, spicier flavors and richer, blackberry-like fruit. Many versions exhibit a hallmark note of eucalyptus, too. Some Shiraz, especially those grown in warmer areas like the Barossa Valley and McLaren Vale, are incredibly dense, laden with dark fruit flavors, oak and tannin, while leaner, more restrained versions come from cooler areas like Western Australia.

at the table

Simple, fruity Shiraz are great for a barbecue with hamburgers, chicken, and sausages, or for saucy ribs. More complex, tannic versions demand heavier food like roasted leg of lamb, prime rib, and thick, charred steaks. The richest, densest bottlings can be enjoyed like a Port after dinner, with a chunk of sharp farmhouse cheddar or aged Gouda.

the bottom line

Simple Shiraz sell for $10 or less; more complex versions range anywhere from $20 to $80. The most famous, Penfolds Grange, sells for around $200.

what to buy SHIRAZ

1997	1998	1999	2000	2001
★★★	★★★	★★★	★★	★★★

recommended wines

1999 Clarendon Hills Moritz, Clarendon　　　★★★★ $$$
dry, medium-bodied, medium tannin, high acidity　drink in 2–12 years
This has the complexity and beauty of a Persian rug, tightly woven with fruit, smoke, minerals, and herbs. It's just one of the impressive wines from this McLaren Vale winery; check out the Grenaches, too.

237

australia reds

1998 Wolf Blass Platinum Label, Barossa Valley ★★★★ $$$
dry, full-bodied, heavy tannin, high acidity   drink now–15 years
Expertly orchestrated, with velvety, dark fruit riding into crescendos of peppery
herb and mineral and harmonizing with notes of melting bitter chocolate.

1999 Mount Horrocks Watervale, Clare Valley ★★★ $$$
dry, medium-bodied, medium tannin, high acidity   drink now–10 years
A beautiful display of graceful red fruit, smoke, and mineral flavors.

1999 Rosemount Estate Balmoral Syrah, McLaren Vale ★★★ $$$
dry, full-bodied, medium tannin, medium acidity   drink now–10 years
Inspired by the wines of France's Rhône Valley, this has smoked meat, earth,
and ripe but restrained fruit flavors.

1999 Blue Pyrenees Estate Reserve, Victoria ★★★ $$
dry, full-bodied, medium tannin, high acidity   drink in 2–10 years
There's no lack of fruit flavors, but the herbs, spice, and almost salty mineral
notes here really sing.

2000 Cape Mentelle Shiraz, Margaret River ★★★ $$
dry, full-bodied, medium tannin, medium acidity   drink now–8 years
Smooth fruit flavors from first sip to last, accented by a note of menthol.

1999 Penfolds Bin 128, Coonawarra ★★★ $$
dry, full-bodied, heavy tannin, medium acidity   drink in 2–10 years
Black is beautiful here, with blackberry, black cherry, and black mineral flavors
filling in this black-as-night red.

1997 Tim Adams, Clare Valley ★★★ $$
dry, full-bodied, medium tannin, medium acidity   drink now–8 years
This offers deep minerals, a breeze of floral and herb scents, and the ripe fruit
flavors that come from bright sunshine.

2000 Brokenwood Rayner, McLaren Vale ★★ $$$
dry, full-bodied, medium tannin, high acidity   drink now–10 years
A wild one, with brambly berry, wild sage and mint, and earthy spice flavors.
Great with roast lamb.

1999 Lindemans Reserve, Padthaway ★★ $$
dry, full-bodied, medium tannin, medium acidity   drink now–8 years
Tasty wine, deep with fruit flavors, a pinch of spice, and earthy, dusty tannin.

2001 Rosemount Estate, South Eastern Australia ★★ $
dry, full-bodied, medium tannin, high acidity   drink now–4 years
Terrific value, with lightly peppery, luscious berry flavors made even sexier
with smoky notes.

2001 Abbey Rock, South Eastern Australia ★ $
dry, medium-bodied, medium tannin, medium acidity drink now–3 years
Strawberries and spice, simple and nice.

WINES WE WISH WE HAD MORE ROOM FOR
2000 Flinders Bay, Margaret River ★★★ $$ dry, full-bodied, heavy
tannin, high acidity, drink in 2–12 years; **2000 Fox Creek Short Row,
McLaren Vale** ★★ $$$ dry, full-bodied, medium tannin, high acidity, drink
now–5 years; **1999 Tahbilk Nagambie Lakes, Central Victoria** ★★
$$ dry, medium-bodied, medium tannin, medium acidity, drink now–6 years;
1999 Owen's Estate, South Australia ★★ $ dry, medium-bodied,
medium tannin, high acidity, drink now–4 years; **2001 Yangarra Park,
South Eastern Australia** ★★ $ dry, full-bodied, medium tannin, medium
acidity, drink now–4 years

CABERNET SAUVIGNON

Shiraz is king in Australia, but that doesn't make Cabernet
Sauvignon any less royal. The grape thrives in Australian soil,
making full-bodied wines with unmistakable blackberry flavors.
They tend to be less tannic than Cabernets from other coun-
tries, and frequently offer mint, chocolate, and coconut flavors
lent by American oak barrels. Coonawarra, in South Australia, is
particularly noted for the earthy flavor acquired by Cabernet
Sauvignon in its startlingly red soils, while Cabernets from
Western Australia are lean enough to draw comparisons to
Bordeaux versions.

at the table
High in fruit flavors and low in tannins, inexpensive Australian
Cabernets are easy-drinking on their own or with burgers. Pair
more concentrated wines with steak *au poivre,* lamb chops, or a
vegetarian shepherd's pie.

the bottom line The price of Australian Cabernet is
rising fast, but many are still available for under $10. Solid-quality,
mid-range Cabernets run about $20, while concentrated, com-
plex examples sell from $30 up to $100.

what to buy CABERNET SAUVIGNON

1997	1998	1999	2000	2001
★★★	★★★	★★★	★★	★★★

recommended wines

1999 Clarendon Hills Sandown Vineyard, Clarendon ★★★★ $$$
dry, medium-bodied, medium tannin, medium acidity drink now–10 years
Berry, lavender, and mineral flavors offer a grace and finesse that Baryshnikov would appreciate.

1994 Tahbilk Reserve, Victoria ★★★ $$$$
dry, medium-bodied, medium tannin, medium acidity drink now–3 years
Mature wine from Australia is hard to find but worth it, as the soft roast fruit, mineral, and light tobacco flavors here demonstrate.

1999 Penfolds Bin 407, South Australia ★★★ $$$
dry, full-bodied, heavy tannin, medium acidity   drink now–10 years
Penfolds' mid-level Cab is square on the mark with a fine balance between fruit and mineral flavors.

1998 Wolf Blass Black Label, Barossa Valley ★★★ $$$
dry, full-bodied, heavy tannin, medium acidity   drink now–12 years
All the exuberance for which Australian wine is known, with big fruit, big chocolate, big mint, and big tannin.

1999 Wynns Coonawarra Estate, Coonawarra ★★★ $$
dry, full-bodied, heavy tannin, medium acidity   drink now–10 years
Grill up a thick steak for this wine, to absorb the heavy tannins and let the juicy berry fruit shine.

2000 Rosemount Hill of Gold, Mudgee ★★ $$
dry, medium-bodied, medium tannin, medium acidity drink now–6 years
Like a York Peppermint Patty, chocolate and mint flavors completely enrobe the fruit. Delicious.

2001 The Rothbury Estate, South Eastern Australia ★ $
dry, medium-bodied, medium tannin, medium acidity drink now–2 years
Abundant berry flavors at a surprisingly low price.

OTHER RED WINES

Though Shiraz is Australia's most distinctive grape, other Rhône varieties like Grenache and Mourvèdre also thrive, producing hearty wines full of fruit, herb, and mineral flavors. In certain cooler areas, Merlot can make rich, velvety wines, though not as successfully as the other Bordeaux native, Cabernet Sauvignon. Pinot Noir is becoming more common, with some great results.

the bottom line Merlot can be had for less than $10, and Pinot Noir for less than $15, but the quality tends to be much better between $20 and $50. Easy-drinking examples of Grenache and Mourvèdre start at $9, both individually and blended together, while more complex versions run $30 to $90.

recommended wines

2000 Rochford Macedon Ranges Pinot Noir, Victoria ★★★★ $$
dry, medium-bodied, medium tannin, high acidity   drink now–8 years
Great Australian Pinot Noir is rare, but here's one filled with finesse.

1999 Charles Melton Grenache, Barossa Valley ★★★ $$$
dry, full-bodied, medium tannin, medium acidity   drink now–6 years
Vivid roasted cherry and mineral flavors announce pure, fun deliciousness.

2000 Joseph Moda Amarone Cabernet Sauvignon-Merlot, McLaren Vale/Coonawarra ★★★ $$$
dry, full-bodied, heavy tannin, medium acidity   drink now–10 years
Italy's Amarone method applied to Cab and Merlot makes one spicy, rich wine.

1998 Pikes Reserve Merlot, Clare Valley ★★★ $$
dry, full-bodied, medium tannin, medium acidity   drink now–8 years
If only all Merlot had the delicious black cherry and mineral goodness of this one.

2000 Hill of Content Pinot Noir, Mornington Peninsula ★★★ $
dry, medium-bodied, medium tannin, medium acidity drink now–8 years
Berry flavors are given depth with mineral and animal notes for a fine Pinot Noir.

2000 Primo Estate Il Briccone Shiraz-Sangiovese, Adelaide Plains ★★ $$
dry, medium-bodied, medium tannin, medium acidity drink now–3 years
A juicy, berry-laden blend of Shiraz and Italian grapes with *abondanza*.

2000 Penfolds Koonunga Hill Shiraz-Cabernet, South Eastern Australia ★★ $
dry, medium-bodied, medium tannin, medium acidity drink now–3 years
An enjoyable vanilla-scented, berry-filled blend.

2001 Rosemount Estate Grenache-Shiraz, South Eastern Australia ★ $
dry, medium-bodied, medium tannin, medium acidity drink now–2 years
Simple, sweet, juicy berry flavors are a match for saucy, spicy barbecue.

new
zealand

Though New Zealand's modern wine industry is barely thirty years old, its vintners put out some of the world's most distinctive wines, from tongue-wagging Sauvignon Blancs to rich, elegant Pinot Noirs. Success has bred more success and explosive growth, so keep your eye on the Kiwis— there's much more good wine to come from this source.

on the label

New Zealand wine labels are easy to decipher since both grape varieties and origin are nearly always listed.

white wines

SAUVIGNON BLANC

In the last decade, New Zealand Sauvignon Blanc has come to define the grape's possibilities as much as France's Sancerre. New Zealand vintners rarely apply oak to their Sauvignon Blanc, allowing the grape's vibrant, distinctive flavors to sing. And distinct they are: with bold flavors that are said to recall citrus, gooseberry, bell pepper, and even cat pee (often euphemized as "boxwood"), it may be hard to imagine the appeal, but they come together for exciting drinking. The most acclaimed examples come from Marlborough on the South Island, although Wairarapa on the North Island puts out exceptional examples, too.

at the table

The green, peppery qualities of New Zealand Sauvignon Blanc give it the rare ability to pair with asparagus, artichokes, and vinaigrette-dressed salads. But don't stop there: it works as well with chicken, fish, and pasta, especially in dishes seasoned with plenty of herbs. And you'd be hard pressed to find a better partner for spaghetti dressed with pesto made from loads of fresh basil, spicy olive oil, and salty pecorino cheese.

the bottom line Popularity and limited supply have driven prices into the $20 range, but it's still possible to find New Zealand Sauvignon Blancs for around $10.

recommended wines

2000 Chancellor Estates Mt. Cass Road, Wairarapa ★★★ $$
dry, medium-bodied, no oak, high acidity   drink now–2 years
A gentle, graceful wine with light notes of fruit, honey, herbs, and minerals.

2001 Cloudy Bay, Marlborough ★★★ $$
dry, medium-bodied, no oak, high acidity   drink now–4 years
Cloudy Bay put New Zealand on the wine map; this grapefruit- and pepper-scented wine demonstrates how.

2001 Goldwater Dog Point Vineyard, Marlborough ★★★ $$
dry, light-bodied, no oak, high acidity   drink now–2 years
Remarkably light on its feet, but heavy on cassis and lime flavors.

2001 Kim Crawford, Marlborough ★★★ $$
dry, medium-bodied, no oak, high acidity   drink now–3 years
As tasty and tangy as mango margarita, full of vervy lime flavors.

2000 Vavasour, Marlborough ★★★ $$
dry, medium-bodied, no oak, high acidity   drink now–2 years
Straight-on kiwi flavors, spiced by green chile and herbs, this is archetypal New Zealand Sauvignon.

2000 Wairau River Reserve, Marlborough ★★★ $$
dry, medium-bodied, heavy oak, high acidity   drink now
Any prejudices against oak in Sauvignon Blanc are removed when it's so well integrated with the orange and apricot flavors.

NECESSITY IS THE MOTHER OF DISTINCTION

Unlike oak-barreled Chardonnays from the U.S. and Australia, New Zealand Chardonnay is rarely described as "buttery." Ironically, the country's dairy farmers are to thank for this distinction. The global downturn in the dairy industry happened to coincide with the ascent of New Zealand's wine industry. One result of the dairy industry's problems was a surplus of temperature-controlled stainless steel tanks. New Zealand's nascent winemakers gave up oak for stainless steel, and turned a cost-cutting move into a distinct advantage, milking the grapes, as it were, for all their luscious, grassy, tropical fruit flavors.

sauvignon blanc new zealand

2001 Isabel, Marlborough ★★ $$
dry, light-bodied, no oak, high acidity drink now–2 years
A fruit salad of melon, tropical, and citrus flavors, with grassy, herbal notes to contrast.

2001 Greenhough, Nelson ★★ $
dry, medium-bodied, no oak, high acidity drink now–3 years
No need to go to an herbalist to cure what ails you. A sip of this herb-laden wine will do the trick.

2001 Mt. Difficulty, Central Otago ★★ $
dry, medium-bodied, no oak, high acidity drink now–4 years
A white with almost red-berry flavors made even more pleasingly funky with herb and animal notes.

2001 Villa Maria Private Bin, Marlborough ★★ $
dry, medium-bodied, no oak, high acidity drink now–2 years
Hits all the notes of Kiwi Sauvignon Blancs for around half the typical price.

2001 Spy Valley, Marlborough ★ $
dry, light-bodied, no oak, high acidity drink now
Light and lively, the tangy papaya and lime flavors of this Sauvignon make a perfect summer pour.

CHARDONNAY

Although New Zealand has more Chardonnay than Sauvignon Blanc planted, Chardonnay for once plays runner-up. While it can make very good wines, New Zealand Chardonnay lacks the uniqueness of its white wine cousin. Thankfully, since most of the Chardonnay is free of oak, even the simplest wines give bright, refreshing flavors; more sophisticated versions offer a minerality that sometimes earns comparisons to Burgundy. Look to Hawke's Bay and Gisborne on the North Island for the best examples.

at the table
With light-bodied, pure fruit flavors and high acidity, New Zealand Chardonnay is versatile enough to stand alone as an aperitif or next to pan-fried brook trout. Match the richer flavors of an oaked Chardonnay with roast salmon, turkey, or chicken. Both versions have the acidity to cut through cream sauces.

the bottom line Quality New Zealand Chardonnay sells for $15 to $40.

recommended wines

2000 Glazebrook, Gisborne ★★★ $$
dry, medium-bodied, light oak, high acidity drink now–5 years
Terrific Chardonnay, almost as aromatic as Riesling, with layers of pineapple, peach, and anise flavors.

2001 Alpha Domus Unoaked, Hawke's Bay ★★★ $
dry, medium-bodied, no oak, high acidity drink now–6 years
There aren't many bargain-priced wines in New Zealand, but this mouthwatering, fruit-and mineral-filled wine qualifies.

1999 Brancott Vineyards Ormond Estate, Gisborne ★★ $$
dry, full-bodied, heavy oak, high acidity drink now–8 years
Heavy oak flavors make for a mouthfilling, spicy, coconut-orange custard of a Chardonnay.

2001 Kim Crawford Unoaked, Marlborough ★★ $$
dry, medium-bodied, no oak, high acidity drink now–5 years
Take your pick: the cork-finished bottle offers lush tropical and baked custard flavors; the screw-topped version, citrus and tropical flavors with intense stoniness. The screw-capped version is no doubt the one that will last the longest in the cellar.

RIESLING & GEWÜRZTRAMINER

In New Zealand's sunny but cool microclimates, Riesling takes on delicious tropical and summer fruit flavors, yet remains light-bodied and full of acidity. Gewürztraminer, Riesling's Alsatian compatriot, also retains excellent balance here, its floral, citrus, and mineral flavors displayed with finesse.

at the table
Both Riesling and Gewürztraminer have the balance to match well with moderately spicy Asian foods, as well as plenty of acidity to stand up to duck, chicken, or smoked ham with a sweet fruit glaze.

the bottom line It's still hard to find New Zealand Riesling or Gewürztraminer in the U.S., but what does make it to our shores tends to sell for $10 to $20. Grab them now, before people clue in to the quality of these wines and the prices go up.

recommended wines

2001 Huia Pinot Gris, Marlborough   ★★★ $$
dry, medium-bodied, no oak, high acidity   drink now–5 years
Nutty flavors are filled out with silky tangerine and mineral notes for a sophisticated take on Pinot Gris.

2001 Martinborough Vineyard Riesling, Martinborough ★★★ $$
dry, medium-bodied, no oak, high acidity   drink now–10 years
Lovely fruit, deep minerality, and an appealing nuttiness make this the equal of most German Rieslings.

2001 Charles Wiffen Riesling, Marlborough   ★★ $
dry, medium-bodied, no oak, high acidity   drink now–10 years
Full-throttle mineral and herb notes join ripe fruit flavors for a Sauvignon Blanc-like Riesling.

2001 Spy Valley Gewürztraminer, Marlborough   ★★ $
dry, medium-bodied, no oak, high acidity   drink now–5 years
With its charming floral aromas and lime- and peachlike fruit, it's hard to find a better Gewürztraminer for the price.

red wines

PINOT NOIR

The most planted red grape in the country, Pinot Noir performs best in cooler wine regions like Martinborough at the south end of the North Island and Central Otago on the South Island. The best can draw comparisons to Burgundy, with their light, velvety texture filled with deep raspberry, blackberry, and herbal flavors.

at the table
Pinot Noir is an extraordinarily versatile wine no matter where it's made, able to marry well with red meats like lamb as well as white meats like pork and veal, not to mention grilled tuna and salmon.

the bottom line Everywhere it's grown, Pinot Noir is on the expensive side. New Zealand versions start around $15 and can run to $70.

new zealand **reds**

recommended wines

2000 Martinborough Vineyard, Martinborough ★ ★ ★ $ $ $
dry, medium-bodied, medium tannin, medium acidity   drink now–6 years
A multitude of fruit, leather, sandalwood, and mineral flavors interact in perfect
harmony.

2000 Greenhough Hope Vineyard, Nelson ★ ★ ★ $ $
dry, medium-bodied, medium tannin, medium acidity   drink now–6 years
Smooth as satin sheets, luxurious yet reserved, the polished flavors of fruit,
mineral, and smoke seem to last forever.

2000 Mt. Difficulty, Central Otago ★ ★ ★ $ $
dry, medium-bodied, medium tannin, medium acidity   drink now–6 years
No difficulty here, the ripe fruit and slight herb flavors slide down like silk.

1999 Jackson Estate, Marlborough ★ ★ $ $ $
dry, medium-bodied, medium tannin, high acidity   drink now–6 years
Ripe, cherry-flavored fruit backed by loads of acidity gives a Burgundian cast
to this fine Pinot Noir.

1999 Brancott Vineyards Reserve, Marlborough ★ ★ $ $
dry, medium-bodied, medium tannin, medium acidity   drink now–5 years
Smoke, meat, sweet fruit, herbs, and spices makes for good, solid Pinot Noir.

OTHER RED WINES

New Zealand Cabernet Sauvignon and Merlot aren't as successful as Pinot Noir, but the best are devoid of the common vegetal
flavors and instead offer silky, medium-bodied, dark fruit flavors.
Look for examples from Hawke's Bay and Wairarapa. Syrah (not
"Shiraz") is reminiscent of wine from the northern Rhône Valley.

at the table

With thirteen sheep to every human, New Zealanders need a
wine to go with lamb. Its Syrah, Merlot, Cabernet, and Bordeaux
blends do just that. They are also terrific with roast venison and
other gamey meats. Vegetarians will want to try them with a wild
mushroom lasagna.

the bottom line Count on paying at least $15 for a
Cabernet or Merlot, and double that for a high-quality blend of
the two. Syrah runs $30 to $40.

recommended wines

1999 Matariki Syrah, Hawke's Bay   ★★★ $$$
dry, full-bodied, medium tannin, medium acidity   drink now–12 years
With smoky cherry, herb, and salt-and-pepper flavors, this evokes the best St-Josephs from France's Rhône.

2000 Millsreef Elsbeth Mere Road Vineyard Syrah,
Hawke's Bay   ★★★ $$$
dry, full-bodied, medium tannin, medium acidity   drink now–10 years
You'll notice the juicy, almost sweet fruit immediately, but the mineral and pepper flavors leave the biggest impression.

1999 Trinity Hill Gimblett Road Cabernet Sauvignon-Merlot,
Hawke's Bay   ★★★ $$$
dry, medium-bodied, medium tannin, high acidity   drink now–15 years
One of New Zealand's best reds, flush with red and dark berry flavors plus minerals and herbs.

2000 Babich Winemaker's Reserve Merlot, Hawke's Bay   ★★ $$
dry, full-bodied, medium tannin, medium acidity   drink in 1–8 years
Immediately appealing fruit and mineral flavors take a little time to gel into something even more special.

1999 Glazebrook Merlot-Cabernet Sauvignon,
Hawke's Bay   ★★ $$
dry, full-bodied, heavy tannin, medium acidity   drink now–8 years
Nothing shy about this red, with its big fruit, chocolate-mint, and oak flavors.

GRAPES VS SHEEP

With tens of millions of sheep in New Zealand, it will take some time for grape growers to muscle sheep ranchers out of the way, but according to a report in the July 2002 issue of *Decanter* magazine, New Zealand meat packers are already blaming the expanding wine industry for a decline in lamb production. However, noting that grapes are usually grown in areas unsuitable to sheep grazing, few winegrowers are convinced they are to blame for the meat industry's losses. Besides, it's in a vintner's best interests to keep the sheep around. After all, what better match for New Zealand Pinot Noir than succulent New Zealand lamb chops?

southern south america

South America has produced wines for nearly 500 years, but its wines didn't make much of a splash in the U.S. until the late 1980s. Back then, they offered voluptuous body and flavor at bargain prices. Now, after tremendous foreign investment and improvements in viticulture and vinification, both quality and price have increased dramatically.

argentina

Not surprisingly in a country with a large population of Spanish and Italian descent, wine has long been an essential part of Argentine life. So essential, in fact, that Argentina is the world's fifth largest wine producer. Most of it is red and rustic, designed for *gauchos* to wash down grilled beef, but happily, a number of vintners are making wines worthy of white-tablecloth dinners.

on the label
Labeling by grape variety and region is the norm in Argentina.

white wines

Argentina's Chardonnays range from light and steely to big and buttery, but the country's most interesting white wines are made from Torrontés, a light, flowery white that grows best in Cafayate, in the far northern region of Salta.

Chile

SALTA

Cafayate

Pacific
Ocean

Argentina

LA RIOJA

Aconcagua

VALPARAISO

Santiago

Casablanca

Puente Alto

Maipo

Maipú

Atlantic
Ocean

Rapel

Luján de Cuyo

BUENOS AIRES

Colchagua

San Rafael

Curicó

Central Valley

Maule

MENDOZA

CONCEPCION

Featured
Wine-Growing
Regions

argentina **whites**

at the table

Torrontés is perfect for sipping by the pool or at the beach, though it also has enough sweet flavors and bright acidity to complement light, spicy dishes like shrimp cocktail or Thai-style sautéed calamari. Oaked Chardonnay is a fine foil for garlicky roast chicken, while steely versions work well with lighter dishes like poached perch or sole.

the bottom line Little-known Torrontés can be found for only $6. Most Chardonnay clocks in under $10, but a few climb into the teens, and at least one sells for $45.

recommended wines

1999 Catena Alta Adrianna Vineyard Chardonnay, Mendoza ★★★ $$$
dry, full-bodied, heavy oak, high acidity drink now–8 years
Toasty, vanilla notes from oak meld with Chardonnay fruit to offer luscious crème caramel flavors.

2000 Alta Vista Cosecha, Mendoza ★★ $
dry, medium-bodied, no oak, high acidity drink now
A blend of local Torrontés with Chardonnay and Chenin Blanc gives juicy tropical fruit flavors made for pleasurable summer nights.

2001 Elsa Semillon-Chardonnay, San Rafael ★★ $
dry, medium-bodied, light oak, medium acidity drink now–3 years
A blend typically found in Australia yields a fragrant floral and citrus-scented wine when made in Argentina.

2001 Pedro del Castillo Chardonnay, Mendoza ★★ $
dry, medium-bodied, no oak, high acidity drink now–2 years
All about freshness, this is like biting into a cold, crisp green apple.

2001 Santa Julia Torrontés, Mendoza ★★ $
dry, light-bodied, no oak, medium acidity drink now
The peach and lime flavors of this Torrontés will refresh even the doggiest days of summer.

2001 Valentin Bianchi Sauvignon Blanc, San Rafael ★★ $
dry, medium-bodied, no oak, high acidity drink now–2 years
Not a pungent style, but full of charming pear and light tropical flavors.

otreds argentina

red wines

With so much cattle, it's no wonder Argentina produces vast quantities of red wine. Inky Malbec, an underperforming grape in its native Bordeaux, sings the lead, with a rich tenor of berry and chocolate flavors harmonized with ripe tannin. Cabernet, Merlot, and, increasingly, Syrah play a strong back-up.

at the table

For Argentina's reds, the simple answer is beef. Inexpensive reds are great with burgers; more substantial versions can take on braised short ribs or roast prime rib. But these wines aren't for carnivores only: try them with baked, tomato-sauced pastas.

the bottom line The days of $6 reds are nearly gone, but there are still a few good wines under $10, and many more around $15. Some deluxe versions reach as high as $85.

what to buy RED WINES

1997	1998	1999	2000	2001
★★★	★★★	★★★	★★	★★

recommended wines

2000 Tikal Jubilo, Mendoza ★★★★ $$$$
dry, full-bodied, heavy tannin, high acidity   drink in 2–12 years
Heavy-duty wine, as intensely flavored as some Napa mountain Cabernets.

2000 Susana Balbo Malbec, Mendoza ★★★ $$$
dry, full-bodied, heavy tannin, medium acidity   drink in 1–10 years
This has a ton of fruit, plus a quarry's worth of mineral and smoke flavors.

**1999 Catena Agrelo Vineyards Cabernet Sauvignon,
Mendoza** ★★★ $$
dry, full-bodied, medium tannin, medium acidity   drink now–8 years
Full berry flavors get a zing from cinnamon and spearmint notes.

2000 Alamos Bonarda, Mendoza ★★ $
dry, full-bodied, heavy tannin, medium acidity   drink now–3 years
Tasty, peppery berry and herb flavors make a strong case for more Bonarda.

argentina **reds**

2000 Elsa Barbera, San Rafael ★★ $
dry, full-bodied, medium tannin, high acidity   drink now–5 years
With Argentina's large Italian population, Italian varieties are fitting, like this smoky, fruity Barbera, great with antipasti.

2000 Laurel Glen Vineyard Terra Rosa Cabernet Sauvignon, Mendoza ★★ $
dry, medium-bodied, medium tannin, high acidity   drink now–5 years
Laurel Glen, responsible for some of California's finest Cabernets, does a good job below the equator, too, with spicy fruit and mineral flavors.

2001 Santa Julia Merlot, Mendoza ★★ $
dry, medium-bodied, medium tannin, medium acidity   drink now–3 years
Ripe strawberry flavors are made more savory with hints of tobacco.

2000 Trumpeter Syrah, Luján de Cuyo ★★ $
dry, full-bodied, medium tannin, medium acidity   drink now–5 years
Smoky berry, herb, and spice flavors make a tasty, everyday quaff.

2001 Don Miguel Gascón Malbec, Mendoza ★ $
dry, full-bodied, medium tannin, medium acidity   drink now–2 years
Bodacious berry and soft, smoky flavors make for simple sipping.

NV Prosperity Red, Mendoza ★ $
dry, medium-bodied, medium tannin, medium acidity   drink now
Popularly priced with a populist engraving on the label, this fruit-and-spice wine is just the thing to get between any working man and his burger.

chile

Until the 1990s, Chilean winemakers generally favored quantity over quality, and produced a sea of decent if uninspiring wine. But a few vintners with a more noble vision and a rush of foreign investors who saw the potential in the country's rich vine lands began to reverse that ratio. Those efforts have allowed Chilean wines to join the pantheon of the world's greats.

on the label

Except for Bordeaux-style blends, Chilean wine labels nearly always list the grape variety. Regional designations are also often included, the most common being the Valle Central, whose 600-miles contain the country's best red wine regions.

white wines

Chile's white wines generally offer good value for the price. Most Chardonnays are medium-bodied with citrus flavors and a touch of oak. Many wines labeled Sauvignon Blanc may in fact be a different grape called Sauvignonasse, but whichever they are made from, they're usually full of green fruit, lemony flavors, and zippy acidity.

at the table
Chilean Chardonnay goes well with the usual suspects: chicken and meaty fish like halibut or monkfish. Sauvignon Blanc's vibrant acidity makes it a great match with shellfish or more delicate finfish like trout or snapper.

the bottom line Though a few lush, California-style Chardonnays climb to $40, most are under $20, and plenty of other white wines cost less than $10.

recommended wines

2000 Concha y Toro Amelia Limited Release Chardonnay, Casablanca Valley ★★★ $$$
dry, full-bodied, medium oak, high acidity drink now–8 years
Very good, very refined Chardonnay, with lemon curd and mineral flavors.

2000 Casa Lapostolle Chardonnay, Casablanca Valley ★★★ $
dry, full-bodied, medium oak, high acidity drink now–8 years
One of Chile's best white wines shows citrus and apple flavors with mineral notes that give it a sophisticated sheen.

2000 Montes Reserve Fumé Blanc Sauvignon Blanc, Curicó Valley ★★★ $
dry, medium-bodied, light oak, high acidity drink now–3 years
These green, grassy, lime flavors will liven up a cocktail party.

2000 Carmen Nativa Garrido Estate Chardonnay, Maipo Valley ★★ $
dry, medium-bodied, medium oak, high acidity drink now–5 years
Complex flavors of baked apple, peach, caramel, and minerals are achieved by using wild yeasts.

2001 Cousiño-Macul Doña Isadora Riesling, Maipo Valley ★★ $
dry, light-bodied, no oak, high acidity   drink now–4 years
If Chile-grown Riesling tastes so rich in minerals, peach, and citrus, one hopes
that they'll grow more of it.

2001 Veramonte Sauvignon Blanc, Casablanca Valley ★ $
dry, light-bodied, no oak, high acidity   drink now
Chill this hard and enjoy its light citrus and pear flavors on a hot afternoon.

red wines

Bordeaux grape varieties, brought to Chile before Bordeaux
vineyards were devastated by the phylloxera louse in the late
1800s, are the most common varieties grown, with Cabernet
Sauvignon in the lead. Carmenère, however, probably makes
Chile's most unique wine, while recent plantings of Syrah show
potential for this Rhône-based grape.

at the table

Simple and fruity, bargain-priced Chilean reds are great pours
for burgers or barbecued chicken. Save more complex wines for
braised oxtails or beef brisket. Elite blends are made for
impressing with rib roasts or venison.

the bottom line Chile has succumbed to market
madness, offering some red wines that tip the scales at $90.
Luckily, really good reds can still be found for $9 to $20.

recommended wines

2000 Almaviva, Puente Alto   ★★★★ $$$$
dry, full-bodied, heavy tannin, medium acidity   drink in 2–15 years
This Cabernet-Merlot ranks among the great wines of the world, with multiple
layers of fruit, mocha, mineral, cedar, and earthy flavors.

1999 Seña, Aconcagua Valley   ★★★ $$$$
dry, full-bodied, medium tannin, medium acidity   drink in 1–10 years
A collaboration between Napa's Mondavis and Chile's Chadwicks brings a
high-powered Cabernet blend with berry, animal, and deep mineral flavors.

2000 Caliterra Arboleda Syrah, Colchagua Valley ★★★ $$
dry, full-bodied, medium tannin, medium acidity   drink now–5 years
A smoldering volcano of spicy fruit, herbs, and minerals.

**2000 Casa Lapostolle Merlot Cuvée Alexandre,
Colchagua Valley** ★★★ $$
dry, full-bodied, medium tannin, medium acidity   drink in 1–10 years
The deep blackberry hue matches the depth of this wine's flavors.

**1999 Concha y Toro Marques de Casa Concha Cabernet
Sauvignon, Puente Alto** ★★★ $
dry, full-bodied, heavy tannin, medium acidity   drink in 1–10 years
Concentrated berry and cassis flavor meet with a concentration of bitter
chocolate and minerals. It's good now; with a little time, it will be even better.

1999 Carmen Reserve Cabernet Sauvignon, Maipo Valley ★★ $
dry, full-bodied, medium tannin, medium acidity   drink now–5 years
Sage and laurel scents infuse the fruit; a terrific match to an herb-laden stew.

**2001 Concha y Toro Casillero del Diablo Carmenère,
Rapel Valley** ★★ $
dry, full-bodied, medium tannin, medium acidity   drink now–4 years
This has juicy, Cabernet-like fruit with palate-awakening mineral flavors.

1999 Dallas-Conté Merlot, Rapel Valley ★★ $
dry, medium-bodied, medium tannin, medium acidity   drink now–3 years
Really good Merlot, with juicy berry flavors and smoked meat notes.

2000 Montes Reserve Malbec, Colchagua Valley ★★ $
dry, full-bodied, medium tannin, medium acidity   drink now–5 years
Malbec is more traditional to Argentina, but this Chilean maker has made a
lovely version with smooth berry flavors.

2000 Santa Rita 120 Merlot, Lontué Valley ★ $
dry, medium-bodied, medium tannin, high acidity   drink now–3 years
With earthy smoked fruit and herb flavors, this almost tastes like it came from
the south of France.

WINES WE WISH WE HAD MORE ROOM FOR
2000 Montes Alpha Syrah, Santa Cruz ★★★ $$ dry, full-bodied, heavy
tannin, medium acidity, drink in 1–6 years; **2000 Calina Reserve Merlot,
Maule Valley** ★★ $ dry, full-bodied, medium tannin, medium acidity, drink
now–3 years; **2000 Los Vascos Reserve Cabernet Sauvignon,
Colchagua** ★★ $ dry, full-bodied, medium tannin, medium acidity, drink in
1–6 years; **2001 Laura Hartwig Carmenère, Colchagua Valley** ★★ $
dry, medium-bodied, medium tannin, medium acidity, drink now–5 years

south
africa

South African wines were once ranked among the world's finest. Since the end of apartheid, the country's innovative winemakers have made great strides toward regaining that status. South Africa today is a wine region to watch.

grapes & styles

Like wine producers in the Americas, Australia, and New Zealand, South Africa grows classic French grape varieties. (Chenin Blanc is traditionally favored for white wines; Pinotage, a unique hybrid of Pinot Noir and Cinsault, for reds.) When it comes to winemaking, however, South African vintners tend to follow the European model that stresses subtlety and expression of *terroir* over the sweet flavor of new oak barrels.

on the label

South Africa's Wine of Origin (WO) system is similar to, though less rigorous than, France's AOC system, in which a wine bearing the name of a region must be 100 percent from that region. Additionally, labels on exported wines nearly always display the name of the grape. The most celebrated wine regions are Stellenbosch, Paarl, and Constantia.

white wines

South Africa's most produced white, Chenin Blanc (often called Steen), offers refreshing summer drinking in both dry and off-dry styles; some versions approach the excellence of France's Loire

Valley Chenin Blancs. Chardonnay, made in a medium-bodied, minerally style, is becoming increasingly prominent, while Sauvignon Blanc gets attention for the over-the-top gooseberry and grassy flavors it achieves here, reminiscent of New Zealand.

at the table

Enjoy Chenin Blanc's soft citrus and melonlike qualities as an aperitif, or with Southeast Asian soups and fish dishes. For Chardonnay's mineral flavors, good acidity, and richer texture, try lobster or flavorful fish like Arctic char. Assertive Sauvignon Blanc can cut through oily fish like mackerel and goes well with chicken roasted with lots of herbs.

the bottom line Chenin Blanc, a tough sell in the U.S., can be found for less than $8, with the most deluxe versions going for around $22. Chardonnays hover between $10 and $35, with the best quality-price ratio tending to fall in the middle. Sauvignon Blanc starts at $8 and rises to $25, though most of it sells for around $16, less than comparable New Zealand versions.

259

recommended wines

**2001 Groot Constantia Sauvignon Blanc,
Constantia** ★ ★ ★ $ $
dry, medium-bodied, light oak, high acidity   drink in 1–8 years
It's rare to recommend aging a Sauvignon Blanc, but this has enough layers of
bitter almond, citrus, cinnamon, and mint flavors to last.

2001 Neil Ellis Sauvignon Blanc, Groenekloof ★ ★ ★ $ $
dry, medium-bodied, no oak, high acidity   drink now–4 years
Flinty, herbal, and full of grapefruit and lime flavors, this is even better than
most Sancerre.

2000 Rustenberg Chardonnay, Stellenbosch ★ ★ ★ $ $
dry, medium-bodied, medium oak, medium acidity   drink now–6 years
A potpourri of sweet apple, citrus, mineral, and floral flavors.

2001 Simunye Sauvignon Blanc, Coastal Region ★ ★ ★ $ $
dry, medium-bodied, no oak, high acidity   drink now–3 years
Spicy pepper and mouthwatering grapefruit flavors demand attention.

2001 Brampton Unoaked Chardonnay, Stellenbosch ★ ★ $
dry, medium-bodied, no oak, medium acidity   drink now–4 years
South African Chardonnay usually offers finesse; this offers ripe pear and
tropical flavors, too.

**2001 Buitenverwachting Rhine Riesling,
Constantia** ★ ★ $
dry, light-bodied, no oak, high acidity   drink now–5 years
A good alternative to Chardonnay, with enjoyable lime and mineral flavors.

**2001 Fleur du Cap Sauvignon Blanc,
Coastal Region** ★ ★ $
dry, light-bodied, no oak, high acidity   drink now–2 years
A green demon of a wine, with green herb, green pepper, lime, and grapefruit
flavors in a zesty package.

2000 Kanu Chardonnay, Stellenbosch ★ ★ $
dry, medium-bodied, medium oak, medium acidity   drink now–5 years
Oak flavors marry well with the ripe fruit and spice flavors.

2001 Nederburg Prelude, Western Cape ★ ★ $
dry, medium-bodied, no oak, high acidity   drink now–4 years
At the start of a fine meal or the end of a long day, this Sauvignon Blanc-
Chardonnay blend offers lively fruit and mineral flavors.

2001 Porcupine Ridge Sauvignon Blanc, Coastal Region ★★ $
dry, medium-bodied, no oak, high acidity drink now–2 years
Sauvignon goes tropical here, with light pineapple and mango flavors, and
only a slight green pepper edge.

2001 Indaba Chenin Blanc, Western Cape ★ $
dry, medium-bodied, no oak, high acidity drink now
Ripe but dry fruit flavors make this a good choice to chill for aperitifs, especially
as a portion of the money spent on the bottle will go to scholarships for aspiring
South African vintners (see box, next page).

red wines

South Africa's red wines can be wonderful: generous sunshine
allows grapes to ripen easily, making full-bodied, fruity wines
that miraculously manage to carry complex smoke and mineral
notes as well. Cabernet, Merlot, and Syrah (called Shiraz in
South Africa, as in Australia) are frequently stellar, but vineyards
have been struck by a virus known as "leaf roll" that can give
wines an unusual vegetal quality. Winegrowers hope replanting
will do away with this scourge. The country's unique hybrid,
Pinotage, is also worth trying: simple versions resemble
Beaujolais Nouveau, but the best offer full-bodied, fruity flavors
with velvety tannins.

at the table
Simple Pinotage, slightly chilled, is great to wash down pizza or
barbecue. Match more complex ones as you would any hearty
red; roast game would be especially appropriate. South African
Cabernets and Merlots can be used in the same way as
American versions, though the wines tend to be earthier and
less forwardly fruity. South African Shiraz is often lighter than its
Australian kin, but it takes on a similiar peppery note that makes
it especially appropriate with spice-crusted meats or winter vegetable tagines.

the bottom line Simple south African reds start
around $7; wines with a little more complexity tend to fall
between $18 and $24. A few trophy wines sell for $40 or more
—not bad considering the prices of trophy wines elsewhere.

recommended wines

1997 Meerlust Rubicon, Stellenbosch ★ ★ ★ ★ $ $ $
dry, full-bodied, heavy tannin, medium acidity   drink now–10 years
A wine that puts South Africa wine in the company of greats: black as night, in color and deep fruit flavors.

1999 Boekenhoutskloof Cabernet Sauvignon, Franschhoek ★ ★ ★ $ $ $
dry, full-bodied, heavy tannin, medium acidity   drink now–6 years
An almost Australian style, with ripe berry flavors, spicy tannin, and a vanilla-coconut edge.

1999 Mont du Toit, Coastal Region ★ ★ ★ $ $ $
dry, full-bodied, medium tannin, medium acidity   drink now–8 years
This is a silk road of smooth fruit and mineral flavors.

SOUTH AFRICA WINE SCHOLARSHIPS

While transition in South Africa from apartheid has gone relatively smoothly, the minority white population maintains control of large sectors of the economy, including the country's wine industry. To date, no black South African owns or runs a South African winery. But moves are afoot to change this. Cape Classics' Indaba brand devotes a percentage of its worldwide sales to scholarship funds for promising black African students who wish to study all aspects of winemaking, from production and viticulture to global marketing. The program is still small—its first recipient, Mr. Mzokhona Mvemve, graduated in December 2001 from the University of Stellenbosch—but according to Cape Classics' president, André Shearer, the program's initiator, with his brother Gary, there are plans to establish an institute that would not only teach winemaking and marketing, but conduct literacy programs for vineyard laborers, and promote health education on issues such as HIV/AIDS and fetal alcohol syndrome. Considering that companies like Disney and Cost Plus have signed significant contracts for Indaba wine, these plans might bear fruit sooner than anyone expected.

1997 Fleur du Cap Cabernet Sauvignon, Coastal Region ★★★ $
dry, full-bodied, heavy tannin, medium acidity   drink now–8 years
What's the Cape Flower? In this wine it's pure lavender, which scents this black berry and mineral-laden wine through and through.

1999 Nederburg Pinotage, Western Cape ★★★ $
dry, full-bodied, medium tannin, high acidity   drink now–5 years
Exuberant Pinotage, with ripe fruit, spice, and the animal edge its fans adore.

1997 Le Bonheur Prima, Stellenbosch ★★ $$
dry, full-bodied, medium tannin, medium acidity   drink now–6 years
Merlot gives lots of soft plum flavors, but Cabernet spices it up.

1999 Rupert & Rothschild Classique, Coastal Region ★★ $$
dry, medium-bodied, heavy tannin, medium acidity   drink now–5 years
Fruit and mineral flavors have a finesse that reflects the Rothschild's Bordeaux influence.

2000 Brampton Cabernet Sauvignon-Merlot, Stellenbosch ★★ $
dry, full-bodied, heavy tannin, medium acidity   drink in 1–8 years
Safari wine, full of smoked meat flavors as well as ripe, peppery berry.

2001 Goats do Roam, Western Cape ★★ $
dry, full-bodied, medium tannin, medium acidity   drink now–2 years
What do you get when you cross Côtes-du-Rhône with a herd of goats? A fun, fruit- and spice-filled wine.

2000 Indaba Cabernet Sauvignon, Western Cape ★★ $
dry, medium-bodied, medium tannin, medium acidity   drink now–4 years
Juicy fruit and slightly smoky flavors, all for a good cause: proceeds from this go to a scholarship fund supporting young black African winemakers.

2000 Spice Route Andrew's Hope Pinotage, Swartland ★★ $
dry, full-bodied, heavy tannin, high acidity   drink now–5 years
Those who scorn Pinotage for its "feral" qualities should give this a try. Ripe fruit, minerals, and none of the funk.

WINES WE WISH WE HAD MORE ROOM FOR
1998 Meerlust Pinot Noir Reserve, Stellenbosch ★★★ $$$ dry, medium-bodied, medium tannin, medium acidity, drink now–6 years; **2000 Fleur du Cap Merlot, Coastal Region** ★★ $$ dry, medium-bodied, medium tannin, medium acidity, drink now–5 years; **1999 Thelema Merlot, Stellenbosch** ★★$$ dry, medium-bodied, medium tannin, medium acidity, drink now–5 years; **2000 Guardian Peak Cabernet Sauvignon-Syrah, Stellenbosch** ★★ $ dry, full-bodied, medium tannin, medium acidity, drink now–6 years

champagne & other sparkling wines

Whether it's a simple California fizzy or a grand Champagne, sparkling wines spell celebration like nothing else. And considering the range of affordable sparklers—from Spain's Cava and Italy's Spumante to America's bounty of sparkling wines—there's every reason to celebrate more often.

at the table

Sparkling wine is a terrific aperitif, but there's no reason to put it away once dinner is served. Try simple, light-bodied styles with dinner salads and light fish; medium-bodied versions with grilled finfish or Dungeness crab. Richer wines can stand up to poultry or even game. Beef lovers should check out Australia's sparkling Shiraz; sweet tooths can choose from many off-dry styles.

champagne

Champagne is a case of making the best of a difficult situation. It's so cool here that the grapes often can't ripen fully. What the grapes lack in sugar, however, they make up for in acidity, which results in a great base for sparkling wines. In Europe, only sparkling wines made in France's Champagne region using the *méthode champenoise* technique can be called Champagne.

grapes & styles

Champagne is typically a blend of Chardonnay, Pinot Noir, and Pinot Meunier. Blanc de Blancs ("white from whites") are 100 percent Chardonnay; Blanc de Noirs are made from Pinot Noir and/or, occasionally, Pinot Meunier. Rosé Champagnes can be made from either Pinot Noir or Meunier, with or without Chardonnay. The color is gained either by allowing the pigment-rich grape skins to steep in the pressed juice or by blending white wine with red.

on the label

Most Champagnes are blends of wines from several vintages to create a consistent house style. Vintage Champagnes are made in years when grapes ripen especially well, about four years in a decade. Most Champagne is dry, but there are variations of sweetness. From driest to sweetest, the categories of Champagne are Brut Zéro (or Brut Nature or Pas Dosé), Extra Brut, Brut, Extra Dry, Sec, Demi-Sec, and Doux.

the bottom line
Expect to pay $24 to $40 for basic, nonvintage wines, $50 to $80 for vintage wines, and well over $100 for the most exalted *cuvées de prestige*.

what to buy VINTAGE CHAMPAGNE

1988	1989	1990	1991	1992	1993
★★★★	★★★	★★★★	★	★★	★★

1994	1995	1996	1997	1998
★★	★★★	★★★★	★★★	★★

recommended wines

1990 Dom Ruinart Blanc de Blancs   ★★★★ $$$$
dry, full-bodied, high acidity
Superb wine, flush with smoky mineral notes and layers of dry citrus zest, apple, and berry flavors.

NV Krug Grande Cuvée Brut   ★★★★ $$$$
dry, full-bodied, high acidity
The ultimate expression of luxurious baked fruit and mineral flavors.

1989 Lanson Noble Cuvée Brut   ★★★★ $$$$
dry, medium-bodied, high acidity
Thirteen years of age make for a mature mélange of mineral and fruit flavors.

1996 Nicolas Feuillatte Cuvée Palmes d'Or Brut Rosé ♟ ★★★★ $$$$
dry, medium-bodied, high acidity
Rosé in full bloom, with exceptionally floral scents and spiced cassis flavors.

1990 Philipponnat Clos des Goisses Brut   ★★★★ $$$$
dry, full-bodied, high acidity
Gorgeous wine, with smoky, caramelized nut and lacquered orange flavors.

1989 Pommery Louise   ★★★★ $$$$
dry, full-bodied, high acidity
Rich and toasty, with mouthfilling apple, nut, and orange flavors.

1995 Veuve Clicquot Ponsardin La Grande Dame Brut ★★★★ $$$$
dry, full-bodied, high acidity
The Grande Dame is an extravagant one, dressed in Versace and a feather boa.

NV Gosset Grand Rosé Brut ♟   ★★★ $$$$
dry, medium-bodied, high acidity
Much went into the bottle design here, but this toasty, nutty rosé would taste
good even if poured from a can.

1993 Moët & Chandon Cuvée Dom Pérignon   ★★★ $$$$
dry, medium-bodied, high acidity
Citrusy, toasty, and ever elegant, with bubbles as bright as the stars in the sky.

NV Bollinger Special Cuvée   ★★★ $$$
dry, medium-bodied, high acidity
Sophisticated scents lead to soft, burnt orange flavors and savory mineral
notes.

1990 Charles Heidsieck Blanc des Millénaires   ★★★ $$$
dry, medium-bodied, high acidity
This elegant wine waltzes through flavors ranging from mineral to citrus,
spice, and candied nut flavors.

NV Jacquesson & Fils Perfection   ★★★ $$$
dry, light-bodied, high acidity
Lavender, lime, and raspberry flavors float as if on gossamer wings of minerals.

NV Jean Milan Carte Blanche Grand Cru Brut   ★★★ $$$
dry, medium-bodied, high acidity
This is so dry it's almost austere, but there's nothing miserly about the toasted
hazelnut and light berry flavors.

1995 Pol Roger Brut Rosé ☺   ★★★ $$$
dry, medium-bodied, high acidity
Roger's copper color alone is worth an award; its finesse and concentrated, dry berry flavors are icing on the cake.

NV Varnier-Fannière Grand Cru Brut   ★★★ $$$
dry, medium-bodied, high acidity
Grand Cru on the cheap, yet these deep orange and mineral flavors are no compromise.

NV Veuve Clicquot Ponsardin Demi-Sec   ★★★ $$$
medium-sweet, full-bodied, high acidity
The perfect wedding-cake wine, with a touch of sweetness complementing the mineraly, orange-honey flavor.

1995 Moët & Chandon Brut Impérial Rosé ☺   ★★ $$$$
dry, full-bodied, high acidity
A very dry rosé, with a lovely light salmon color and slightly singed cedar and berry flavors.

NV Deutz Brut Classic   ★★ $$$
dry, light-bodied, high acidity
Sophisticated orange and mineral flavors dance brightly to a tune of Sherry-like nuttiness.

NV Louis Roederer Brut Premium   ★★ $$$
dry, full-bodied, high acidity
Stone-dry Champagne,with tart green apple flavors paved with minerals.

NV Nicolas Feuillatte Kosher Mevushal Brut   ★★ $$$
dry, medium-bodied, high acidity
A good choice even if you're not keeping kosher, with apple-honey cake flavors lifted by fine mineral notes.

NV Piper-Heidsieck Brut Rosé ☺   ★★ $$$
dry, full-bodied, high acidity
Most rosé Champagnes are full of fruit, but this is focused on sandalwood, spice, and lots of minerals.

NV Veuve Clicquot Yellow Label Brut   ★★ $$$
dry, full-bodied, high acidity
Always reliable, with rich citrus and apple flavors balanced by high acidity.

NV G.H. Mumm Cordon Rouge Brut   ★ $$$
dry, full-bodied, high acidity
Long the standard for affordable sophistication.

other sparkling wines

Almost every wine-producing country makes sparkling wine. They may not have the same cachet as Champagne, but examples from other French regions as well as from Italy, Spain, and the U.S. can come close in quality. Delicious bubblies are also made in Austria, Germany, and the Southern Hemisphere.

france

Sparkling wines made outside of Champagne with *champenoise* techniques are labeled *méthode traditionnelle.* These wines normally employ local grape varieties, and depending on regional customs, are often called *Crémant* or *Mousseux.*

the bottom line Non-Champagne French sparklers can be outstanding bargains at $10 to $25.

recommended wines

**NV Domaine Collin Blanquette de Limoux,
Languedoc-Roussillon** ★★★ $
dry, full-bodied, medium acidity
As good as Champagne for a lot less.

NV Champalou Vouvray Brut, Loire ★★ $$
dry, medium-bodied, high acidity
Vouvray's seductive charms are translated into bubble form, with inviting peach, cassis, and tangerine flavors balanced by high acidity.

NV Willm Brut Crémant d'Alsace ★★ $$
dry, medium-bodied, medium acidity
Alsace's wines are aromatic whether still or sparkling. Essences of flowers and tart apples prove the point.

italy

Italy has a great tradition of Spumante wines, particularly in the north. Most employ the *metodo classico* of Champagne. Those from Lombardy's Franciacorta region are the best. Moscato d'Asti is less serious and lightly sweet; less serious still is Prosecco, made near Venice, where it's traditionally drunk from tumblers.

the bottom line Prosecco and Moscato run about $10. Some impressive Franciacorta Bruts cost $30 to $60.

recommended wines

NV Bellavista Cuvée Brut, Franciacorta ★★★ $$$
dry, medium-bodied, medium acidity
One of Italy's best sparklers, with crisp, tangy apple flavors.

1997 Bellavista Gran Cuvée Brut Rosé, Franciacorta ♥ ★★★ $$$
dry, full-bodied, medium acidity
The rare flavor of wild strawberries is light, but it makes a statement.

NV Ferrari Brut, Trento ★★★ $$
dry, medium-bodied, high acidity
Mousse-like, nutty pear and lime flavors have finesse and class.

2001 Bellenda Prosecco di Conegliano Valdobbiadene, Veneto ★★★ $
dry, medium-bodied, high acidity
More elegant than most Prosecco, this is lively with herb, lime, and mineral notes.

NV Soldati La Scolca Brut, Gavi ★★ $$$
dry, medium-bodied, high acidity
These honeysuckle and peachy lime flavors will cure any afternoon blues.

NV Mionetto Prosecco Brut Spumante, Veneto ★★ $
dry, medium-bodied, high acidity
Ripe summer fruit flavors have a surprising—and delicious—smokiness.

NV Zardetto Prosecco Brut, Veneto ★ $
dry, light-bodied, high acidity
This light and zingy wine will add a Venetian holiday air wherever you drink it.

spain

Spain's sparkling Cavas used to be more notable for low prices than quality, but the latter has risen dramatically while prices remain low.

the bottom line While $6 specials exist, $10 to $15 buys more interesting wines.

recommended wines

NV Parxet Titiana Brut Nature   ★ ★ ★ $ $
dry, medium-bodied, high acidity
Beautiful Cava, with fine bubbles through a rare lushness of apricot and floral flavors framed by minerals.

1998 Marqués de Gelida Brut   ★ ★ ★ $
dry, full-bodied, high acidity
With candied apple, cassis, and marzipan flavors, this has the complexity of many Champagnes, for far less.

1999 Mont Marçal Brut Reserva   ★ ★ ★ $
dry, medium-bodied, high acidity
Uncommonly floral, with enjoyable citrus and mouthwatering minerality.

1999 Huguet Gran Reserva Brut Nature   ★ ★ $ $
dry, medium-bodied, high acidity
More impressive than most Cava, with ripe citrus flavors that gain depth from powdery mineral notes.

NV Jaume Serra Cristalino Brut   ★ ★ $
dry, full-bodied, high acidity
California Chardonnay lovers looking to add sparkle to their lives will be pleased with this, with citrus and buttered popcorn flavors.

NV Sardà Brut   ★ ★ $
dry, medium-bodied, medium acidity
A Cava with tiny, fine bubbles and honeyed citrus flavors with a quinine edge.

NV Freixenet Cordon Negro Brut   ★ $
dry, medium-bodied, high acidity
An always reliable sparkler to celebrate the everyday.

united states

California still dominates in price and prestige, but sparkling wine is made all over the U.S., from New York to Washington State to New Mexico. Many are made using the classic *méthode champenoise,* and the best of them compare favorably with all but the finest Champagne.

the bottom line Quality American sparklers range from $9 to $75, with very good quality between $12 and $25.

recommended wines

1996 Schramsberg J. Schram, Napa Valley ★★★★ $$$$
dry, full-bodied, high acidity
Light berry and citrus flavors are imbued with subtle smokiness. Superb.

**1997 Iron Horse Russian Cuvée,
Sonoma County/Green Valley** ★★★★ $$$
dry, medium-bodied, high acidity
Simply wonderful, with an enchanting herbal quality amongst the ripe fruit and hazelnut flavors.

1990 Lenz Cuvée RD, North Fork ★★★★ $$$
dry, full-bodied, high acidity
This complex and finely finessed sparkler is one of the best in the U.S.

1996 Roederer Estate L'Ermitage Brut, Anderson Valley ★★★★ $$$
dry, full-bodled, hlgh acldity
The citrus and berry flavors here are so delicious they could have distracted the Romanoffs during the storming of the Winter Palace.

**1995 Domaine Carneros by Taittinger Le Rêve Brut,
Carneros** ★★★ $$$$
dry, medium-bodied, high acidity
The finesse of excellent Champagne with the ripeness of California fruit.

1989 Argyle Extended Tirage Brut, Willamette Valley ★★★ $$$
dry, full-bodied, high acidity
Mixed berries and cream, this verges on sweet, but stays dry, augmented by unexpected acidity.

**1997 Wölffer Christian Wölffer Cuvée,
The Hamptons/Long Island** ★★★ $$$
dry, medium-bodied, high acidity
A lot of Wölffer's Hamptons neighbors can afford the most expensive Champagne, but why bother, when the spicy fruit flavors of this are so good.

NV Chandon Étoile Rosé, Napa County/Sonoma County ♥ ★★ $$$
dry, full-bodied, high acidity
This seduces with fresh strawberry and toast flavors.

1996 Handley Cellars Brut, Anderson Valley ★★ $$$
dry, medium-bodied, high acidity
California's Anderson Valley is recognized as being especially suited to making sparkling wines. No argument here.

1999 Schramsberg Crémant Demi-Sec, California ★★ $$$
off-dry, medium-bodied, high acidity
Enjoy the spicy berry flavors with Asian dishes, or with fruit.

NV Jepson Blanc de Blancs, Mendocino County ★★ $$
dry, medium-bodied, high acidity
Really ripe and toasty, this does Mendocino proud.

1999 Korbel Natural, Russian River Valley ★★ $
dry, medium-bodied, high acidity
One of the best from Korbel, the biggest producer of wine using the Champagne method in California.

NV Pacific Echo Brut, Mendocino County ★ $$
dry, medium-bodied, high acidity
Light and lively citrus flavors from a company owned by Veuve Clicquot.

NV Piper Sonoma Blanc de Noir, Sonoma County ★ $$
dry, medium-bodied, high acidity
Spicy, candied fruit flavors balanced by high acidity for casual celebrations.

other producers

In Europe, look to Germany and Austria for some great Sekt made from Riesling. Excellent bubbly is made in Australia, in white versions as well as the unique, deep red, sparkling Shiraz. Elsewhere in the Southern Hemisphere, South Africa, New Zealand, and Argentina also offer very good sparklers.

the bottom line South American sparklers cost around $8 to $12. Australia has a few wines in that category, but also offers higher-quality wines for $20 to $45, as well as sparkling Shiraz from $16 to $45. Good South African and Austrian bubblies run just under $20, and while there are a few Germans in the under-$20 range, luxury bottlings can cost $30 to $70.

recommended wines

1994 Georg Breuer, Rheingau, Germany ★★★★ $$$
dry, medium-bodied, high acidity
Absolutely superlative. Exceptionally dry, exceptionally mineral, and exceptional citrus and dry honey flavors.

NV Fox Creek Vixen, McLaren Vale, Australia ♥ ★★★ $$
dry, full-bodied, high acidity
Don't let the blood-red color shock you: this Shiraz, Cab Franc, and Cab Sauvignon sparkler has all the flavors (and tannin) of a still wine, lightened by the bubbles.

NV Greg Norman Estates Sparkling Chardonnay-Pinot Noir, Australia ★★ $$
dry, medium-bodied, high acidity
Named for golfer Greg Norman, this apple and mineral wine is just right for toasting at the end of 18.

NV Pierre Jourdan Brut, South Africa ★★ $
dry, medium-bodied, high acidity
South Africa offers a bone-dry, mineral-laden wine.

NV Chandon Brut Fresco, Argentina ★ $
dry, full-bodied, high acidity
Wherever Chandon goes, it makes good wine. This pleases with a toasty, fat, and orange quality.

NV Krimskoye Semi-Sweet Red Champagne, Ukraine ♥ ★ $
medium-sweet, medium-bodied, high acidity
Red sparkling wines, especially those that taste like red cherry, pomegranate, and crushed rose, might be an acquired taste, but it's certainly worth a try.

1999 Seaview Brut, South Eastern Australia ★ $
dry, medium-bodied, high acidity
A good, value-priced, citrus and mineral sparkler with a touch of sweetness.

fortified &dessert wines

Whether it is dry Fino Sherry before dinner or a sweet Sauternes afterward, fortified and dessert wines are ideal for framing a fine repast. Many can also be enjoyed throughout the meal.

fortified wines

As the name implies, fortified wines have been strengthened by the addition of alcohol, usually neutral grape spirits. The extra alcohol helps preserve the wines, an important consideration in warm climes. Depending on when it is added, the alcohol can also affect the sweetness of the final wine. The best-known fortified wines are Sherry, Madeira, and Port.

sherry

From the chalky soil around Jerez in the south of Spain come some of the most unique, if least appreciated, wines in the world. Styles range from bone-dry with palate-awakening verve, to tooth-achingly sweet and unctuous.

grapes & styles

Most Sherry is made from Palomino grapes, though the sweetest styles are often made from or with the addition of Pedro Ximénez or Moscatel grapes. There are two basic categories, Fino and Oloroso, each with its own subcategories:

Fino Sherry develops its yeasty, floral, slightly nutty character from *flor,* an oxygen-stifling yeast that grows on the wine's surface as it matures. **Manzanilla** denotes a Fino aged in Sanlúcar de Barrameda, an area near the sea that is especially hospitable to *flor.* These wines often have a fresh, salty flavor evocative of a sea breeze. **Amontillado** is a Fino that has been left to age after the oxygen-blocking *flor* dies. Oxidation adds a nutty character to the wines' inherent minerality. Most Amontillados are dry. **Pale Cream** Sherries are Finos sweetened with Pedro Ximénez wine or grape juice concentrate.

Oloroso Sherry is aged without *flor.* Thus exposed to oxygen, it develops nutty and sometimes tobacco aromas and flavors and a dark amber hue. A few dry Olorosos exist, but most are sweet. **Cream** Sherries are Olorosos sweetened with Pedro Ximénez wine. **Palo Cortado** is a rare type of Oloroso that happens to develop *flor.* Dark in color, it falls between an Amontillado and an Oloroso in flavor.

Pedro Ximénez is made from grapes of the same name grown in the Montilla-Moriles region outside Jerez. While a PX (as it's commonly referred to) wine is technically not a Sherry, several Sherry houses make them. Nearly all PX wines are thick, sweet as treacle, and full of dried fruit flavors.

at the table

Dry Finos make a fine aperitif, especially with olives or anchovies. Richer dry Olorosos are great with creamy soups, Serrano ham, or braised chicken. Pair sweeter versions with chocolate cake or date bread. Pour PX over vanilla ice cream.

the bottom line Sherry is terrifically underpriced. Many bottles are offered below $12; those from top producers run only a few dollars more. Older wines or special blends can range from $20 to $125.

recommended wines

1975 Bodegas Toro Albalá Don PX Gran Reserva   ★ ★ ★ ★ $$$
sweet, full-bodied, high acidity
More than a quarter century in barrel brings spectacular fig, burnt sugar, tangerine, and thyme flavors to this sticky-sweet Sherry.

fortified wines **sherry**

Hidalgo Pastrana Amontillado Viejo ★★★★ $$$
dry, full-bodied, high acidity
A single-vineyard Sherry totally imbued with toasted nut, dry orange peel, and polished mineral flavors.

Bodegas Dios Baco Cream ★★★ $$
sweet, full-bodied, high acidity
Sweet but not treacly flavors are made more complex with nut and mint notes.

Gonzalez Byass Apóstoles Muy Viejo Palo Cortado ★★★ $$
medium-sweet, medium-bodied, medium acidity
Velvety *dulce de leche* flavors meet with dry apricot and orange spice.

Gonzalez Byass Matusalem Muy Viejo Oloroso Dulce ★★★ $$
sweet, full-bodied, high acidity
The roasted coffee and nut flavors are as delicious as the beautiful chestnut color promises.

Hidalgo La Gitana Manzanilla ★★★ $
dry, light-bodied, high acidity
Ideal Manzanilla, light as a butterfly, with a briny, sea-breeze freshness and nutty pear flavors. Great value.

Hidalgo Napoleón Amontillado ★★★ $
dry, medium-bodied, medium acidity
Almond brittle flavors with great finesse make this one to savor over a long evening.

Bodegas Dios Baco Fino ★★ $$
dry, medium-bodied, high acidity
Unique Fino, as bone-dry and mineral-filled as one expects, but also weighty and woody.

Lustau Don Nuño Dry Oloroso ★★ $$
dry, medium-bodied, medium acidity
Exceptionally smooth, with almond butter richness and smoky mineral notes.

Gonzalez Byass Tío Pepe Palomino Extra Dry Fino ★★ $
dry, light-bodied, high acidity
Salty nut and apple flavors make for fine Fino to chill and serve before dinner with roasted almonds and manchego cheese.

Lustau Papirusa Light Manzanilla, Sanlúcar de Barrameda ★★ $
dry, light-bodied, high acidity
Refreshing and light, this charms with apple blossom and herb aromas and palate-provoking mineral flavors.

madeira

The fortified wines of Madeira, a Portuguese island off the coast of Morocco, are undeservedly ignored today. This is a shame, as Madeira wines, like Sherry, come in styles highly suited for before, during, and after a meal.

grapes & styles

The best Madeiras are labeled by grape variety. Sercial makes the driest wines, while Verdelho, Bual, and Malmsey (Malvasia) grapes give sweeter wines. If the grape variety is not specified, the wine is usually made from inferior varieties and is often labeled "Rainwater." Most Madeiras are nonvintage wines. Designations of approximate age (such as "five years old") refer to the youngest wine in the blend. "Solera" Madeiras indicate the vintage year of the oldest wine in the blend. High-quality Madeira can age almost indefinitely.

at the table

Sercials and Verdelhos go well with salty hors d'oeuvres like olives, almonds, or smoked fish. Madeira is a classic match for thick winter soups. The high acidity and rich sweetness of Buals and Malmseys are terrific with crème brûlée or marzipan cookies.

the bottom line Rainwater Madeiras run $10 to $15; superior five-year-olds, $17 to $25. Prices escalate with age: decades-old Madeira goes for $100 or more.

recommended wines

1968 D'Oliveira Reserve Bual ★★★★ $$$$
medium-sweet, full-bodied, high acidity
Like the best fruitcake possible, with spiced dry apricot, nut, and orange flavor (no maraschino cherries) in a bottle.

Broadbent 10 Year Malmsey ★★★ $$$
medium-sweet, full-bodied, high acidity
Definitive Madeira, full of toasted filbert and dried orange peel flavors and a sweep of herb notes.

fortified wines **madeira**

Cossart Gordon 5 Year Bual ★★★ $$
medium-sweet, full-bodied, medium acidity
Pungent herb qualities course through the dried orange and spice flavors.

Justino's 10 Year Malmsey ★★ $$$
medium-sweet, full-bodied, high acidity
Piquant and herbal, this has the attractive aromas of ripe apricots and straw.

Blandy's 5 Year Sercial ★★ $$
off-dry, medium-bodied, medium acidity
This driest of the noble Madeira varieties offers unusual mineral, dry herb, and light, dry apricot flavors.

Blandy's 5 Year Verdelho ★★ $$
medium-sweet, full-bodied, high acidity
Delightful dry apricot and mineral flavors finish on peppery flower notes.

1995 Broadbent Colheita ★★ $$
medium-sweet, full-bodied, high acidity
A young, vintage Madeira, full of peppery dried fruit flavors.

Leacock's Rainwater ★ $
medium-sweet, medium-bodied, high acidity
The thrill of smoky Madeira at a nice price.

port

Popularized by British merchants in the late 1600s, Port wines are a perennial favorite among wine lovers.

on the label

Since more than forty grape varieties can go into Port, the style of the wine, rather than the variety, is mentioned on the label. There are several categories: **White Port** is a refreshing aperitif from white grapes. Serve chilled. **Ruby Port** is the most common Port, a simple blend of wines aged for two or three years. **Reserve** or **Vintage Character Port** are blends of Ruby Ports that have been aged for four to six years to acquire more intense flavors. These wines often carry proprietary names like Warre's Warrior or Graham's Six Grapes. **Late Bottled Vintage (LBV) Ports** are from a good-but-not-great vintage, aged for four to six years in barrels. They offer some of the attributes of Vintage Ports, but they don't require further aging once bottled. **Vintage Ports** are blended from the best red grapes of a single vintage that has been declared exceptional (perhaps three out of ten) and held in oak casks for two to three years before bottling, Vintage Ports require years, even decades, of aging before their potential is realized. **Single Quinta Vintage Ports** are vintage wines from single vineyards ("quintas"). They are treated in the same manner as Vintage Ports, with two or three years in cask before bottling. **Tawny Ports** get their tawny color and dried fruit and nut flavors from an extended time in oak barrels. The finest Tawnies are labeled with the average age of the wine in the bottle, usually five to forty years. **Colheita Ports** are Tawny Ports that are mostly from a single vintage and aged a minimum of seven years, though they are often kept for as long as ten, twenty, or even fifty years.

at the table

Chilled White Port makes a nice aperitif, especially with a splash of tonic and a twist. Ruby Ports are simple accompaniments to berry cobblers. Echo the flavors of a Tawny with desserts containing dried fruits and nuts. Vintage Port is classically paired with strong salty cheeses like Stilton and cracked walnuts.

the bottom line Ruby Ports run $10 to $20; LBVs between $18 and $30. Young Vintage Ports sell for $35 to $85. Single Quinta Ports often run about half the price of the same house's Vintage Port. Tawny Ports with age designations represent good value: ten-year Tawnies run $25 to $35 and increase in price with age, reaching $100 or more for forty-year-olds.

recommended wines

1999 Quinta do Crasto Vintage　　　　★ ★ ★ ★ $$$$
sweet, full-bodied, medium acidity
Luscious as luscious can be, with blackberry liqueur richness

Taylor Fladgate 30 Year Tawny　　　　★ ★ ★ ★ $$$$
medium-sweet, medium-bodied, high acidity
Fabulous in every way, from its subtle caramel undertones and Seville orange bitterness, to its profound smoky mineral flavors.

1997 Fonseca Vintage ★★★ $$$$
medium-sweet, full-bodied, medium acidity
Complex blueberry, orange peel, herb, and spice flavors come together in a luxuriously textured wine. Age for a decade.

Ramos Pinto Quinta do Bom Retiro 20 Year Tawny ★★★ $$$$
sweet, full-bodied, medium acidity
There's an almost bitter herbal quality to this wine, but the orange and berry flavors sweeten things up: a nice balance for the end of a meal.

1998 Cockburn's Quinta dos Canais Vintage ★★★ $$$
sweet, full-bodied, high acidity
This Single Quinta wine may not be as sumptuous as a blended Vintage Port, but with pomegranate and spice, tamarind and berry, and deep earthy flavors, it is no less fine.

1976 Smith Woodhouse Colheita Single Year Tawny ★★★ $$$
medium-sweet, medium-bodied, high acidity
A rare single-vintage Tawny Port, with lashes of herb and dried apricot flavors.

1992 Warre's Late Bottled Vintage ★★★ $$
medium-sweet, full-bodied, medium acidity
Layer upon layer of flavor: cherry, berry, and pomegranate cemented together with spicy tannin.

Dow's 10 Year Tawny ★★ $$
medium-sweet, medium-bodied, medium acidity
Vanilla-rum aromas pour out of the bottle when opened, but they take a back seat to the orange-spice and light berry flavors.

Taylor Fladgate Chip Dry White Port ★ $$
dry, light-bodied, medium acidity
Dry citrus and light green apple flavors make for a good aperitif, well-chilled. It's also good with a splash of tonic and a twist.

Cockburn's Fine Ruby ★ $
sweet, full-bodied, high acidity
Good, basic Port, with lightly tannic and spicy cherry flavor.

PORTS WE WISH WE HAD MORE ROOM FOR
1997 Broadbent Vintage ★★★ $$$$ medium-sweet, full-bodied, high acidity; **Ferreira Dona Antonia Personal Reserve** ★★★ $$ medium-sweet, medium-bodied, high acidity; **1997 Osborne Late Bottled Vintage** ★★ $$ medium-sweet, full-bodied, medium acidity; **Warre's Warrior Special Reserve** ★★ $ sweet, full-bodied, high acidity; **Graham's Six Grapes** ★ $$ sweet, full-bodied, medium acidity

dessert wines

Dessert wines can provide the perfect coda to a fine meal. Whether a light, fizzy Italian Moscato or a golden, honeyed French Sauternes, dessert wines revive the palate like a brilliant autumn day awakens the spirit after the lethargy of summer.

sauternes & similar wines

It may not sound ideal, but Sauternes, France's famed dessert wine, gets its inimitable flavor from a mold. *Botrytis cinerea,* or "noble rot," is what gives these sweet, peach- and tropical fruit-filled wines their smoky, spicy, honeyed nuances. The wines are based on Semillon, with Sauvignon Blanc and Muscadelle added. Neighboring regions such as Cadillac and Loupiac offer similar wines often at a fraction of the price. Wines labeled Barsac are from a subregion of Sauternes.

In France's Loire Valley, Chenin Blanc (also called Pineau here) makes similarly golden wines heavy with honey and summer fruit flavors. Those from Coteaux du Layon and Montlouis are good, but the best come from Quarts de Chaume, Savennières, Vouvray, and Bonnezeaux.

California, South Africa, and Australia also produce golden, Sauternes-like wines.

at the table

Sauternes and Sauternes like wines are classically paired with foie gras or blue cheeses, though they can be an indulgent sip on their own or after dinner with fresh or baked fruit desserts.

the bottom line
Sauternes start at $25 and rise to around $325 for the most revered example, Château d'Yquem. Fortunately, half bottles are common. Similarly styled wines from nearby Loupiac, Cadillac, Gaillac, and Monbazillac run $12 to $25 (a few special bottles climb over $100), but only the best approach Sauternes in quality. Half bottles of excellent Loire Valley dessert wine run $18 to $75, while the best California versions can reach $60. Australian "stickies" offer great value at $15 to $60.

what to buy SAUTERNES

1991	1992	1993	1994	1995
★	★	★	★★	★★★

1996	1997	1998	1999	2000
★★★	★★★	★★★	★★★	★

recommended wines

1999 Château Suduiraut, Sauternes, Bordeaux, France ★★★★ $$$$
sweet, full-bodied, high acidity
From the thick-and-sticky school of Sauternes comes a baroque wine full of nectarous fruit and spice flavors.

1998 Dolce Late Harvest Wine, Napa Valley,
California ★★★★ $$$$ (375 ml)
sweet, full-bodied, high acidity
An ambrosial wine with orange, spice, floral, and musky flavors blessed by California's sunshine.

1997 Domaine Huet Le Haut-Lieu Moelleux, Vouvray, Loire Valley,
France ★★★★ $$$
off-dry, full-bodied, high acidity
This spectacular wine from one of the Loire's most revered names has loquat jam flavors all over it, joined by spicy mineral notes.

1995 Nederburg Auction Selection Edelkeur Noble Late Harvest
Chenin Blanc, Paarl, South Africa ★★★★ $$$ (375 ml)
dry, full-bodied, high acidity
Fascinating berry and spicy, dry apricot flavors have the truffle-oil earthiness that comes from botrytis.

2000 Paumanok Late Harvest Sauvignon Blanc, North Fork,
Long Island, New York ★★★ $$$
sweet, full-bodied, medium acidity
A sip of this silken, dry pear- and fig-flavored wine brings Long Island's Gold Coast to the North Fork.

2000 Domaine François Chidaine Clos Habert, Montlouis,
Loire Valley, France ★★★ $$
medium-sweet, full-bodied, high acidity
Full of fruit and mineral enjoyment, this affordable Loire wine can't be beat at the price.

2000 Domaine Baumard, Coteaux du Layon, Loire Valley, France ★★ $$
medium-sweet, medium-bodied, high acidity
The most modest of Baumard's line-up (their Quarts de Chaume is spectacular) offers clean, lean peach and lime flavors with nervy acidity.

muscat

Known for its heady floral scent, juicy fruit, and musklike flavors, Muscat grows in nearly every wine-producing country. While the grape can be used for dry wines, it usually appears as a sweet wine. Different techniques are used to attain different styles:

Late-Harvest wines are made from grapes picked late in the fall, when they have attained a very high degree of sugar. Most wine-producing countries make late-harvest wines. Some terrific examples are from Samos, Greece. Lighter and more refreshing are the fizzy Moscato d'Asti wines from Italy's Piedmont.

Passito wines are a specialty of Italy (particularly the isle of Pantelleria) made from late-harvested grapes that have been dried on straw mats before pressing.

Vin Doux Naturel (VDN) is a term applied to wines in the south of France that receive a dose of neutral spirit to stop fermentation while the sugar level is still high. The resulting wines, such as Muscat de Beaumes-de-Venise, are higher in alcohol than non-fortified dessert wines, yet do not feel heavy.

at the table
The lightest Muscats, like Moscato d'Asti, are refreshing after dinner with fresh fruit. Slightly richer fortified Muscats are delicious with custard desserts or creamy cheeses. Match the caramel notes of heavy Muscats like those from Samos or Passito versions with nut tarts or almond biscotti.

the bottom line Compared to prized Passitos costing $18 and up per half bottle, Moscato d'Asti is a bargain at $10 to $20 for a full bottle. Samos wines sell for $7 to $15 a full bottle. Muscats from Beaumes-de-Venise and Rivesaltes range from $9 to $29 for a full bottle.

recommended wines

**De Bartoli Bukkuram, Moscato di Pantelleria, Sicily,
Italy** ★ ★ ★ $$$$ (500 ml)
sweet, full-bodied, high acidity
Pantelleria's Arab heritage wafts through this wine in scents of dry fruit, sweet
spice, and marzipan.

**2000 Abbazia di Novacella Moscato Rosa, Alto Adige,
Italy** ★ ★ ★ $$$ (375 ml)
medium-sweet, medium-bodied, high acidity
A rare red Muscat, scented with violets and flavored with dry berry, smoke,
and mineral notes.

**2000 Domaine de Coyeux, Muscat de Beaumes de Venise,
Rhône Valley, France** ★ ★ ★ $$ (375 ml)
sweet, medium-bodied, high acidity
Flower and honey flavors have an acidity that makes them buzz with a bee-
hive's worth of palate action.

2001 Marenco Scrapona, Moscato d'Asti, Piedmont, Italy ★ ★ ★ $$
medium-sweet, light-bodied, high acidity
Moscato d'Asti always charms, but the light floral and lime flavors of this one
make the knees go weak.

**2000 Sarda-Malet, Muscat de Rivesaltes, Languedoc-Roussillon,
France** ★ ★ ★ $$ (375 ml)
medium-sweet, medium-bodied, high acidity
A spark-plug of a wine, with honey and lime blossom flavors enlived by vibrant
acidity.

Kourtaki Muscat, Samos, Greece ★ $
sweet, full-bodied, medium acidity
Lazy, golden wine for lazy nights.

riesling

Every year, producers in Germany, Austria, and Alsace—where
the finest dry Rieslings are grown—hope that some of their
grapes will ripen enough to make sweet wines. In Germany and
Austria, the least lush of the sweet wines are marked *Auslese*. A
step up are *Beerenauslese* (BA) wines, which might also offer a

smoky flavor derived from the botrytis mold. The most intense are labeled *Trockenbeerenauslese* (TBA). But while these wines take on intense citrus, tropical fruit, and honey flavors, they often retain strong acidity, which makes them ageworthy as well as refreshing. Alsatian vintners mark their late-harvest wines *Vendange Tardive* (VT), and wines from botrytis-infected grapes *Sélection de Grains Nobles* (SGN). California, New York, Washington State, and Australia also make superb sweet Rieslings.

at the table

Simple fruit tarts or ripe summer fruit are excellent matches for delicate dessert Rieslings, though the most luxurious versions, such as SGN, BA, and TBA, are best savored on their own.

the bottom line Leaving grapes on the vine to ripen longer than normal tempts fate: strong winds, heavy rain, hail, early frost, or hungry wild animals can destroy fragile grapes in minutes. Prices reflect the risks. Half bottles of Alsatian VT wines start at $35 and reach $100 or more; the SGN range is nearly double that. German and Austrian Auslese wines start at $35, and prices rise with the level of sweetness. California, New York, and Australia offer fine dessert Rieslings for $14 to $25 (some reach up to $50), while Washington State versions cost $10 to $15.

recommended wines

2000 Domaine Zind-Humbrecht Clos Windsbuhl Vendange Tardive, Alsace, France ★★★★ $$$$
medium-sweet, full-bodied, high acidity
Power with a delicate touch, as dried lime, pear, herb, and mineral flavors envelop the tongue.

1999 Georg Breuer Rüdesheim Berg Rottland Goldkapsel Auslese, Rheingau, Germany ★★★★ $$$ (375 ml)
medium-sweet, medium-bodied, high acidity
Botrytis's phantom effects flow through elegant tropical and lemony flavors.

2000 Long Vineyards Botrytis, Napa Valley, California ★★★★ $$ (500 ml)
sweet, full-bodied, high acidity
The only California Riesling exported to Germany. Any questions?

2001 Mount Horrocks Cordon Cut, Clare Valley,
Australia ★ ★ ★ ★ $$ (375 ml)
sweet, full-bodied, high acidity
Absolutely hedonistic, but measured so the tropical fruit flavors never become
too overwhelming.

1999 Wairau River Botrytised Reserve, Marlborough,
New Zealand ★ ★ ★ $$$ (375 ml)
sweet, full-bodied, high acidity
As pungent with sweet herb and tropical fruit flavors as Marlborough's
Sauvignon Blancs.

ice wine/eiswein

If leaving grapes on the vine long into autumn to get extra ripe
isn't risky enough, trying to leave them there until the first freeze,
without the development of any mold, benevolent or otherwise,
is the ultimate wine thrill. The frozen grapes are then pressed
while frozen, extracting the luscious juice while leaving the
frozen water behind. The result is an intense but delicate wine
that captures the essence of the grape. It's a German and
Austrian tradition that is now attempted by vintners around the
world. Although most ice wines are made from Riesling, some
are made from Scheurebe and Grüner Veltliner. Vintners in
Canada, New York, and Washington State also make ice wine
from Riesling, Chenin Blanc, and Vidal when conditions are
right. Following the lead of iconoclastic winemaker Randall
Grahm, some California vintners don't wait for perfect conditions. They just put their late-harvest grapes in the freezer.

at the table
Ice wines tend to be so intense they don't need any accompaniment, but if dessert is called for, make it simple and not too
sweet: pound cake, poached pears, or fresh fruit will do.

the bottom line Because of the great risks, German
and Austrian ice wines are expensive, ranging from $30 to $300
per half bottle. Canadian ice wine is almost as expensive at $30
to $85. Washington State ice wines rarely achieve great distinc-
tion, but at about $25, there's little reason to complain.

recommended wines

**2001 Selbach-Oster Zeltinger Himmelreich Riesling,
Mosel-Saar-Ruwer, Germany** ★★★★ $$$$ (375 ml)
sweet, medium-bodied, high acidity
Floral as a bed of rose petals, filled up with ripe apricot and spice flavors.
Beautiful wine.

**2001 Joseph Phelps Vineyards Eisrébe, Napa Valley,
California** ★★★★ $$ (375 ml)
sweet, medium-bodied, high acidity
A luscious herb and flower extravaganza with citrus undertones.

**1999 Inniskillin Riesling, Niagara Peninsula,
Canada** ★★★ $$$$ (375 ml)
sweet, medium-bodied, high acidity
How pineapple flavors get to Canada is a mystery—but so are the intense flavors of this wine.

**2000 Henry of Pelham Vidal, Niagara Peninsula,
Canada** ★★★ $$$ (375 ml)
sweet, medium-bodied, high acidity
Vidal's spicy nature takes over here, with tropical flavors providing a background.

**2001 Kiona Chenin Blanc, Red Mountain,
Washington State** ★★★ $$ (375 ml)
sweet, full-bodied, high acidity
Thoroughly delicious, with dried apricot flavors and a seductive spiciness.

ICE THIEVES

In the movies, jewel thieves have been known to call the diamonds in their heist "ice." In the winter of 2001, Bernhard Breuer, of the Rheingau's Weingut Georg Breuer, discovered a new use for the term. With temperatures dropping, Breuer went to check in on the carefully selected grapes he had left on the vines with the intention of making ice wine, only to discover that they had been illicitly harvested. A police investigation was conducted, with no success. "Whoever did this had the makings of a very luscious dessert wine," said Breuer, who also added that the reward he posted has gone unclaimed. "And no one has even sent me a bottle of the result."

other white dessert wines

Hungary's extraordinarily long-lived Tokaji wines are made by a unique method that combines a dry base of still white wine with a mash of botrytis-infected grapes (*aszú* in Hungarian). Each bin of mash is called a *puttonyo,* and the sweetness of the wine is denoted by how many *puttonyos* of mash went in. Eszencia is the ultimate Tokaji, made from the juice that oozes from the grapes crushed only by the pressure of their own weight. Austria's Ausbruch wines are made in the same way as Tokaji.

In Alsace, Gewürztraminer, Muscat, and Pinot Gris are sometimes made into *Vendange Tardive* (VT) and *Sélection de Grains Nobles* (SGN) wines. Any number of grapes can be made into *Beerenauslese* and *Trockenbeerenauslese* wines in Germany and Austria. In Italy, Passito wines are also made in Tuscany and Umbria (mostly from Trebbiano grapes), where they are called Vin Santo, and in the Veneto, where they are called Recioto wines.

at the table

Drink these sweet wines alone, or as you would others of their kind. Vin Santo is classic with crunchy almond biscotti. Tokaji's spicy, apricotlike flavors are especially delicious with apricot-filled crepes or crème brûlée.

the bottom line

Four- and five-*puttonyo* Tokaji Aszús sell for $20 to $65 per 500 ml, while the rarer Eszencia costs well over $100. Alsatian VT wines start at around $35; SGN wines at $60, and both can skyrocket above $100. Auslese wines from Germany and Austria range from $40 to $100. Good Vin Santo and white Recioto wines run $20 to $75; some exceptional Vin Santos reach $145.

recommended wines

1994 Trimbach Sélection de Grains Nobles Gewurztraminer, Alsace, France   ★ ★ ★ ★ $ $ $ $
sweet, full-bodied, high acidity
Magnificently lush, with spiced, honeyed, tropical fruit flavors.

other whites dessert wines

1993 Château Pajzos 5 Puttonyos, Tokaji Aszú,
Hungary ★★★★ $$$ (500 ml)
sweet, full-bodied, high acidity
This Hungarian seduces with smooth-talking dry apricot, hibiscus, and peppery orange flavors.

1997 Gini Re Nobilis, Recioto di Soave, Veneto,
Italy ★★★★ $$$ (375 ml)
sweet, full-bodied, high acidity
One of Italy's best, this has intense, electric fruit and spice flavors with an unforgettable edge.

2000 Maculan Torcolato, Breganze, Veneto,
Italy ★★★★ $$$ (375 ml)
sweet, full-bodied, high acidity
A classic, with sweet fruit given a toasted-corn nuttiness that comes from oak-barrel aging.

2000 Navarro Late Harvest Vineyard Select Gewürztraminer,
Anderson Valley, California ★★★★ $$ (375 ml)
sweet, medium-bodied, high acidity
Luscious tangerine and citrus blossom flavors have a piquant, almost salty minerality.

1999 Walter Filiputti Picolit, Friuli, Italy ★★★ $$$$ (500 ml)
medium-sweet, medium-bodied, medium acidity
Exceptionally smooth and lightly spiced with quince marmalade flavors, this is just delicious.

2000 Kracher Cuvée Beerenauslese, Neusiedlersee,
Austria ★★★ $$$ (375 ml)
sweet, full-bodied, high acidity
This is the most basic offering from the king of Austrian sweet wines. It only gets better from here.

1995 Villa La Selva Vigna del Papa Vin Santo, Tuscany,
Italy ★★★ $$$ (500 ml)
medium-sweet, full-bodied, high acidity
Worthy of a pope, this offers the flavors of heaven and earth in its sunny fruit flavors and earthy minerality.

2001 Weingut Kruger-Rumpf Scheurebe Auslese, Nahe,
Germany ★★★ $$$
medium-sweet, medium-bodied, high acidity
Scheurebe's funky nature is on display in this aromatic show of fruit and truffle flavors.

dessert wines **other whites**

1999 Clos Lapeyre Sélection, Jurançon, France ★★★ $$ (375 ml)
sweet, full-bodied, high acidity
With wines like this nutty, spicy, mango-flavored elixir, Jurançon deserves
more fame.

**1996 Cieck Alladium Caluso Passito Erbaluce, Piedmont,
Italy** ★★ $$$ (375 ml)
sweet, full-bodied, high acidity
The grape's name, Erbaluce, sums up the flavors: herbs, sweet and bitter, and
sun-dried fruit. Fine wine.

**2000 Bodegas Gutiérrez de la Vega Casta Diva, Alicante,
Spain** ★★ $$ (500 ml)
sweet, full-bodied, high acidity
A taste of Alicante in wild herb scents and orange and almond flavors.

WHITE DESSERT WINES WE WISH WE HAD MORE ROOM FOR
**2001 Messmer Burrweiler Altenforst Gewürztraminer Spätlese,
Pfalz, Germany** ★★★ $$$ medium-sweet, medium-bodied, high acidity;
**1999 Didier Champalou Cuvée des Fondraux, Vouvray, Loire Valley,
France** ★★★ $$ off-dry, full-bodied, high acidity; **2001 Geyser Peak
Reserve Late Harvest Riesling, Dry Creek Valley, California** ★★★
$$ (375 ml) sweet, full-bodied, high acidity; **2001 Hermann J. Wiemer
Late Harvest Johannisberg Riesling, Finger Lakes, New York**
★★★ $$ off-dry, medium-bodied, high acidity; **2001 Joseph La Magia
Botrytis Riesling-Traminer, Eden Valley, Australia** ★★★ $$ (375
ml) sweet, full-bodied, high acidity; **1998 Montes Late Harvest
Gewürztraminer-Riesling, Curicó Valley, Chile** ★★★ $$ (375 ml)
sweet, full-bodied, high acidity; **1999 Domaine des Trés Cantous
Muscadelle Doux, Gaillac, France** ★★★ $ (500 ml) sweet, full-bod-
ied, medium acidity; **2001 Coppo Moncalvina, Moscato d'Asti,
Piedmont, Italy** ★★ $$ medium-sweet, medium-bodied, high acidity;
1997 Massandra Red Stone White Muscat, Crimea, Ukraine ★★ $$
(500 ml) sweet, full-bodied, high acidity

other red dessert wines

Port is not the only sweet red wine. Grenache is the base of two
rich, purple fortified wines from Roussillon in southern France,
Banyuls and Maury. And from northeastern Italy comes the lighter,
bittersweet Recioto della Valpolicella, made from the same sorts
of grapes that go into Valpolicella, but dried before pressing.

at the table

Banyuls and Maury have lush berry flavors that pair well with chocolate, though they are also good with cheese. Recioto della Valpolicella matches well with plum compote or spice cake.

the bottom line Banyuls and Maury run between $20 and $50. Rarer Recioto wines cost $70 to $100 or more.

recommended wines

1998 Domaine de la Casa Blanca, Banyuls, Languedoc-Roussillon, France ★★★★ $$
sweet, full-bodied, high acidity
Spectacular. Sweet cherry, dried lavender, and powdery mineral flavors are built for a long life.

Mas Amiel Cuvée Spéciale 10 Ans d'Age, Maury, Languedoc-Roussillon, France ★★★ $$$
off-dry, medium-bodied, medium acidity
Here's what an obsessed confectioner must dream of at night: delicious dry plum, cherry, fig, almond, and bitter chocolate flavors.

1999 Bonny Doon Vineyard Recioto of Barbera, Monterey County, California ★★★ $$ (375 ml)
medium-sweet, full-bodied, medium acidity
What's next? Inspired by Veneto's Amarone, Randall Grahm crafts a wine with distinct blackberry, chocolate, and bitter mineral flavors.

1996 M. Chapoutier Banyuls, Languedoc-Roussillon, France ★★★ $$ (375 ml)
medium-sweet, full-bodied, medium acidity
Rather than the typical plum-and-spice model, this offers mature flavors of dried berries, leather, and herbs.

1998 Lucas Late Harvest Zinfandel, Lodi, California ★★ $$$ (375 ml)
medium-sweet, full-bodied, medium acidity
Zinfandel grapes are partially dried on mats to give this wine its intense, chocolaty berry flavors.

Keo Commandaria St. John, Cyprus ★ $
sweet, full-bodied, medium acidity
Claimed to be the oldest wine in the world, this is like a thick, affordable Madeira.

food & wine pairing chart

	antipasti; mezes; salty, assertive foods; hors d'oeuvres	foie gras	sausages; charcuterie	soups; salads	egg dishes
Light, simple whites unoaked Chardonnay; California and South Africa Chenin Blanc; most Italian whites; Mediterranean blends; Muscadet; basic German Riesling; white Rioja; Sauvignon Blanc; Vinho Verde	●			●	●
Fragrant, medium-bodied whites Albariño; Australian blends; white Bordeaux; Loire Chenin Blanc; Gewürztraminer; German Kabinett Riesling	●	●		●	●
Rich, full-bodied whites oaked Chardonnay; white Burgundies; Pinot Gris; Austrian Riesling & Grüner Veltliner; aged Semillon; Scheurebe; Viognier		●			
Light, fruity reds & rosés France's Beaujolais, Cabernet Franc (Bourgueil), & simple Languedoc reds; basic Freisa, Nebbiolo, & Sangiovese; all rosés	●		●		
Medium-bodied, slightly tannic reds Agiorgitiko; simple Bordeaux; Cabernet Franc (Chinon); Sangiovese from Chianti Classico; Côtes-du-Rhône blends; Dolcetto; Grenache; Merlot; Pinot Noir; Portuguese reds			●		
Rich, dense, tannic reds Aglianico; Barbaresco; Barolo; France's Bordeaux, Rhône Valley, & Southwest reds; high-end New World Cabernets & Syrah/Shiraz; Malbec; Zinfandel			●		
Sparkling white wines Cava, Champagne, Crémant, Prosecco, other sparkling wines		●	●	●	●

There's no single perfect wine for any given dish. In fact, the possibilities are nearly infinite. Use this handy Food & Wine Pairing Chart to help you sort through the options and make delicious matches—at home, in wine shops, and in restaurants.

pasta, rice & other grains			fish & seafood		poultry & game birds		pork & veal	
light; summery; vegetable-based	rich; mushroom- or truffle-based	baked; tomato or cheese sauces	mild varieties; light sauces	rich varieties; heavy sauces	chicken; turkey	duck; game birds	herbed or with savory sauces	fruit-based sauces
●			●		●			
●			●		●			
	●			●	●	●	●	●
	●	●		●	●	●		●
	●	●				●	●	
		●				●	●	
●	●		●	●	●	●	●	●

food & wine pairing chart

	beef: steaks, stews, ribs, etc.	lamb, venison, game meats		asian & curry dishes	
		herbed or with savory sauces	fruit-based sauces	fish; seafood; vegetables	meat; lentils; root vegetables
Light, simple whites unoaked Chardonnay; California and South Africa Chenin Blanc; most Italian whites; Mediterranean blends; Muscadet; basic German Riesling; white Rioja; Sauvignon Blanc; Vinho Verde				●	
Fragrant, medium-bodied whites Albariño; Australian blends; white Bordeaux; Loire Chenin Blanc; Gewürztraminer; German Kabinett Riesling				●	
Rich, full-bodied whites oaked Chardonnay; white Burgundies; Pinot Gris; Austrian Riesling & Grüner Veltliner; aged Semillon; Scheurebe; Viognier				●	●
Light, fruity reds & rosés France's Beaujolais, Cabernet Franc (Bourgeuil) & simple Languedoc reds; basic Freisa, Nebbiolo, & Sangiovese; all rosés					●
Medium-bodied, slightly tannic reds Agiorgitiko; simple Bordeaux; Cabernet Franc (Chinon); Sangiovese from Chianti Classico; Côtes-du-Rhône blends; Dolcetto; Grenache; Merlot; Pinot Noir; Portuguese reds	●	●			
Rich, dense, tannic reds Aglianico; Barbaresco; Barolo; France's Bordeaux, Rhône Valley, & Southwest reds; high-end New World Cabernets & Syrah/Shiraz; Malbec; Zinfandel	●	●	●		
Sparkling white wines Cava, Champagne, Crémant, Prosecco, other sparkling wines		●	●	●	●
Dessert wines, white Ice Wine, Muscat, Riesling, Sauternes, Tokaji, Vin Santo					
Dessert wines, red Banyuls, Maury, Port, Recioto della Valpolicella					

food & wine pairing chart

barbecue; burgers; pizza	vegetarian dishes			cheeses		desserts		
	stews; gratins	grilled tofu or vegetables	artichokes; asparagus	mild	strong	fruit-based; poundcake	creams; custards; soufflés	chocolate; nuts; coffee
		●	●	●				
		●		●				
		●	●	●				
●	●	●		●				
●	●	●		●	●			
	●				●			
		●	●			●		
				●		●	●	
								●

295

bargain wine finder

Good value was a key consideration when making recommendations for this book. Following is an index of wines whose quality (★) to price ($) ratio makes them exceptional values.

WHITE WINES

★ ★ ★ ★ $ $

Bonny Doon Vineyard Viognier, CA, 35

Boutari Kallisti, Santorini, Greece, 220

Chehalem Reserve Pinot Gris, Willamette Valley, OR, 64

Coldstream Hills Reserve Chardonnay, Yarra Valley, Australia, 233

Domaine Agathe Bursin Pinot Blanc, Alsace, France, 86

Domaine Huet Clos du Bourg Sec, Vouvray, France, 117

Domaine Tempier Rosé, Bandol, France, 129

Mietz Sauvignon Blanc, Sonoma County, CA, 29

Movia Turno, Brda, Slovenia, 223

Qupé Reserve Bien Nacido Chardonnay, Santa Maria Valley, CA, 24

R. López de Heredia Viña Gravonia, Rioja, Spain, 183

Robert Weil Estate Riesling Kabinett Halbtrocken, Rheingau, Germany, 204

Rutz Cellars Maison Grand Cru Chardonnay, Russian River Valley, CA, 24

von Othegraven Kanzem Altenberg Riesling, Mosel-Saar-Ruwer, Germany, 204

Wisching Iphöfer Kronsberg Scheurebe Kabinett Trocken, Franken, Germany, 208

★ ★ ★ ★ $

Gai'a Ritinitis Nobilis, Retsina, Greece, 220

Hermann J. Wiemer Chardonnay, Finger Lakes, NY, 76

Navarro Vineyards Dry Gewürztraminer, Anderson Valley, CA, 32

★ ★ ★ $

Alpha Domus Unoaked, Hawke's Bay, New Zealand, 246

Antonio Esteves Ferreira Soalheiro Alvarinho, Vinho Verde, Portugal, 196

Au Bon Climat Bien Nacido Vineyard Pinot Gris-Pinot Blanc, Santa Barbara County, CA, 33

Beckmen Vineyards Estate Sauvignon Blanc, Santa Ynez Valley, CA, 30

Bethel Heights Vineyard Pinot Gris, OR, 65

Bucci Verdicchio dei Castelli di Jesi Classico, Le Marche, Italy, 173

Can Feixes Blanc Selecció, Penedès, Spain, 190

Casa Lapostolle Chardonnay, Casablanca Valley, Chile, 255

Chappellet Dry Chenin Blanc, Napa Valley, CA, 33

Château de la Colline Sec, Bergerac, France, 142

Château de la Ragotière Muscadet sur Lie, Sèvre-et-Maine, France, 119

Claiborne & Churchill Alsatian-Style Riesling, Central Coast, CA, 33

Cune Monopole, Rioja, Spain, 184

Curtis Heritage Blanc, Santa Barbara County, CA, 33

Di Stefano Sauvignon Blanc, Columbia Valley, WA, 69

Domaine de l'Oratoire St-Martin, Côtes-du-Rhône, France, 137

Domaine de la Pépière Clos de Briords Muscadet sur Lie, Sèvre-et-Maine, France, 119

Domaine Les Hautes Noëlles Muscadet sur Lie, Côtes de Grandlieu, France, 119

Dr. Fischer Ockfener Bockstein Riesling Kabinett, Mosel-Saar-Ruwer, Germany, 205

Fitz-Ritter Dürkheimer Spielberg Chardonnay Spätlese, Pfalz, Germany, 208

Foris Gewürztraminer, Rogue Valley, OR, 64

Gini, Soave Classico Superiore, Italy, 158

Heinrich Seebrich Niersteiner Oelberg Gewürztraminer Spätlese, Rheinhessen, Germany, 208

Hermann J. Wiemer Dry Johannisberg Riesling, Finger Lakes, NY, 76

Karthäuserhof Estate Riesling, Mosel-Saar-Ruwer, Germany, 205

Kavaklidere Selection Beyaz Narince de Tokat, Turkey, 228

Kourtaki Assyrtiko, Santorini, Greece, 220

Ktima Kyr-Yianni Samaropetra, Florina, Greece, 220

L'Ecole Nº 41 Barrel Fermented Semillon, Columbia Valley, WA, 69

La Cadalora Traminer Aromatico, Trentino, Italy, 148

Macari Sauvignon Blanc, North Fork, NY, 76

Martínez Bujanda Conde de Valdemar Finca Alto de Cantabria, Rioja, Spain, 184

Montes Reserve Fumé Blanc Sauvignon Blanc, Curicó Valley, Chile, 255

Navarro Vineyards Dry Muscat Blanc, Mendocino, CA, 33

Navarro Vineyards Sauvignon Blanc, Mendocino, CA, 30

Navarro Vineyards White Riesling, Anderson Valley, CA, 35

Oak Knoll Pinot Gris, Willamette Valley, OR, 64

Olivier Leflaive Les Sétilles, Bourgogne, France, 106

Ott Sélection Les Domaniers Rosé, Côtes de Provence, France, 129

Palmer Vineyards Gewürztraminer, North Fork, NY, 77

Paumanok Semi-Dry Riesling, North Fork, NY, 77

Peconic Bay Winery Riesling, North Fork, NY, 77

Penfolds Thomas Hyland Chardonnay, Adelaide Hills, Australia, 233

Pikes Riesling, Clare Valley, Australia, 235

Pojer e Sandri Palai Dolomiti Müller-Thurgau, Alto Adige, Italy, 147

Sibyl Riesling Qualitätswein, Nahe, Germany, 206

Tahbilk Marsanne Nagambie Lakes, Central Victoria, Australia, 236

Tenuta Beltrame Chardonnay, Friuli, Italy, 147

von Othegraven Maria v. O. Riesling, Mosel-Saar-Ruwer, Germany, 206

Weingut Dr. von Bassermann-Jordan Estate Riesling Trocken, Pfalz, Germany, 206

Weingut Eugen Wehrheim Niersteiner Orbel Riesling Spätlese, Rheinhessen, Germany, 206

Weingut Pfeffingen Estate Dry Riesling, Pfalz, Germany, 206

Wölffer Rosé, The Hamptons, NY, 77

RED WINES

★★★★ $ $

Au Bon Climat La Bauge Au-Dessus Bien Nacido Vineyard Pinot Noir, Santa Maria Valley, CA, 50

Chappellet Merlot, Napa Valley, CA, 46

Joseph Swan Vineyards Lone Redwood Ranch Zinfandel, Russian River Valley, CA, 54

Le Domaine Magellan Les Murelles, Vin de Pays de Côtes de Thongue, France, 126

Louis Jadot Château des Jacques La Roche, Moulin-à-Vent, France, 113

Rochford Macedon Ranges Pinot Noir, Victoria, Australia, 241

Rosenblum Cellars Rockpile Road Vineyard Zinfandel, Dry Creek Valley, CA, 54

Rutz Cellars Maison Grand Cru Pinot Noir, Russian River Valley, CA, 50

★★★ $

Beckmen Vineyards Cuvée Le Bec, Santa Barbara County, CA, 59

Bodegas Bretón Loriñon Crianza, Rioja, Spain, 186

Bodegas Castaño Solanera Monastrell, Yecla, Spain, 192

Castel di Salve Priante Salento Rosso, Apulia, Italy, 179

Château Bousquette, St-Chinian, France, 126

Château d'Oupia, Minervois, France, 127

Château La Coustarelle Grande Cuvée Prestige, Cahors, France, 142

Concha y Toro Marques de Casa Concha Cabernet Sauvignon, Puente Alto, Chile, 257

Domaine du Mas Cremat, Côtes du Roussillon, France, 126

Domaine Nôtre Dame de Cousignac, Côtes-du-Rhône, France, 139

Fleur du Cap Cabernet Sauvignon, Coastal Region, South Africa, 263

Globus, Ribatejo, Portugal, 198

Hedges CMS, Columbia Valley, WA, 71

Hill of Content Pinot Noir, Mornington Peninsula, Australia, 241

Hogue Genesis Blue Franc-Lemberger, Columbia Valley, WA, 73

Kavaklidere Selection Kirmizi Oküzözü d'Elazig, Turkey, 230

Le Terrazze Rosso Cònero, Le Marche, Italy, 174

Nederburg Pinotage, Western Cape, South Africa, 263

Quinta do Crasto, Douro, Portugal, 198

names you can trust

Some importers consistently offer excellent wines. If the name of one of these importers is on the label, you can bet that the wine is good for its type:

Australian Premium Wine Collection Boutique wines from Australia.

Cape Classics South African estates.

Chartrand Imports Excellent French and Italian wines, many organic.

Classical Wines Fine selections from Spain and Germany, often at excellent prices.

Marc de Grazia Selections New-wave Italian wines.

Robert Kacher French wines at bargain prices.

Leonardo LoCascio Selections Italian wines with regional character.

Louis/Dressner Selections Excellent finds from underappreciated regions of France and Portugal.

Kermit Lynch Wine Merchant King of the small, *terroir*-oriented French producers.

Eric Solomon/European Cellars High-quality, well-priced wines from France, Italy, and Spain.

Tempranillo Imports Superb Spanish wines.

Terry Theise Champagne, Austrian, and German wines from quality small producers.

Vias Imports Traditional and cutting-edge Italian wines.

Vin Divino Great Austrian and Italian wines.

Vineyard Expressions French wines from small producers, with an accent on organic, low-sulfate, and bio-dynamic wines.

index of wines

index

index

index

index

e

index

a

index

index

index

n

index

index

index

STAR WARS

REY TO THE RESCUE!

Written by Lisa Stock

Written and edited by Lisa Stock
Designer Anna Pond
Senior Designer Clive Savage
Pre-production Producer Marc Staples
Producer Alex Bell
Managing Editor Sadie Smith
Managing Art Editor Ron Stobbart
Publisher Julie Ferris
Art Director Lisa Lanzarini
Publishing Director Simon Beecroft

For Lucasfilm
Editorial Assistant Samantha Holland
Image Archives Newell Todd and Gabrielle Levenson
Art Director Troy Alders
Story Group Leland Chee, Pablo Hidalgo, Rayne Roberts, and Matt Martin

First American Edition, 2017
Published in the United States by DK Publishing
345 Hudson Street, New York, New York 10014

Page design copyright © 2017 Dorling Kindersley Limited
DK, a Division of Penguin Random House LLC
16 17 18 19 10 9 8 7 6 5 4 3 2 1
001–298000–Jan/17

© & ™ 2017 LUCASFILM LTD.

A catalog record for this book is available from the Library of Congress.

ISBN 978-1-4654-5581-9 (Hardcover)
ISBN 978-1-4654-5580-2 (Paperback)

DK books are available at special discounts when purchased in bulk for sales promotions, premiums,
fund-raising, or educational use. For details, contact: DK Publishing Special Markets, 345 Hudson Street,
New York, New York 10014
SpecialSales@dk.com

Printed and bound in China

A WORLD OF IDEAS:
SEE ALL THERE IS TO KNOW

www.dk.com
www.starwars.com